D0520295

# EAST BAY HERITAGE

# EAST BAY HERITAGE
## A Potpourri of Living History

by

**Mark A. Wilson**

photography by

**Robert Breuer**

with line drawings by  
**Ann Johnson**

and maps by  
**Nancy Warner**

A California Living Book

This book is dedicated to my parents,
who taught me to look for beauty in the world.

First Edition
Copyright ©1979 California Living Books
The San Francisco Examiner Division of the
Hearst Corporation. Suite 223, The Hearst
Building, Third and Market Streets, San
Francisco, California 94103

Printed in the United States of America.
Design/Production by David Charlsen
ISBN 0-89395-026-2
Library of Congress Catalog Card Number 79-51144

# Contents

# Acknowledgments

Of all those people who in some way were helpful in creating this book, my partner, Ann Johnson, deserves my first thanks. She did the line drawings, and her love, patience, and understanding made the whole book possible. Robert Breuer, whose superb photographs grace these pages was also indispensable in his creative suggestions and enthusiasm for this project. To the two women who typed the entire manuscript, Esther Golde and Shirley Ramacher, I will be eternally grateful. And to Valerie Winemiller, a friend who helped greatly to develop the concept in its early stages, I give my deepest appreciation.

A number of individuals and organizations offered tremendous assistance by collecting the research for various chapters in this book. First and foremost among them were Anthony Bruce and Leslie Emmington of the Berkeley Architectural Heritage Association, with whom I have enjoyed working for many years and who most generously helped me document much of the material on Berkeley. Stephanie Manning of the Oceanview Neighborhood Preservation Association also gave her time unstintingly to research the Oceanview chapter. Many thanks also to Ray Suderman and to the other members of the Brooklyn Neighborhood Preservation Association, who enthusiastically provided much data for the sections on East Oakland. Other individuals and associations helped by gathering factual material for the many tours in this book, and I have duly noted their contributions in the individual tour notes.

Countless friends, relatives, and acquaintances gave me invaluable assistance through their interest, encouragement, and suggestions along the way. My father and my stepmother, Sally, both read the early versions of the book and offered me their loving faith as well as their constructive criticism when I needed it most. To Rich Campbell and all my other friends from the staff and student body at Skyline High School in Oakland, my thanks for encouraging and assisting the early efforts of a then-budding writer. To all my adult school and junior college students who took an interest in the creation of the book and offered their helpful suggestions, thank you for putting up with the occasional vicissitudes of an author under pressure. And a special note of thanks to Beverly Standifer for her friendship and moral support during a crucial stage in this project.

Finally, I wish to thank Hal, Jay, Jill, and all the other wonderful people on the staff of California Living Books who had enough confidence in this idea to put their professional efforts into helping it become a reality.

Mark Wilson
Berkeley, California
August 1979

# A Note on Historic Preservation

*Oakland, 12th at Broadway, c. 1869*

America may not have great medieval cathedrals or grand, Renaissance Era cities, but we do have a wealth of incredibly varied architectural styles that span several centuries. In recent years, the movement to preserve our historic buildings and the esthetic integrity of our older neighborhoods has steadily gained converts across the nation. As the urban culture we once prized now threatens to engulf us, more and more citizens are recognizing that we need to preserve whatever evokes a more serene past and nourishes the weary spirit of the modern city dweller.

The ability of older buildings to offer spiritual sustenance is their real attraction. But should we need additional justification for ensuring the survival of older structures, we can find many economic and practical reasons. Considering that nearly every kind of resource is in short supply these days, and that these shortages place limitations on our society, often we can no longer *afford* to destroy the existing buildings in our inner cities and towns in favor of building new ones. As city planners discover that movie palaces can be converted into opera houses and train sheds into exhibition centers, older buildings are being "recycled" into modern uses.

But beyond the practical justifications, something inside us demands that we preserve worthy examples of our past life-styles. A growing desire for a sense of cultural identity and stability compels us, in this all-too-mobile society, to hold onto some tangible evidence of the world of our ancestors. To counteract the cultural conformity that is fast becoming the norm, people are beginning to seek out the interesting and unusual to add the spice of variety to their lives. In an environment choked with human-made ugliness, we all feel the need at times to surround ourselves with beauty and refresh our spirits.

This is not to say that every interesting old building must be saved, or even that every good example of an architectural style — say, Italianate-style rowhouses — must be kept intact, no matter what the other uses to which its site might be put. We have to strike a reasonable balance between the past and the present to insure a high quality of life for the future. But although we don't need to protect all old buildings, we must preserve the esthetic quality of old neighborhoods. Then we can use these as yardsticks with which to compare the present; to teach history to our young; to foster respect and admiration for craftsmanship and beauty; to illustrate the contributions of past generations; and to bring enjoyment to future generations. We simply cannot permit the alternatives — they are too dehumanizing. For instance, several of Louis Sullivan's buildings once stood in downtown Chicago. Now, only two remain. We can ill afford to repeat this tragedy with the remaining treasures of our historic architecture. Indeed, *every* community that possesses such irreplaceable cultural resources must take steps to ensure their continued existence.

# Introduction

To discover a beautiful old building is a unique joy. Happily, an ever-growing number of people are having this experience. We can all derive pleasure from the sight of weathered, wooden shingles in the mellow afternoon sun, or of robustly rendered, carved details on a Queen Anne Victorian house. And as we enjoy these visual delights, our appreciation for them grows; we seek out more such sights, and in turn our esteem for them grows still more.

This book evolved out of just such a desire for exploration and the thrill of discovery. After several years of roaming the streets of various communities in search of architectural beauty, I decided that my lack of a sufficient background in the subject kept me from fully experiencing the structures at which I was looking. I believed then, as I do now, that it is always helpful to have a fairly specific idea of just what it is we are seeking. If we have knowledge of the field, we can more easily understand and appreciate the objects we find along the way. To fill that need, this book is designed as a tool for anyone — layperson or expert — who wishes to share in the delights of exploring the historic architecture along the eastern portion of the San Francisco Bay.

Beginning with a brief overview of the history and development of architecture in the East Bay from 1800 to 1950, this book offers a series of keyed maps with descriptions, many drawings, and photographs of noteworthy old buildings in more than a score of East Bay communities. Most of the structures included have never been mentioned in any other text. You can use the descriptive, illustrated guide to the varius styles of architecture that were popular in this area before 1950 to recognize the general types of historic buildings found in the East Bay. And, if you are a more serious student, you will find a chronologically arranged list of some 1,200-odd structures, giving style, address, date, and architect (when known), as well as an annotated reading list and information on local architectural organizations and reference sources.

If beauty is truly in the eye of the beholder, then the more beholders of a given kind of beauty, the more likely that such beauty will be preserved for others to enjoy. The encouragement of preservation is really the ultimate purpose of this book. For if we do not preserve the beauty we have created around us, then what will become of our environment? Only through the survival of such notable remnants of an earlier era can we today still truly touch the past.

*Berkeley, Durant and Ellsworth Streets, c. 1885*

# Part I

## A Brief History of Architecture in the East Bay: 1800–1950

*Fourteenth Street, Oakland, looking west; c. 1869.*

# Chapter 1

# East of the Golden Gate

Nearly everyone agrees that architecture reflects the character and aspirations of the people who practice it. But a building is more than merely a reflection of people's character traits; it is a microcosm of the culture from which it came, a solid piece of evidence that testifies to what life was like for the society that built it. An old or historic structure lets us understand what the world was like before we were in it. Few other objects provide such helpful (and enjoyable) tools for us to use in our search for personal and cultural roots.

In this sense, the communities that lie along the eastern edge of the San Francisco Bay are wealthy indeed, for they possess an uncommon variety and quality of architecture that spans nearly two centuries. From the adobe-and-beam structures of the first Spanish missionaries in the late eighteenth century, through the romantic fantasies-in-wood of the prosperous nineteenth-century settlers, to the truly revolutionary new styles developed by great architects in this century, no urban area in the United States offers more to the student of history and art.

Before the arrival of the first white people, the Costanoan Indians built their own structures. These conical-shaped "huts" were built of poles tied together at the top, covered with brush, and banked with earth around the base for support.[1] Such simple, straightforward, and utilitarian dwellings conformed as well as any modern structure to Louis Sullivan's great dictum, "Form follows function." None of these huts survived many years past the first Spanish settlement.

The Spanish settlers of the late eighteenth century introduced the first "design-oriented" buildings to the California landscape — the California missions. Borrowing construction techniques from the Indians of the Southwest, the builders of these churches rendered in relatively crude form the elements of the Spanish Baroque style imported from the mother country. Limited by the materials at hand, these structures had no possibility (and no need) of being as fashionable and ornate as their earlier counterparts in Central and South America. Built only of adobe-brick walls, wood-beamed ceilings, and clay-tile roofs, these "pioneer" churches nonetheless incorporated some degree of conscious design; each mission looked different from the next.

The first Spanish settlement in the East Bay occurred at what is now Mission San Jose in 1797. There, Father Lasuen set up a mission that eventually grew into the wealthiest of all the Spanish ecclesiastic holdings. The original church had a chapel with a never-finished bell tower to the left of its nave and several outbuildings arranged in the traditional quadrangle, or cloister, pattern. Only one of these buildings, the friars' dormitory, survived the earthquake of 1869; it still stands today. Built between 1810 and 1820, Mission San Jose is by far the oldest structure remaining in the East Bay.[2]

The next significant Spanish settlement in the East Bay began two decades later, when Don Luis Maria Peralta was granted a huge tract of land as a reward for his years of military service at the Presidio in San Francisco. This sizeable grant included all of what is now Albany, Berkeley, Oakland, Emeryville, Alameda, and part of San Leandro.[3] Peralta soon divided the land among his sons, and each one set up his own spacious rancho with an adobe house and tanning shed to make use of their various herds of cattle (cattle was the main "industry" in Spanish and Mexican California). Unfortunately, none of these early dwellings has survived to the present day.

However, two other adobe buildings in the area still stand. The older of the two is the oldest private dwelling in the East Bay today: the single-story Vallejo Adobe in Niles, built in 1843 by Jose de Jesus Vallejo to secure his claim to the

*Vallejo Adobe, Niles Fremont Tour A-10*

Rancho Arroyo de Alameda.[4] Standing on the grounds of the California Nursery along Niles Canyon Road, the Vallejo Adobe's thick, heavily buttressed walls have managed to survive the ravages of time in remarkably good shape. The other structure from this period is the two-story, verandaed Martinez Adobe, constructed in 1848 on the grounds of what is now the John Muir Estate in Martinez. It was originally the main building on the 18,000-acre Rancho El Pinole, granted to Ignacio Martinez in 1824.[5]

The East Bay's extant architectural heritage from the Spanish and Mexican periods is indeed a fragile one. The few structures that remain from before the Gold Rush are made priceless by their very scarcity. But equally important is their lasting influence on the architectural styles of later generations of East Bay residents. We will discuss this topic later on.

# Chapter 2

## The Gilded Era

When the Anglo-American settlers arrived after 1846, the East Bay suddenly met up with the Victorian Age (and all the ostentation that went with it). The first of these "gringo" settlers came to the area as squatters on the great ranchos, after striking out in the gold fields.[6] They pitched tents or built simple shacks to live in while they expanded their "claims" and thought up ways to profit from the floodtide of settlers they were certain would follow. Within the next few years, most of today's communities along the East Bay had taken root as the nuclei of the great cities and towns they would eventually become. Easterners first settled in Benicia in 1847, in Oakland in 1849, in Vallejo and Alameda in 1850, in Hayward and San Leandro about the same year, and in Piedmont and West Berkeley (then called Oceanview) in 1852.[7]

These early American settlers brought with them the architectural styles they had known in their native states east of the Mississippi River, where the Romantic notions and picturesque penchants of the Victorian Era were in full bloom. A few of their earliest structures were built in the pre-Victorian Greek Revival mode, a style popularized by Thomas Jefferson in the early 1800s, which essentially involved designing the front of a building in imitation of a Greek temple, in wood or brick. The only full-blown Greek Revival structure remaining in the area is the Old State Capitol Building in Benicia, erected in 1852 at First and West G streets.[8] Its imposing facade sports two huge brick columns, stuccoed over to look like stone.

At the time of the western Gold Rush, however, back east the medieval-inspired Gothic Revival style was all the rage. Mark Twain's caustic observation that the culture of the ante-bellum South was suffering from "the Sir Walter [Scott] disease" was equally true when it came to architecture in the rest of the nation. Imported from England in the 1830s and '40s, the Gothic Revival craze transformed America's landscape: wooden imitations of medieval cathedrals dotted the area, as did steeply gabled cottages whose eaves were lined with delicately carved scrollwork, after the fashion of Tudor houses in the "olde country." Oakland was the first settlement in the East Bay to boast of one such confection. In 1849, Moses Chase built the first frame house — a small cottage with a high-peaked roof — in the infant town, and shortly thereafter he improved it by adding several more gables and a porch embellished with Gothic trimming.[9] Today, the Chase cottage has long since disappeared, but a number of other early Gothic Revival buildings remain in the East Bay. The oldest among them (and one of the oldest wood-frame buildings extant in the area) is the Walch Cottage at 235 East L Street in Benicia. It was built in 1849 from prefabricated sections brought by ship from New England — a common practice of the early settlers.[10] Oakland's oldest existing structure is the Parish Hall of St. James Episcopal Church, erected in 1858 on East 12th Street, a modest but finely executed exercise in the wooden, Gothic Revival church mode.[11] Vallejo also has a number of neo-Gothic Victorian buildings that date from the 1850s and '60s, when it developed as a naval port. But by far the most splendid and impressive example of Gothic Revival in the East Bay is Mosswood Cottage, built in 1864 by the Moss family near the current intersection of Broadway and MacArthur in Oakland. The future-conscious Mayor Frank K. Mott preserved Mosswood Cottage for future generations by insisting that the city purchase the house and land around it and maintain it as a park. This came to pass in 1912.[12]

As the Gothic Revival fad began to wane after the Civil War, a proliferation of other Victorian architectural styles took hold of the public's imagination in rapid succession, each one calculated to satisfy the appetite of the times for the

*Mosswood Cottage, Oakland Tour A-31*

13

*Anthony House, Alameda Tour A-2*

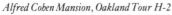

*Alfred Cohen Mansion, Oakland Tour H-2*

picturesque by borrowing various historic motifs. On the heels of the Gothic craze came the Italianate style. Derived from the towered palaces of Renaissance Italy, it was first introduced in America in the 1850s by eastern architects as the Tuscan villa. Easily the most dignified of all the Victorian styles, Italianate houses combined a Classical formalism with a relatively moderate degree of ornamentation. They were characterized by tall, narrow windows that usually curved at the top and were trimmed with decorative woodwork, and by carved brackets along the roofline and angled bays projecting from their facades. The full Italianate villa also had a squared tower or cupola in the center and a columned porch topped by a balcony. The most outstanding surviving examples of this style in the East Bay are the Meek Estate (c. 1869) on Hampton Road in San Lorenzo; Oakland's Pardee Mansion (1868) at 11th and Castro Streets and Camron-Stanford Mansion (1876) on Lake Merritt; and the Anthony House (1876) in Alameda. The Italianate mode adapted so well to the tastes of the Victorian Era that it was used for many a fasionable home for more than a generation after its introduction, as evidenced by the villa-like design of the John Muir House in Martinez, built in 1884.

No sooner had the Italianate villa captured the scene than a new style, the so-called Stick cottage — the first truly invented by American architects — came into vogue (about 1870). Visually related to the Gothic Revival style, with its usually high-peaked gables and decorated eaves, Stick houses sometimes even aspired to the status of villas by including a squared corner tower in their design. But the prime feature of all Stick-style houses was the vertical strips of wood applied for decorative effect to their surfaces above and below windows and along each corner. In their purest form, these buildings were the least ornate of the Victorian modes. But they seldom remained pure, nor did anything else in the Gilded Era.

In the later 1870s, a number of Bay Area architects came up with the novel idea of combining the Stick style with various decorative motifs (sunburst patterns, incised floral panels) borrowed from the furniture of the famed English designer, Sir Charles Eastlake.[13] Wholly without Sir Charles' blessing (indeed, to his great displeasure), these local architects created a style all their own; appropriately enough, it was dubbed "Stick–Eastlake." The most prominent among these "young Turks" of the late-Victorian architectural scene was the Bay Area firm of Samuel and Joseph Newsom, whose Stick–Eastlake villas and cottages (along with constructions based on many of their other designs) decorated the budding communities of northern California in the late nineteenth century. A number of the Newsom brothers' outstanding buildings still survive in Alameda and East Oakland. One of the most fascinating in the Stick–Eastlake vein is an 1887 cottage located at 2304 9th Avenue in Oakland.[14] Other noteworthy examples of this style are the 1889 Niehaus Villa at 7th Street and Channing Way in Berkeley; a circa-1876 house in an impressive setting on West H Street in Benicia; and the magnificent, perfectly maintained Alfred Cohen Mansion at 1440 29th Avenue in East Oakland, built between 1882 and 1884 and now preserved by the city as a designated historic landmark.

As the Victorian Age drew to a close, the mania for carved-wood decoration and applied ornament reached its logical extreme in the last truly Victorian style (or, more accurately, culmination of styles): the outlandish Queen Anne. An 1884 edition of the *California Architect and Building News* probably summed up this late "flowering" of a Romantic-minded era most succinctly. In an imaginary conversation between an architect and his client (which actually could have taken place, given the temper of the times), a builder brings an architect his own set of plans for approval before deciding whether to hire the architect to oversee the construction of his dream house — a common procedure for wealthy homebuilders in those days. A brief discussion of the design of the building then ensues:

ARCHITECT: *Well, I declare, that is a pretty fair house plan for an amateur — only you have no space for stairways and closets. Did you make it yourself?*

BUILDER: *Yes, but the only thing that puzzles me is to know what style of cottage it is. It is not Gothic, nor Italian, nor—*

ARCHITECT: *No, it is absolutely nothing. As to style, it is merely a meaningless hodgepodge — to be frank with you.*

BUILDER: *Well, what shall I call it? Have you no names for hodgepodges?*

ARCHITECT: *Oh! Yes! We call 'em Queen Annes!*[15]

The Queen Anne "style" reigned supreme from the early 1880s through the mid '90s. Its most imposing feature, a castle-like corner tower (usually round), soon came to dominate the skyline of affluent residential neighborhoods throughout the East Bay. Even the person of more modest means could often afford to indulge in the stylistic fancies of Queen Anne by building a high-peaked cottage and decorating it with a personal arrangement of fish-scale shingles, spindlework along the porch, sawn-wood floral patterns, and perhaps a stained-glass window or two, all of which could be obtained at the nearest planing mill. Among the best examples of the "full" Queen Anne house still existing in East Bay towns are the elegant 1889 Boudrow House at 1836 Oxford Street in Berkeley; a relatively refined 1888 version by the Newsom brothers, at 1806 10th Avenue in East Oakland; the 1891 Fish Mansion in Benicia; and two superbly ornamented homes of the later '80s that face each other across the intersection of Willow and San Jose streets in Alameda (see cover photo). To look at these fantastic buildings is to stare in open-mouthed amazement. For better or for worse (depending on your point of view), the Victorian Era simply *had* to come to an end eventually. After all — where could it have gone from there?

*Willow and San Jose Streets, Alameda Tour B-22*

# Chapter 3

## The East Bay Comes of Age

Even before the "wondrous" nineteenth century ended, many Americans began to react against "foreign" influences in their art and culture and to turn instead, in their search for a stronger national identity, toward what they felt were more basic indigenous values. As has always been the case throughout recorded history, a certain fin de siècle feeling began to set in during the waning years of the century. During the 1890s, the growing popularity of the so-called Colonial Revival movement architecturally reflected this gradual shift in the public's mood. By 1901, when the Victorian Era officially ended, the Colonial Revival mode had replaced most of the remnants of European historicism in at least the common person's domestic architecture. House design began to conform (if loosely) to a pattern inspired by the eighteenth-century, late-Colonial-Era Georgian style. Columned porticos adorned the entrances of homes; Palladian windows were set into clapboarded or shingled walls. The most common variation of this style was a two-story "box" with decorative pilaster strips along each corner and a central dormer window projecting from a low-angled or "hipped" roof. Speculators and developers began to produce large numbers of such houses in the now-mushrooming residential sections that were growing up along the newly laid streetcar lines in older East Bay cities. Blocks of these houses were built in the flatlands of Oakland and Berkeley (many can still be seen in their original, unaltered state) and in many of the turn-of-the-century neighborhoods: the newly born Richmond; Alameda; Emeryville; Vallejo; and Benicia. Of the homebuilders who followed the Colonial Revival trend, the wealthier ones could afford such added amenities as Art Nouveau stained glass, diamond-pane leaded windows with beveled glass, friezes with carved wood or molded terra-cotta garlands, and a full two-story colonnade to lend an air of monumental dignity to their sumptuous abodes. The best-known East Bay Colonial Revival mansion is the Dunsmuir House, built in 1898 in the Oakland Hills near what is now Knowland State Park. Surrounded by magnificently kept grounds, it is owned by the City of Oakland, which uses it as a convention center and also opens it to the public for special events.[16] Some of the other noteworthy homes in this style are the Lindblom House at Hillegass and Parker streets in Berkeley (1898); the graceful McReary home on Durant Avenue in Berkeley (1904); a temple-like mansion at 1819 7th Avenue in East Oakland (1905), and a delightful, New England-inspired, neo-Georgian house at 1428 Union Street in Alameda (c. 1905).

During this same period in California, a new, popular movement arose in architecture that gave the building art in the Bay Area a unique and distinct flavor. Part of a wider "back to nature" trend in the nation as a whole, this movement developed an architectural style that, in its most common domestic form, became known as "California Craftsman." These houses were generally single- or one-and-a-half-story bungalows that had low, dormered roofs usually sloping toward the street, and wide windows to let in lots of light. The California Craftsman style rejected the affectation and "false" decoration of the Victorian Era, choosing instead an esthetic effect based on the use of "natural" materials (primarily, unpainted wood in its various forms — shingles, clapboarding, exposed beams at the roofline, and unadorned porch posts). For structural and esthetic purposes, other natural materials were also favored — for example, dressed stone for foundations or porch walls, and rough-looking klinker brick (rejects from kilns) on chimneys and often in pillars to support the wide, overhanging eaves. Because untreated wood paneling was used heavily — perhaps with a touch of Colonial Revival decorative carving in the wainscotting or along the fireplace mantel — interiors were usually quite dark. Colonial motifs often

*Dunsmuir House, Oakland Tour H-35*

existed in the form of exterior detail, as well — primarily, leaded glass in windows and Georgian dentils carved into projecting cornice lines above doors. These homes were meant to be designed and constructed by their owners, and indeed many were. Craftsman bungalows abounded throughout the East Bay, which was essentially their native ground. Among the best examples are a one-and-a-half-story home standing on the northwest corner of Cedar and Milvia streets in Berkeley (c. 1905); a very large house at 205 MacArthur Boulevard in North Oakland (1909);[17] and a rambling residence built by a Danish immigrant named Hjul at 705 Grand Avenue in Alameda (1905–1920).

*Hjul House, Alameda Tour A-28*

As charming and refreshing as the owner-built Craftsman home was, the creation of a truly unique, indigenous tradition required the special genius of the great local architects of that era. In fact, the so-called California bungalow (in all its various forms) actually gave many of the architectural giants of the turn-of-the-century East Bay the foundation for many of their early designs — giants like Bernard Maybeck, Julia Morgan, John Hudson Thomas, Ernest Coxhead, and John Galen Howard. All these immensely creative individuals were themselves influenced by and participants in a revolutionary new trend in domestic design that was based on the long, low-lying houses of a young, unorthodox prodigy from Chicago named Frank Lloyd Wright. Just before and after 1900, Wright developed a system of home design that completely opposed the vertical emphasis and applied ornamentation of the Victorian Era. Instead, it stressed clean, horizontal lines and large areas of glass in order to integrate the house with its physical surroundings — to blend in with its landscaping and to allow sunlight, breezes, and pleasing aromas from outside to enter the living quarters freely. Wright and his followers came to be known as the Prairie School of architecture, and most of the great architects practicing in the East Bay at that time adopted at least some of its design elements.

To be sure, these radical new ideas received opposition, primarily from architects who practiced in the various Period Revival modes, such as the ever-popular English Tudor Revival, which more than held its own with wealthy homebuilders of the early 1900s. This resistance to fundamental change (the

American architectural tradition of historic derivation had always been accepted) was expressed quite vociferously by Horace G. Simpson, a staunch advocate of Tudor Revival and a partner in the highly successful San Francisco firm of Simpson and Wood. In the February 1916 issue of the locally published professional magazine, *Architect and Engineer*, Simpson declared:

> *There is also a sort of style imported from the Middle West and consisting chiefly of plate glass and horizontal lines, which enjoys a wide vogue and a quite inexplicable reputation for originality. Without doubt our domestic architecture is suffering from the taint of egotism in the designers which causes them to express their own peculiarities rather than the uses of the building and personality of its occupants.*[18]

But such pompous criticism did not deter the innovative architects who borrowed from the Prairie School and added "their own peculiarities" to create the First Bay Tradition. Of all East Bay architects, the one most directly influenced by the Prairie style was John Hudson Thomas, a young man who had studied the techniques of Frank Lloyd Wright early in the twentieth century. The Loring House at 1730 Spruce Street in Berkeley, one of Thomas' early (1914) designs, bears a striking resemblance to Wright's most revolutionary designs of the same period. In two of Thomas' other well-known commissions, the Kelly House at 455 Wildwood Avenue in Piedmont (1910) and the Merrill House at 10 Hillcrest Court in Berkeley (1911), he mixed elements of the Prairie School (horizontal lines and wide, overhanging eaves) with his own interpretation of Califonria's Mediterranean and Bungalow modes.

Ernest Coxhead, an Englishman who came to the Bay Area in the late 1880s,[19] was truly one of the creators of the area's Brown Shingle movement. By adopting the building materials of the shingled cottages of his native land and combining them with his own unique design concepts and an admixture of Early American and English Renaissance motifs, Coxhead helped spur the local architectural effort that, in the early twentieth century, became known collectively as the First Bay Tradition. Two of Coxhead's designs, an early one and a late one, illustrate the range and variety that he expressed within the same basic

*Christian Science Church, Berkeley Tour G-1*

stylistic mode. The early design (1892–1894) was the Greenlease House, a brown shingle home at 1726 Santa Clara Street in Alameda,[20] which mixed seventeenth- and eighteenth-century details. His last shingled design (1906) was the boldly simple and forceful Torrey House at 10 Canyon Road in Berkeley.

Among those who led the ranks of the First Bay Tradition, the most prominent were two incredibly prolific yet diverse personalities: Bernard Maybeck and Julia Morgan. Born in 1862, Maybeck[21] was the son of a German woodcarver. He was virtually a hermit, and in many ways his work reflected more of the artist and craftsman than of the professional architect. Trained at the École des Beaux Artes in Paris in the 1880s, Maybeck moved to the Bay Area from New York in the early '90s.[22] At that time, the "back to nature" movement was just beginning, prompted by such groups as the Hillside Club in Berkeley, a gathering of artists, architects, and esthetes dedicated to the creation of natural order and beauty. Maybeck soon joined this club. He adapted the new form of the California bungalow to his own woodcraftsman's love of "earthy" materials and penchant for historic detail, thereby creating a personal form of architecture that was to influence his colleagues heavily for nearly forty years. Although no two of Maybeck's buildings are much alike, each radiates an enduring beauty achieved by the use of natural materials, the impressive arrangement of interior space, and (as with the designs of Wright, his contemporary) a harmony of line that makes each structure seem to be an integral part of its environment. These highly pleasing qualities of Maybeck's work can be seen readily in such outstanding examples as his Christian Science Church at Dwight and Bowditch in Berkeley (1910); his brown-shingled Town and Gown Club at Dana Street and Dwight Way in Berkeley (1899); and the "Swiss Chalet" he built in 1907 atop a prominent site in the Berkeley hills at 1325 Arch Street for University of California (U.C.) anthropology professor Charles Kroeber.[23] The Christian Science Church, generally considered to be Maybeck's masterpiece, displays all his great creative abilities to the utmost: it mixes elements of six historic styles and adroitly uses such modern "industrial" materials as poured concrete, asbestos tiles, and factory sash windows.

Julia Morgan was in every way the equal of Maybeck, her mentor and personal friend. Only now is she (rightfully) coming to be regarded as one of the great geniuses of twentieth-century American architecture; up until about ten years ago, the general public had hardly heard of her. An incredibly prolific and energetic professional, Morgan designed over 800 structures in her forty-odd years of active work,[24] ranging from William Randolph Hearst's San Simeon Castle to modest, single-story, Brown-Shingle-style bungalows. Born in 1872 and raised in Oakland, she received her degree from the École des Beaux Arts in 1902, the first female to graduate from that prestigious school.[25] Returning to the Bay Area, she immediately began working with the University of California Architect's Office under John Galen Howard, helping him design many of the Berkeley campus' Beaux Arts neo-Classical buildings, including the Greek Theater and the main University Library. By 1905, however, she began to break out on her own and design homes for wealthy clients in the nearby communities of the East Bay.

A fastidious and painstaking perfectionist, Morgan personally oversaw most of the details on the construction sites of her many projects. She handled the monumental proportions of the Beaux Arts tradition magnificently, but it is probably for the warm, intimate, and thoroughly livable qualities of her tastefully designed domestic architecture that she is most admired.

*Schneider-Kroeber House, Berkeley Tour B-14*

*St. John's Presbyterian Church, Berkeley Tour G-19*

The varied types of structures she designed throughout the East Bay bear witness to this great architect's amazing range. Her modest, Mediterranean-flavored Starr House at 216 Hampton Road in Piedmont (1911) contrasts dramatically with her impressively scaled, neo-Classic Hearst's Gymnasium for Women on the U.C. campus (1927); and her supreme exercise in the Craftsman mode, St. John's Presbyterian Church at Derby and College in Berkeley (1908), poses an equally effective contrast to the Italian-Renaissance-style City Club on Durant Avenue in Berkeley (1928), which conjures up images of Florentine splendor. Even a fleeting glimpse of such well-designed structures shows why Julia Morgan is considered a major creative force in the First Bay Tradition.

To be sure, many other highly creative local architects of that day helped shape the great twentieth-century Bay Area movement. John Galen Howard, the founder of the School of Architecture at U.C. Berkeley and best known as a master of Beaux Arts Classical-Revival designs, created many major buildings in that mode for the university: the University Library (1907–1917); the Hearst Mining Building (1902-1907); Wheeler Hall (1912-1917); and the Campanile 1914-1917), to name a few. But Howard could design innovative domestic structures, utilizing natural materials, just as capably. North Gate Hall (1906) and the Naval Architecture Building (built in 1914 and recently saved from demolition by the university) are his two greatest triumphs in this mode. In these First-Bay-Tradition buildings, he used the Brown Shingle mode to integrate the site and the interior space, and he handled it masterfully. Cloin Court, an early (1908) U.C. residence hall at Ridge Road, and his own house at 1401 LeRoy Avenue (1912) in the Berkeley foothills[26] further demonstrate Howard's abilities in this vein.

A great many other noteworthy architects contributed their talents, as well, to the First Bay Tradition. This movement continued on into the early 1930s, and before it ended it spread across the West and even managed to affect many of the architects practicing in the relatively staid and tradition-oriented East.

# Chapter 4

# Skyscrapers and Norman Villages

When it came to early-twentieth-century commercial architecture, the East Bay — like every other urban American community — followed the lead of a group of Chicago architects who created an entirely new type of structure: the skyscraper. As early as 1884, a young Windy City architect named William LeBaron Jenny hit upon the idea of using a steel framework as a "skeleton" to support the weight of the walls on a ten-story building for the Home Insurance Company. Thus was born the first high-rise office building. Over the next several years, Chicago architects expanded upon Jenny's idea and created ever-higher monuments to the triumph of modern engineering. The most successful of these "Chicago School" designers was Louis L. Sullivan, who coined a dictum that summed up the underlying concept behind all modern architecture: "Form follows function." Curiously, Sullivan and his contemporaries rarely followed this maxim completely; instead, they invariably chose to cloak their commercial structures in decorative historic motifs.

The architects who designed the first skyscrapers in the East Bay were no exception to this trend. Oakland's City Hall at Washington and 14th streets (1911–1914) probably best exemplifies the wedding of historically inspired exterior design and modern steel-frame construction. Standing sixteen stories tall on its metal skeleton, this Beaux Arts neo-Classic building bears such hallmarks of that style as massive columns across the entrance, allegorical sculpture in the form of eagles (symbolizing Government) perched atop the balcony above the third floor, and a set-back arrangement of the facade into several receding sections, topped by a Classic-Baroque-style octagonal clock tower.

Other good examples of steel-frame buildings with historic motifs are John Galen Howard's 315-foot-tall, Italian-Renaissance-style Campanile on the U.C. Berkeley campus (completed in 1917); Oakland's old Union Savings Building at 13th and Broadway, built in Renaissance style and one of the oldest skyscrapers in the East Bay (c. 1900); the French-Chateau-style Cathedral Building at the intersection of Broadway, Telegraph Avenue, and 16th street in Oakland (1913);[27] and the Colonial-Revival-style early high-rise at Addison and Shattuck in Berkeley, built for the Mason — MacDuffie Realty Company (1906).

During the Victorian Era, medieval Europe often was turned to for architectural inspiration. At the turn of the century, it became the source of another historically oriented style: the Romanesque Revival. During the early Middle Ages, Romanesque was the style of cathedrals and castles in Europe, prior to the rise of the Gothic style. New England architect Henry H. Richardson introduced it to America in its revived form in the 1870s, whereupon it was used frequently for churches, public buildings (such as city halls), large-scale commercial structures, and many of the wealthiest private homes.

The main features of Romanesque Revival were taken directly from its Old World origins: half-round brick or stone arches with molded rims above them; rusticated (or carved) stone at the foundation, often used for the entire facade; rounded or squared corner towers; and stained glass. Romanesque Revival did not reach California until 1886, when it was chosen for the style of the still-intact First Unitarian Church at 14th and Castro streets in Oakland. This impressively scaled structure (now a state historic site) has a huge, squared bell tower at one corner and a rounded turret at the other. It also has rusticated stone along the lower portion of its walls, a round-arched entrance, and some of the finest stained-glass windows to be found in the western United States. Aside from its architectural value, the church also played an important role in California's history: Bret Harte, Jack London, and Frank Norris all spent time there (but they

*Cathedral Building, Oakland Tour A-8*

*Old Southern Pacific Depot, Berkeley Tour K-2*

weren't always attending services). Isadora Duncan did one of her first public dance performances inside its walls, and the UNESCO chapter of the United Nations was founded in one of its meeting rooms in 1945.

The Romanesque mode quickly spread to other churches, such as Oakland's fortress-like First Baptist Church at 21st and Telegraph (1903–1906), and solid-stone First Christian Science Church (1899) at 17th and Franklin streets. Brick was used to construct the Romanesque-style Alameda City Hall at Alameda and Oak streets (1896), as well as such neo-Romanesque commercial buildings as the old Masonic Hall at Alameda Avenue and Park Street in Alameda (1890s), and the Barker Block at Shattuck Avenue and Dwight Way in Berkeley (1904).

Spanish California provided the material for an equally popular local movement: the Mission Revival. What began in the 1890s as simply renewed interest in the history and restoration of the largely ruined remains of California missions had, by the turn of the century, grown into a full-fledged architectural boom; and embellished versions of early Spanish missions went up all over California. St. Mark's Cathedral at Bancroft Way and Ellsworth Street in Berkeley (1902) and the Masonic Temple at 15th and Harrison in Oakland (1903) show the more impressive renderings of this style. The modified Mission form was even applied to railroad stations, such as the Southern Pacific Railway Depot at 3rd and University Avenue in Berkeley, built in 1913 and now a restaurant.

Another style that appeared in California around 1900 and remained popular into the 1930s was the Spanish Colonial Revival style, sometimes loosely referred to as the Mediterranean Revival. This mode, applied most commonly to private residences, borrowed heavily from the adobes and haciendas of Latin America and early California. It adapted such aspects of Mediterranean-style architecture as clay-tile roofs, open-beamed projecting balconies, and stucco-covered walls in pastel colors. Depending on a person's social status, individual versions of such houses could range from a lavish scale, such as the home that Ernest Coxhead designed for Phoebe Hearst at 2368 LeConte Avenue in Berkeley (1900) and the finely ornamented Spanish Colonial house at 320 Hampton Road in Piedmont (c. 1920),[28] to the mass-produced, Spanish-Colonial-style "adobe" bungalows along the 600 block of East 20th Street in Oakland (1920s). The influence of the California Mediterranean Revival movement became so far-flung that it spread as far east as Kansas City, Missouri. There, incongruous-looking Mission Revival shopping centers of the 1920s sport false bell towers and mock-adobe walls.

The trend of adapting past architectural styles to create a desired historic effect reached a zenith in the 1920s and '30s. Indeed, the years between the end of

World War I and the beginning of World War II can be called the era of the Period Revivals. Reproducing specific historic styles fairly accurately, by and large, Period Revival buildings catered to the longing of most Americans for a sense of cultural and historic identity, an identity that was becoming increasingly difficult to maintain in a rapidly changing society.

Although the homebuilder of this time had access to an almost limitless variety of Period Revival styles, a few modes were used most commonly — Georgian Colonial, English seventeenth-century Jacobean, French Provincial, Italian Gothic, and the immensely popular English Half-Timbered, or Tudor Revival. Many of the great First Bay Tradition architects were equally adept at designing Period Revival houses for clients who desired their own personal bit of the past. Julia Morgan rendered a fine example of a Georgian Colonial home on a grand scale at 1 Eucalyptus Road in Berkeley (1919). And her Women's City Club at 2315 Durant Avenue in Berkeley (1927) is a magnificent exercise in the Italian Gothic mode. John Hudson Thomas helped materialize a wealthy client's fantasies by designing a medieval Spanish castle whose fortified walls overlook the entire Bay from its craggy site at 2900 Buena Vista Way in Berkeley hills (1928).

Tudor and Jacobean Revival houses abound throughout the East Bay, but some of the most impessive examples can be found in Piedmont. The whitewashed, early-Jacobean-style Uhl House at 304 Hillside (c. 1913), and the incredibly huge Tudor Revival mansion at 55 Sea View Drive (c. 1920) reflect the ostentation of many of these homes.

Occasionally, Period Revival architects ignored rigid historic accuracy in favor of humor and spontaneity. The Half-Timberd mode was the style most often chosen for this purpose, and the usually amusing result was dubbed the Hansel and Gretel, or Mother Goose style. Thornberg (sometimes called Normandy) Village, designed in 1927 by the artist William R. Yelland and situated between 1817 and 1839 Spruce Street in Berkeley, provides an outstanding illustration of the extremes to which this so-called style could be carried. Crazily exaggerated sagging roofs and whimsical, carved-wood gargoyles give the impression of a living Walt Disney cartoon.

*Thornberg (Normandy) Village, Berkeley Tour B-1*

# Chapter 5

## From Big Bust to Baby Boom

At the same time that most private residences were imitating older styles of architecture, a relatively new and bold type of design was being used on commercial and public buildings of the 1920s and '30s — Art Deco. Originating in France as an outgrowth of the curved lines and geometric shapes of the earlier Art Nouveau movement, Art Deco was spurred by the discovery of the fabulous art treasures found in the tomb of the Pharaoh Tutankhamun during a 1922 expedition to Egypt. In that sense, Art Deco began as a sort of modified Egyptian Revival style, using figurines in profile as friezes and brightly colored glazed tile as decorative surfaces. It also borrowed heavily from Babylonian (stepped pyramidal shapes and projecting slabs on wall surfaces), Byzantine (mosaic panels), and even Classical architecture (stylized pilasters at corners and occasional columns flanking entranceways).

But at least as important as what Art Deco borrowed was what it introduced: striking geometric shapes and patterns, such as zigzag friezes and fountain-spray motifs as finials; many "modern" industrial materials like chrome, aluminum, and plastic panels, used primarily for interior decoration on stair railings, sculpture, and light fixtures; and a celebration of life in the modern industrial world, using panels, friezes, and mosaics to depict working men and women in various roles, often amid the machines and tools of twentieth-century technology.

Many of the Art Deco motifs were applied to skyscrapers of the '20s and '30s. Oakland's Financial Center Building at 14th and Franklin streets (early 1930s) is a case in point, with its facade of alternating vertical slabs, a frosted-glass hanging light fixture set in aluminum framing above the door, and Babylonian rams' heads at both corners of the entrance arch. There is no better example of the Art Deco Era's use of glazed terra cotta in the East Bay than I. Magnin's Department Store at 20th and Broadway in Oakland (1931).[29] The facade is sheathed in gleaming green tile and black marble.

The Berkeley Public Library at Shattuck Avenue and Kittridge Street, designed in 1930 by the great East Bay Art Deco architect James Plachek, presents an imposing facade of Babylonian-style slabs, zigzag friezes around the top of each wall, and large, eye-level, incised panels with ancient, garbed figures depicting Culture and Learning. The old clothing store now known as the Oakland Floral Depot, located at the northeast corner of 19th and Telegraph streets (c. 1930), has a marvelously flamboyant design of dark-blue glazed tile, topped by cast-aluminum fountain-spray motifs.

But the ultimate of the Art-Deco-style buildings were the great movie "palaces" of that era, and Oakland still possesses two of the finest ever built on the West Coast. The Fox Theater, at the southwest corner of 19th and Telegraph (1928), is sadly empty at this time and faces an uncertain future. Nonetheless, it still retains an air of delightful fantasy and awe about it, with its Hindu-style tower, ornate Islamic inlaid tilework, and its heavy scrollwork and curved, stainless-steel pillars around the box office and entranceway.

The Art Deco style reached its East Bay zenith, however, in Oakland's Paramount Theater. Designed by the renowned San Francisco architect Timothy Pfleuger (of Miller and Pfleuger) in 1931, this huge building, located at 21st and Broadway, recently was restored and reopened. Now it houses the Oakland Symphony. In originally making this theater a showpiece of everything Art Deco had to offer and then some, no expense was spared. The front entrance has a fifty-foot-high marquee, flanked by a huge, Byzantine-style mosaic of two "puppet-masters" controlling smaller figures depicting various roles in the entertainment industry. To stand in the lobby is to be almost overwhelmed by the

*Public Library, Berkeley Tour F-18*

array of stunning decorative details. These range from Egyptian-style friezes of nearly nude female figures and polished-chrome railings to a gigantic, phallic-shaped, frosted-glass light fixture above the entrance doors. Indeed, as many visitors have been overheard to say, it is all almost "too much." But it is fascinating nonetheless.

During the Depression years of the mid and late '30s, the federal government got nto the act: under the New Deal's Works Progress Administration program (the W.P.A.), the government built its own version of Art Deco structures. These buildings were labeled, appropriately enough, "W.P.A. Moderne," since they were a modified version of the Streamlined Moderne mode. Streamlined Moderne was itself essentially a "cleaned-up" version of Art Deco, emphasizing the structure's geometric lines and masses rather than adding on a wealth of decoration. Streamlined Moderne retained such early-Art-Deco elements as zigzag friezes and glazed terra-cotta tile, but added innovations like curved corners, porthole windows, and thick glass "bricks" set into wall surfaces. The W.P.A. Moderne style focused on the working class; and W.P.A. artists used murals, mosaics, and bas-relief sculpture to show the everyday activities of the common people for whom these buildings were designed. The use of heavy concrete pilasters between windows and of wide friezes along the roofline revealed the strongly neo-Classic bent of W.P.A. Moderne.

One charactcristic W.P.A. Moderne edifice is El Cerrito High School's main building at Ashbury and Eureka avenues. Designed with heavily Classic lines, it was constructed (1939) of poured concrete. With their sweeping lines ending in curved corners and prominent relief-sculptures extolling the virtues of art and learning, Berkeley High School's shop wing (1938–1940) and Florence T. Schwimley Auditorium (1942–1946) are typical W.P.A. structures. These buildings, located on Addison Street between Milvia and Grove, were designed by the firm of Gutterson and Corlett.

Two other outstanding Moderne buildings that were built with W.P.A. funds and designed by Charles Plachek are the Alameda County Courthouse at 14th and Lakeside in Oakland (1935), and the Farm Credit Building at Milvia and Center streets in Berkeley (1938). Both combine neo-Classic, plastered facades

*Paramount Theatre, Oakland Tour A-2*

*Berkeley High School Auditorium, Berkeley Tour F-16*

and stepped-pyramidal forms. In the later '30s and '40s, Streamlined Moderne was quite popular for small-scale commerical establishments and the most avant-garde homes. The Balaam Brothers' store, at 1350 Powell Street in Emeryville (1940),[30] is an exaggeration of this mode, with its sharply rounded corners and an outsized porthole window. The Anthony House at the intersection of LeConte and Hearst Streets in Berkeley (1939) takes full advantage of its triangular-shaped lot: its boldly curving design resembles a captain's bridge on an oceanliner. Many elements of the Streamlined Moderne remained in use through the late '40s and even well into the '50s.

With the end of World War II and the onslaught of mass-produced culture that resulted from the ensuing baby boom, American architecture turned severely away from the historically oriented styles and decorative quality to which it had adhered for so long. The decline of individual craftsmanship, the rising costs of construction, and a growing desire to be surrounded with the newest and most "modern" structures possible led to the growth and development of an architectural esthetic that held strictly to Louis Sullivan's famous dictum. Form followed function, and local, national, and international architects brought the East Bay new forms of building design: the Bauhaus skyscraper, the Corporate International style, the Pavilion mode, Concrete Brutalism, the ranch house, the post-and-beam house, and, most recently, the cutout vertical box. All these belong more to the realm of contemporary architecture than of historic architecture.

*Anthony House, Berkeley Tour C-20*

Before we explore existing historic buildings in the East Bay, let's hear a word or two in defense of the study and appreciation of the structures described in this book.

Many architectural critics tend to denigrate most of the buildings erected in America in the nineteenth and early twentieth centuries as "derivative" architecture — that is, as merely modified or recycled versions of European and Asian prototypes. If this label is accurate, then all of western architecture, for the last 2,000 years, is just as derivative. The Romans borrowed (and sometimes copied directly) from the Greeks, whom they conquered and assimilated. The early-medieval Romanesque style owed many of its motifs to the architecture of Imperial Rome. The Gothic cathedral combined elements of the earlier Romanesque with the Islamic invention of the pointed arch. Renaissance architecture was essentially a revival of the design principles of Ancient Greece and Rome, in modified form. Colonial and Early American buildings relied heavily on older European models. Even such "fathers" of early modern architecture as Frank Lloyd Wright and Bernard Maybeck appropriated many of their most characteristic motifs from the centuries-old traditions of Japanese domestic architecture. In the final analysis, the value of an old building doesn't really depend on whether it conforms to some modern critic's arbitrary esthetic standard, but rather on whether it has the enduring power to show us, to help us understand, indeed to let us *feel* what the world was like for those who came before.

# Notes

1   Walter Bean, *California: An Interpretive History* (New York: McGraw-Hill, 1968), p. 6.

2   Kurt Bauer and Hugo Rudinger, *Architecture of the California Missions* (Berkeley: University of California Press, 1958), p. 194.

3   Elinore Richey, *The Ultimate Victorians* (Berkeley: Howell-North Books, 1971), p. 14.

4   *Ibid.*, p. 143.

5   Augusta Fink and Morley Maer, *Adobes in the Sun* (San Francisco: Chronicle Books, 1972), p. 79.

6   *Ibid.*, p. 136.

7   Richey, *Ultimate Victorians*, p. 14.

8   Joseph Baker, *History of Alameda County* (Chicago: S.J. Clarke Co., 1914).

9   Richey, *Ultimate Victorians*, p. 32.

10  David Gebhard *et al.*, *A Guide to Architecture in San Francisco and Northern California* (Santa Barbara, Calif.: Peregrine Smith, Inc., 1971), p. 308.

11  *Ibid.*, p. 295.

12  Richey, *Ultimate Victorians*, p. 40.

13  *Ibid.*, p. 84.

14  Gebhard, *Guide to Architecture*, pp. 194–295.

15  Richey, *Ultimate Victorians*, p. 95.

16  *Ibid.*, p. 135.

17  Gebhard, *Guide to Architecture*, p. 289.

18  *Architect and Engineer*, San Francisco, February 1917 issue, p. 53. Available at the Environmental Design Library, University of California, Berkeley.

19  Leslie Freudenheim and Elisabeth Sussman, *Building with Nature: Roots of the San Francisco Bay Region Style* (Santa Barbara, Calif.: Peregrine Smith, Inc.), p. 36.

20  Gebhard, *Guide to Architecture*, p. 306.

21  Esther McCoy, *Five California Architects* (New York: Reinhold Publishing Co., 1960) p. 2.

22  *Ibid.*, p. 5.

23  Gebhard, *Guide to Architecture*, p. 244.

24  Douglas Davis, "Women as Architects," *Newsweek*, 7 march 1977, p. 79.

25  Richey, *Ultimate Victorians*, p. 166.

26  Gebhard, *Guide to Architecture*, p. 248.

27  *Ibid.*, p. 285. Also the *Oakland Revisited* exhibit at the Oakland Museum, March 1977 to May 1977.

28  Gebhard, *Guide to Architecture*, p. 306.

29  *Ibid.*, p. 285.

30  *Ibid.*, p. 275.

# Part II

## Major Styles of Historic Architecture in the East Bay

*Old State Capitol Building, Benicia Tour- 23*

## Spanish and Mexican Era: 1776–1848

1 — Spanish Colonial Styles, c. 1790s–1850s

     Dating from the Spanish and Mexican periods of early California history, these structures include the Mission San Jose and a handful of adobe houses. The style is basically thick adobe walls, latticed windows, and post-and-beam construction on overhanging rooflines. Later adobes, like the Martinez Adobe on the John Muir Estate in Martinez, often have "Monterey"-style second-floor balconies.

Drawing 1:   Spanish Colonial Style
                  c. 1790s–1850s

SQUARE-LATTICED WINDOWS

HIPPED ROOF

"MONTEREY"-STYLE DOUBLE-BALCONIED VERANDA

## Victorian Era: 1837–1901

2 — Greek Revival, c. 1840s–1860s

     A relatively small number of Greek Revival structures remain from the settlements that came with the Gold Rush Era. These buildings share the basic characteristic of a front resembling a Greek temple, with a triangular, pedimented roofline and columns or pillars across the facade. California's best example of this style is the Old State Capitol in Benicia, which has a refined, neo-Classic design.

Drawing 2:   Greek Revival
               c. 1840s–1860s

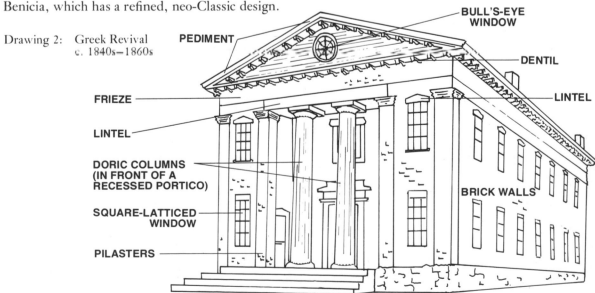

PEDIMENT

BULL'S-EYE WINDOW

DENTIL

LINTEL

FRIEZE

LINTEL

DORIC COLUMNS (IN FRONT OF A RECESSED PORTICO)

BRICK WALLS

SQUARE-LATTICED WINDOW

PILASTERS

3 — Gothic Revival, c. 1840s– ±1900

Gothic Revival, the first truly Victorian style, borrowed from the Gothic churches and houses of medieval Europe. The main features of this style are pointed, arched windows and/or doors; high-peaked gables; and, usually, lacy trim in the form of bargeboards on the edges of gables, and tracery carving over doors and windows. Many wooden and brick churches throughout the East Bay used this style, which, as in the St. Francis de Sales Cathedral in Oakland, usually has tall, tapering spires and stained-glass windows. A handful of Gothic Revival houses still stand in the area. The best example is Oakland's Mosswood Cottage.

Drawing 3:  Gothic Revival
          c. 1840s–1900

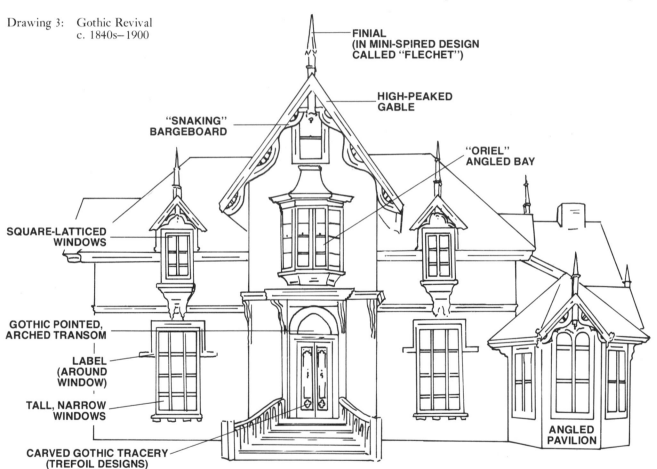

FINIAL
(IN MINI-SPIRED DESIGN
CALLED "FLECHET")

HIGH-PEAKED
GABLE

"SNAKING"
BARGEBOARD

"ORIEL"
ANGLED BAY

SQUARE-LATTICED
WINDOWS

GOTHIC POINTED,
ARCHED TRANSOM

LABEL
(AROUND
WINDOW)

TALL, NARROW
WINDOWS

CARVED GOTHIC TRACERY
(TREFOIL DESIGNS)

ANGLED
PAVILION

4 — False-Front "Pioneer" House, c. 1860– ±1890

These early-Victorian wood-frame houses (often called cottages) resemble the New England ones that many of the pioneer settlers had left behind them, but in addition these houses have a rectangular, flat extension of the facade above the roofline. The term "Pioneer box" refers to houses that are similar but lack the false front and usually have a pedimented or hipped roof. The decorative trim on such houses consists of hoods or "shelf molding" above the doors and windows, and, often, of brackets along the cornice line below the false front. Pioneer houses often also have raised basements, below the main floor. Berkeley's Oceanview neighborhood has an excellent example on 5th Street.

Drawing 4: False-Front "Pioneer" House
c. 1860–1890

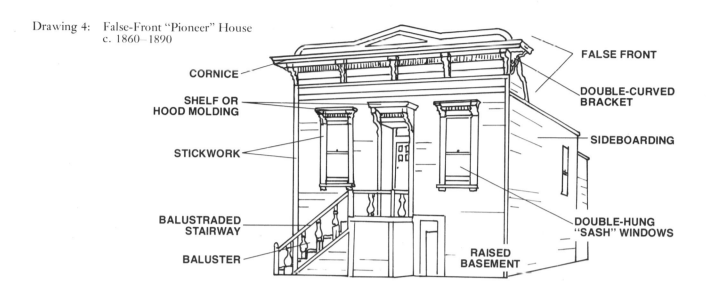

CORNICE

SHELF OR
HOOD MOLDING

STICKWORK

BALUSTRADED
STAIRWAY

BALUSTER

FALSE FRONT

DOUBLE-CURVED
BRACKET

SIDEBOARDING

DOUBLE-HUNG
"SASH" WINDOWS

RAISED
BASEMENT

5 — Bracketed Italianate House

This mode was one of the most popular and therefore most numerous of all the Victorian styles. Bracketed Italiate homes borrowed Italian Renaissance motifs — for example, tall, narrow, round-arched windows; columned porticos; low-hipped roofs; and, often, quoins at the corner. The houses invariably are made of wood, with double-curved brackets on the cornice and angled or slanted bay windows. The Anthony House in Alameda is a superb example.

Drawing 5: Bracketed Italianate
c. 1865–1890

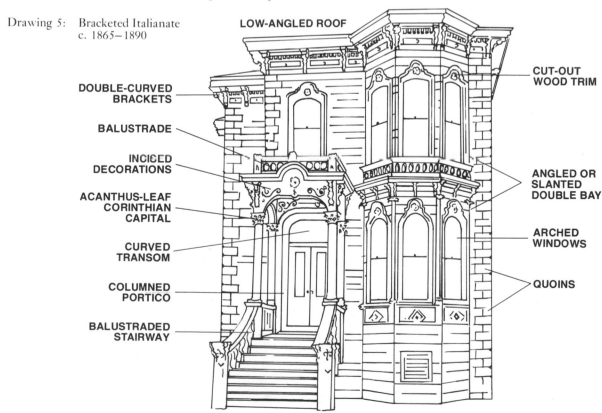

LOW-ANGLED ROOF

DOUBLE-CURVED
BRACKETS

BALUSTRADE

INCISED
DECORATIONS

ACANTHUS-LEAF
CORINTHIAN
CAPITAL

CURVED
TRANSOM

COLUMNED
PORTICO

BALUSTRADED
STAIRWAY

CUT-OUT
WOOD TRIM

ANGLED OR
SLANTED
DOUBLE BAY

ARCHED
WINDOWS

QUOINS

### 6 — Raised-Basement Cottage, c. 1865–±1885

Similar to Pioneer houses, these homes have Italianate-style trim, triangular pediments in the roofline, and raised basements. Less ornate versions are often called "workingman's cottages." A good example stands at Dana and Parker streets in Berkeley.

Drawing 6:   Raised-Basement Cottage (Italianate Style)
c. 1865–1885

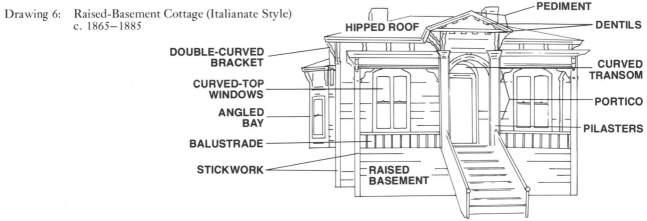

### 7 — Italianate Villa, c. 1860–±1885

These large, often mansion-sized homes resemble the Bracketed Italianate style, but also have a squared tower or cupola above the roofline. Generally more ornate than their less ostentatious counterparts, they usually have triangular pediments on the roofline and/or porch and very ornately decorated porticos, as well as quoining at the corners. The Pardee Mansion in Oakland is one of the best remaining illustrations in the East Bay.

Drawing 7:   Italianate Villa
c. 1860–1885

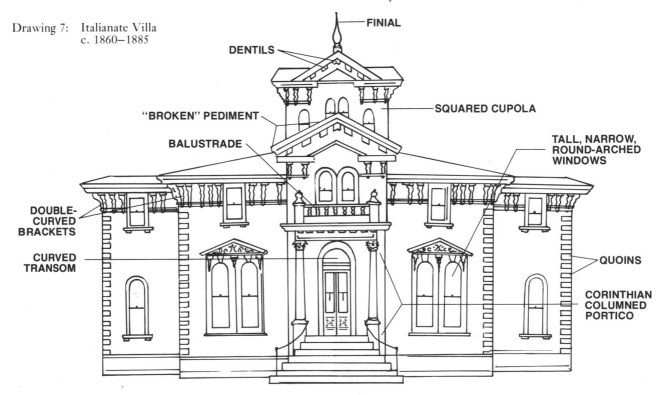

8 — Stick Style, c. 1870–±1895

Stick-style houses have a basically squared, vertical structure with strips of wood planking along the corners and above the windows and doorways (stickwork). The bay windows and tall porticos are squared or boxy, and brackets are usually at 90-degree angles. This mode is the simplest and least ornate-looking of all the later Victorian styles. A good example can be found at 750 Pacific Street in Alameda.

Drawing 8:  Stick Style
c. 1870–1895

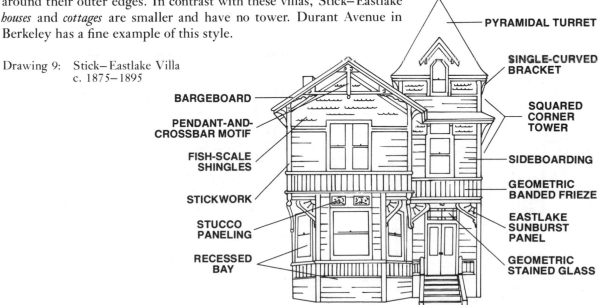

9 — Stick–Eastlake Villa, c. 1875–±1895

These imposing square-towered houses combine stickwork trim and vertical lines with Eastlake decorative motifs (borrowed from the English designer, Charles Eastlake): carved or incised floral panels, machine-cut geometric friezes, and sunburst panels. Stained-glass windows also are common, generally with "geometric," multicolored panes around their outer edges. In contrast with these villas, Stick–Eastlake *houses* and *cottages* are smaller and have no tower. Durant Avenue in Berkeley has a fine example of this style.

Drawing 9:  Stick–Eastlake Villa
c. 1875–1895

10 — Queen Anne Style, c. 1880–1900

This style was the Victorian Era's last and most ornate style. Exuberant wooden confections combine numerous motifs from earlier Victorian styles, such as bargeboards along high-peaked gables; stickwork; sunburst panels; stained-glass windows; and cut-out floral panels with such Queen Anne elements as spindles on the porch, fish-scale shingles, "scenic" stained-glass windows, and recessed corner bays. The Queen Anne cottage has most of these features but no tower. The large Queen Anne house or "towered villa" has rounded corner towers topped by spires, most commonly in a "witch's-hat" shape. The Boudrow House in Berkeley is a superb illustration.

Note: Victorian buildings often combine elements of two or more distinct styles in one design, thus creating "Queen Anne/Eastlake" or "Stick/Italianate" styles.

Drawing 10:  Queen Anne Tower House
c. 1880–1900

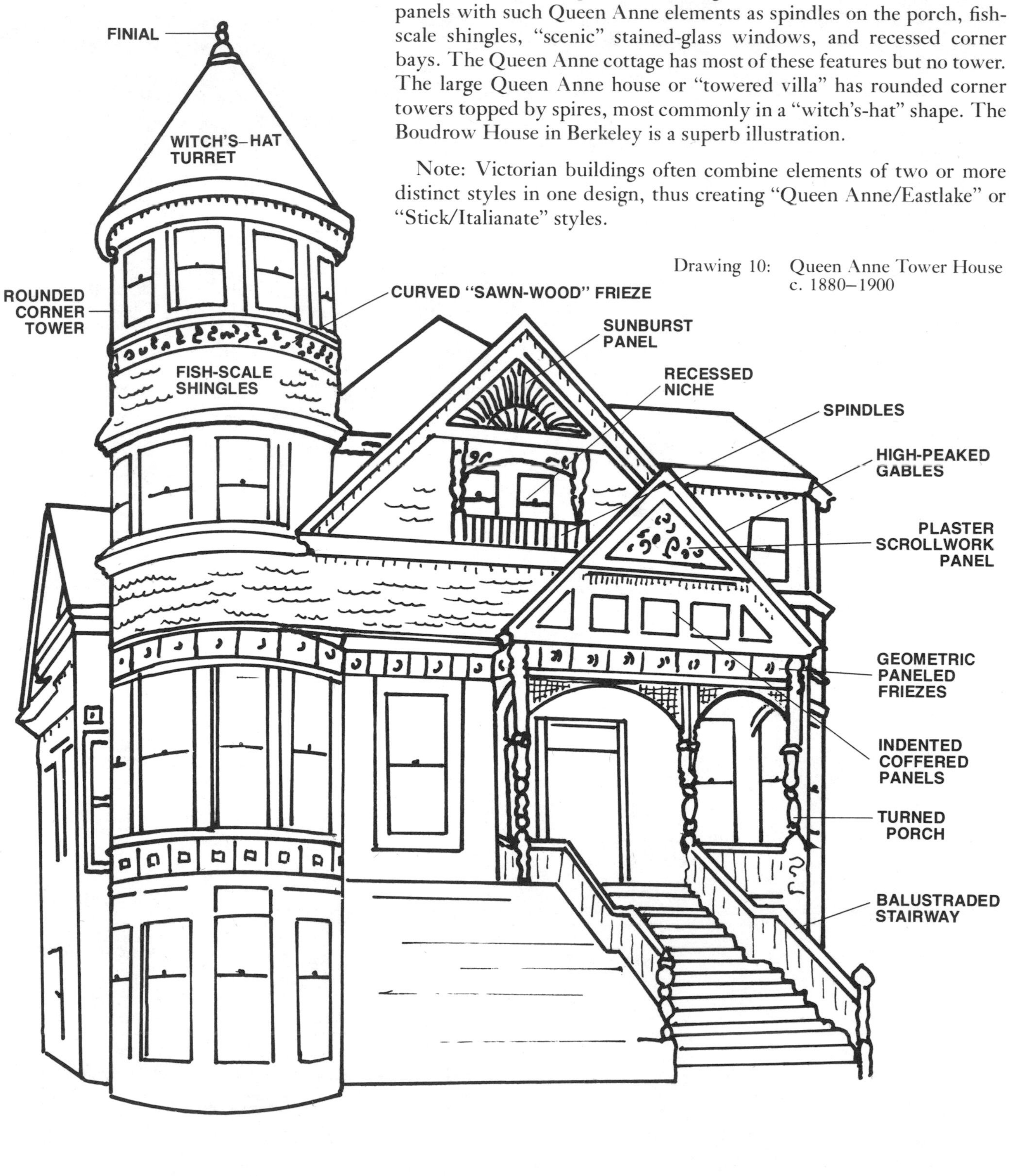

FINIAL

WITCH'S–HAT TURRET

ROUNDED CORNER TOWER

CURVED "SAWN-WOOD" FRIEZE

SUNBURST PANEL

RECESSED NICHE

SPINDLES

HIGH-PEAKED GABLES

PLASTER SCROLLWORK PANEL

FISH-SCALE SHINGLES

GEOMETRIC PANELED FRIEZES

INDENTED COFFERED PANELS

TURNED PORCH

BALUSTRADED STAIRWAY

## Transitional Era: c. 1890–1915

11 — Romanesque Revival, c. 1886– ±1915

Taken from the heavy stone structures of early medieval Europe, this style was used primarily for churches and commercial buildings. The walls are of thick, "rusticated" stone or red brick, and the rounded arches usually have concentric ridges or rims around their outer edges. Churches in the Romanesque Revival style invariably have squared and/or rounded corner towers, semicircular apses set into their walls, and large stained-glass windows (often, these are round in shape and are called "rose" windows). A fine example of a church in this style is the Christian Science Church at 17th and Franklin streets in downtown Oakland.

Drawing 11: Romanesque Revival
c. 1886–1915

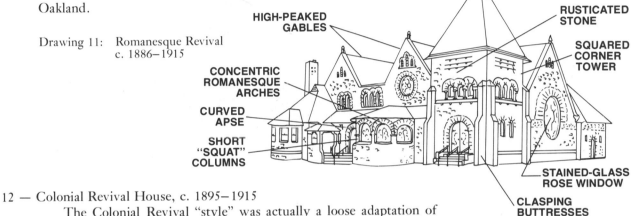

12 — Colonial Revival House, c. 1895–1915

The Colonial Revival "style" was actually a loose adaptation of various Early American styles and motifs. The most popular form of this style was the boxy, hipped-roof Colonial Revival house, which generally was decorated with: Palladian windows; pilasters at the corners; clapboarding and/or shingling on the facade; leaded- and/or stained-glass windows; and columned porticos, often topped with balustrades. The McReary House on Durant Avenue in Berkeley exemplifies this style.

Drawing 12: Colonial Revival House
c. 1895–1915

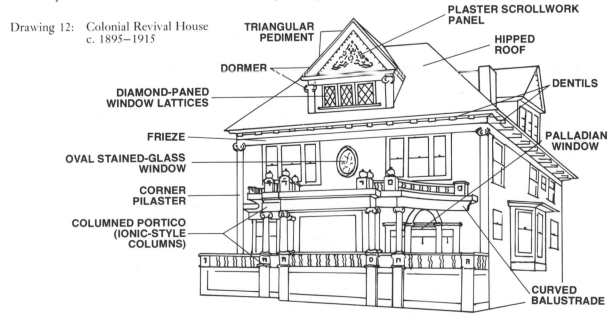

13 — High-Peaked Colonial Revival House, c. 1895–1915

      This transitional form of the Colonial Revival house, has a steeply pitched main gable; slanting dormers on the sides; small corner porticos; balustraded or Palladian windows in the gable; and shingling on the upper surfaces and clapboarding on the lower ones. A house on Bonita Street in Berkeley shows this style effectively.

Drawing 13:   High-Peaked Colonial Revival
c. 1895–1915

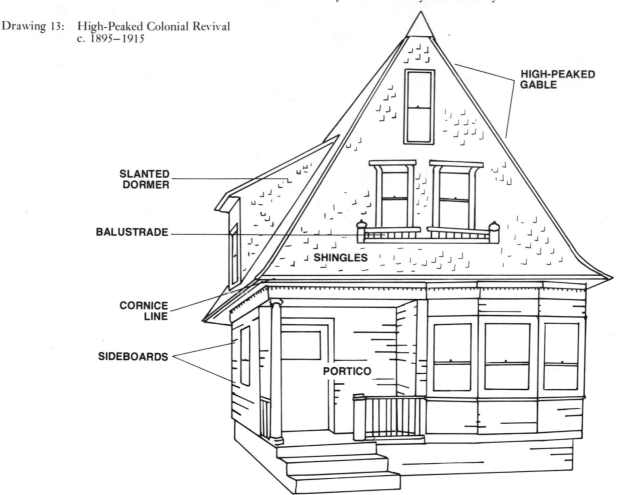

HIGH-PEAKED GABLE

SLANTED DORMER

BALUSTRADE

SHINGLES

CORNICE LINE

SIDEBOARDS

PORTICO

14 — Craftsman Bungalow, c. 1890–±1920

      These modest-sized houses (the word "bungalow" refers to a one- or a one-and-a-half-story house) have a rustic, woodcrafted look about them that comes from their use of natural materials. They generally have roofs sloping towards the street, with a dormer window in the middle; exposed beaming along the eaves; brown-shingled walls; and wood, stone, or brick pillars along the front porch. The owners themselves often were the designers. A typical example of a Craftsman bungalow is located at Milvia and Cedar streets in Berkeley.

    Note: The Brown Shingle and First Bay Tradition styles combine the materials and construction techniques of Craftsman bungalows with each architect's own original design features. As a result, each First Bay Tradition building is unique.

Drawing 14: Craftsman Bungalow
c. 1890–1920

**CENTRAL DORMER**

**SLOPING ROOFLINE WITH OVERHANGING EAVES**

**UNPEELED REDWOOD LOGS**

**EXPOSED RAFTERS**

**OVERLAPPING CLAPBOARDS**

15 — Beaux Arts Neo-Classic, c. 1890– ±1925

Originating in Paris at the École des Beaux Arts, this school of architecture used neo-Classic Renaissance motifs, usually on large public buildings built of stone or brick and constructed with steel frames. The facades invariably have receding wings (alternating planes), and are decorated with allegorical or symbolic sculptures and sometimes inscriptions. John Galen Howard's Hearst Mining Building, on the U.C. campus, is a superb example.

Drawing 15: Beaux Arts
c. 1890–1925

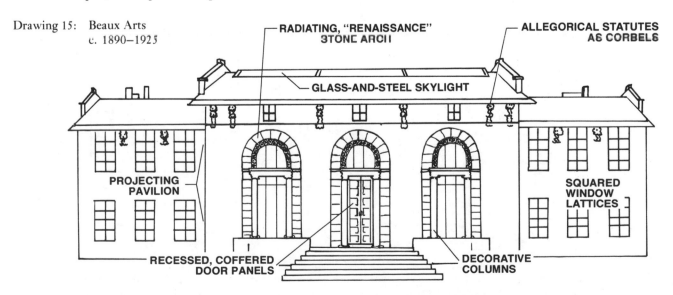

**RADIATING, "RENAISSANCE" STONE ARCH**

**ALLEGORICAL STATUTES AS CORBELS**

**GLASS-AND-STEEL SKYLIGHT**

**PROJECTING PAVILION**

**SQUARED WINDOW LATTICES**

**RECESSED, COFFERED DOOR PANELS**

**DECORATIVE COLUMNS**

Drawing 16:   Mission Revival
              c. 1900–1940

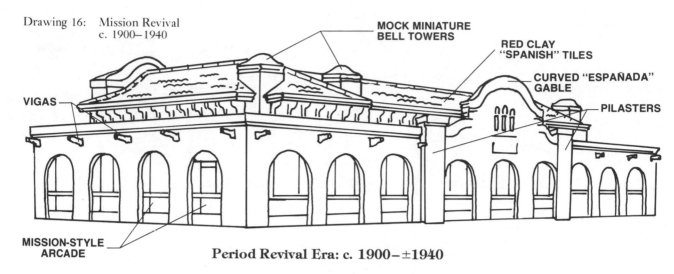

MOCK MINIATURE
BELL TOWERS

RED CLAY
"SPANISH" TILES

CURVED "ESPAÑADA"
GABLE

PILASTERS

VIGAS

MISSION-STYLE
ARCADE

**Period Revival Era: c. 1900–±1940**

16 — Mission Revival Styles, c. 1900–1940

Several historic styles were adapted from the various Mediterranean cultures, including Italian, Spanish, and Spanish Colonial styles. Mediterranean styles often were used on bungalows, and the major characteristics are pastel-colored stucco walls; round-arched windows and/or doors; and red clay-tile roofs. One of the most popular Mediterranean Revival styles in California was the Mission Revival, which used mock bell towers, curved española gables, exposed rafter beams (vigas), and usually an arcade along one or more sides. The old Southern Pacific Railroad Depot in Berkeley exemplifies this style.

Drawing 17:   Tudor Revival
              c. 1910–1940

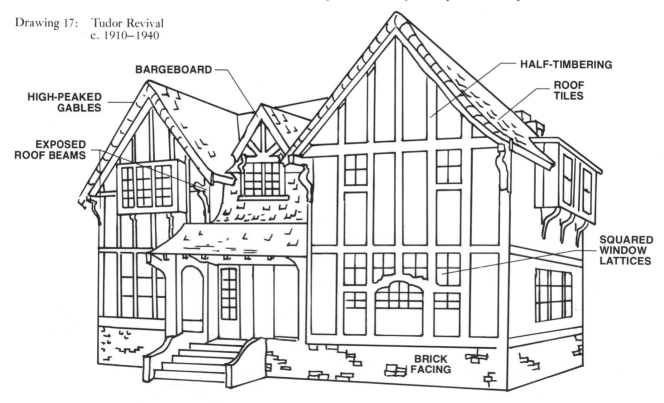

BARGEBOARD

HALF-TIMBERING

ROOF
TILES

HIGH-PEAKED
GABLES

EXPOSED
ROOF BEAMS

SQUARED
WINDOW
LATTICES

BRICK
FACING

17 — Tudor Revival Style, c. 1910–1940

The most popular Period Revival style for well-to-do home builders, Tudor Revival was borrowed from sixteenth-century house designs. The prominent features are the high-peaked gables and half-timbered facade; leaded-glass windows, bargeboards, and brick facing are also common. A nice example is located at 35 Parkside Avenue in Berkeley.

Drawing 18:  Georgian Revival
           c. 1910–1940

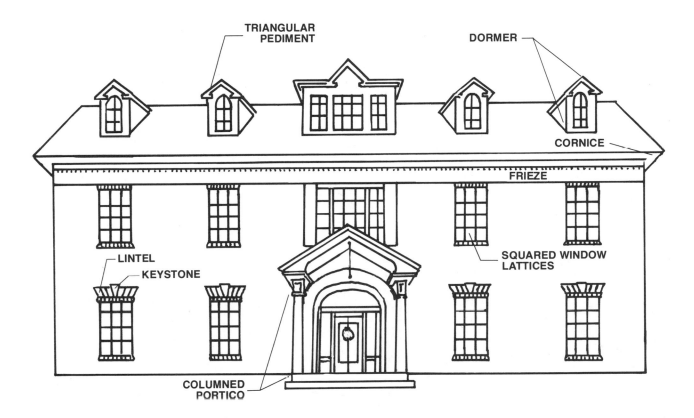

18 — Georgian Revival Style, c. 1910–±1940

More historically "correct" than their Colonial Revival predecessors, these buildings (usually homes or churches, sometimes commercial structures) essentially copied the American Georgian Colonial style. They have either gambrel (double-angled) or high-peaked gables, latticed windows with shutters, dormers in the roof, and pedimented porticos in front of the entryway. Lintels above windows and Palladian doorways and/or windows were sometimes used, as well. Julia Morgan's fine design for a house at 1 Eucalyptus Road in Berkeley shows this style very well.

**Early Modern Era: c. 1906–1950**

19 — Prairie Style, c. 1906–±1930

Sometimes called Prairie School, this style was derived from an early prototype design that Frank Lloyd Wright published in the *Ladies' Home Journal* in 1906. Used almost exclusively on houses around the East Bay, the Prairie style is distinguished by its plain, rectangular surfaces, horizontal overall lines, and flat or low-pitched roofs with wide, extending eaves. The facades of these houses are stucco, and simple, geometric stucco patterns were set within the chimney and/or porch and rectangular panels in the window panes, as well as often in panels set between the windows. One of the prime examples in the area is John Hudson Thomas' Loring House on Spruce Street in Berkeley.

Drawing 19:   Prairie Style
            c. 1906–1930

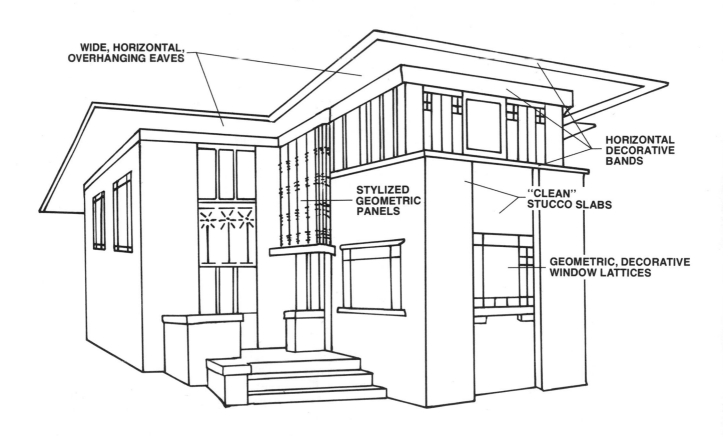

WIDE, HORIZONTAL, OVERHANGING EAVES

HORIZONTAL DECORATIVE BANDS

STYLIZED GEOMETRIC PANELS

"CLEAN" STUCCO SLABS

GEOMETRIC, DECORATIVE WINDOW LATTICES

20 — Art Deco and Streamlined Moderne Styles, c. 1925–1950

The Moderne structure was designed to suggest the new, "clean" design of a technical twentieth-century society, with perhaps a heavy dose of the exotic thrown in. In the Art Deco or Zigzag Moderne style, the entry was usually ornate, and the facade, with its projecting vertical slabs, was decorated with Egyptian, Babylonian, Aztec, Islamic, and/or Hindu motifs. The Streamlined Moderne was "cleaned up" Art Deco — curved edges, and, across the facade, straight horizontal lines and the use of such modern industrial materials as reinforced concrete, glass bricks, and aluminum. The Alameda Theater, designed by Pfleuger and Miller, is an excellent example of the Art Deco style with Streamlined Moderne elements.

Drawing 20:  Zigzag Moderne
c. 1925–1950

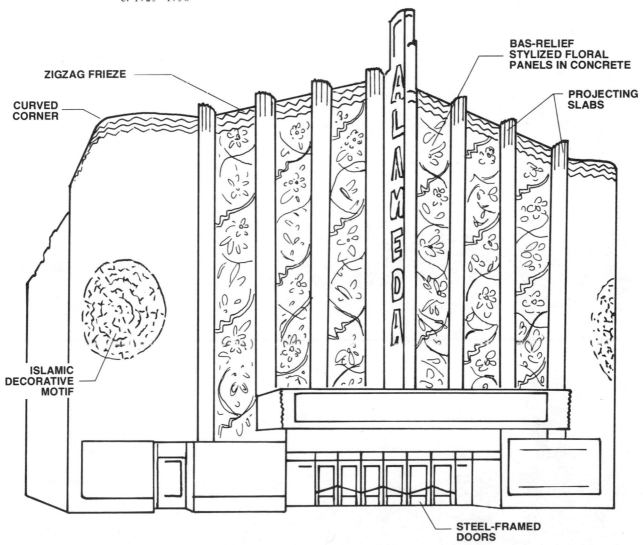

BAS-RELIEF
STYLIZED FLORAL
PANELS IN CONCRETE

PROJECTING
SLABS

ZIGZAG FRIEZE

CURVED
CORNER

ISLAMIC
DECORATIVE
MOTIF

STEEL-FRAMED
DOORS

# Part III

## Self-Guided Tours of Historic Architecture in the East Bay

*Lake Merritt/County Court House, Oakland Tour E-12*

# List of Areas Covered

**Alameda (5 Tours)**
>Tour A: Franklin Park Area
>Tour B: Gold Coast
>Tour C: Downtown
>Tour D: East End
>Tour E: West End

**Albany (1 Tour)**

**Benicia (1 Tour)**

**Berkeley (11 Tours)**
>Tour A: Victorian North Berkeley
>Tour B: North Berkeley Foothills
>Tour C: Northgate
>Tour D: "Nut Hill"
>Tour E: University of California Campus
>Tour F: Downtown
>Tour G: South Campus
>Tour H: College Homestead Area
>Tour I: Claremont Area
>Tour J: Ocean View
>Tour K: Southwest Berkeley

**Emeryville (1 Tour)**

**Fremont (2 Tours)**
>Tour A: Niles District
>Tour B: Mission San Jose

**Hayward (1 Tour)**

**Kensington–Thousand Oaks (1 Tour)**

**Oakland (8 Tours)**
>Tour A: Downtown
>Tour B: Preservation Park–Victorian Row
>Tour C: Oak Center
>Tour D: West Oakland
>Tour E: Lake Merritt
>Tour F: Brooklyn Area
>Tour G: San Antonio Park Area
>Tour H: Fruitvale

**Piedmont (3 Tours)**
>Tour A: Central Piedmont
>Tour B: North Piedmont
>Tour C: Upper Piedmont

**Richmond (1 Tour)**

**Vallejo (1 Tour)**

One word of etiquette before you start your tour—unless the book entry tells you otherwise, the homes contained in these listings are private. You can look to your heart's content from the sidewalk, but please respect the privacy of the inhabitants. Now get out your hiking shoes! And have a wonderful feast for the eyes.

# Alameda

Population: 72,000. First settled: 1851, at the east end of the island. Incorporated: 1872. Area: 23 square miles. Architectural characteristics: Although the predominant historic building styles are Victorian, the gamut from Gothic Revival to Queen Anne and Colonial Revivals is run. In addition, a number of fine, brick Romanesque Revival churches and community buildings are found in the downtown area. Period Revival homes (primarily Tudor and Georgian) and large, brown-shingled houses also prevail in the central area of town.

## Areas Covered by Walking Tours

A: Franklin Park Area
B: Gold Coast
C: Downtown Area
D: East End
E: West End

Long known as a "treasure-trove" of Victorian architecture, Alameda undeniably has the finest collection of nineteenth-century houses in the East Bay. From its stunningly ornate Queen Anne mansions along San Jose and San Antonio streets to its dignified little raised-basement Italianate cottages near Park Street, this unique community contains outstanding examples of nearly every architectural genre that ever played a part in the Victorian pageant.

As with so many other East Bay towns, Alameda's first European settlement was a part of the Luis Peralta Rancho between 1820 and the Gold Rush. Yankee settlers built the first wood-frame houses around the east end of the island in 1851. A remarkable survivor of that early pioneer stage is a prefabricated Gothic Revival cottage built about 1852, which stands today at 1238 Versailles Avenue.

Although the post-Civil-War Era saw steady growth throughout the island, the greatest boom occurred during the 1870s, when the major railroad lines arrived in the area and regular ferry services across the Bay was instituted. By the turn of the century, Alameda was a major bedroom community for wealthy and middle-class families, drawing from San Francisco large numbers of professional men who settled primarily in what was known as the Gold Coast along the island's central-western edge. A real estate ad in the November 1906 issue of *Overland Monthly Magazine* enticed new residents to the growing town with this charming query: "Wouldst have thy children's cheeks like roses? Wouldst have them healthy and happy? Then live in Alameda, 'The city of homes' (across the bay from San Francisco)."

Alameda continued to grow in a steady and organized manner until the naval shipyards of World War II brought massive residential development. Despite the impact of the wartime boom and the tract housing projects that followed in the 1950s and '60s, most of Alameda still retains its pleasant Victorian residential quality. A strong preservation and restoration movement has sprung up over the past decade, and to it we owe the survival of so much fascinating nineteenth-century architecture in Alameda, as well as the opportunity to enjoy it by taking walking tours of the island.

## Tour Notes

# Franklin
# Park Area

The neighborhood around Alameda's Franklin Park near the center of the island has the distinct character of a well-preserved, nineteenth-century midwestern town. The park itself is lined on three sides by nearly intact blocks of late-Victorian and early-twentieth-century houses whose brightly decorated facades come in a wide variety of architectural styles. Grand Street, to the east of the park, is named appropriately, since it has some of the largest and finest Victorian houses in the city. Despite early real estate promotions in the 1860s, the development of this area really got underway in the late 1870s, once railroad and ferry service networks connected Alameda with all other parts of the Bay Area. An elegant reminder of that era is the Anthony House at 1630 Central Avenue (1876), one of the East Bay's best examples of a large Bracketed Italianate house. Residential construction in this neighborhood increased greatly during the 1880s and '90s, and by 1900 the area was fairly well built up. Today, among these beautiful, tree-lined streets, you can find a wealth of late-nineteenth-century and turn-of-the-century residences in all the picturesque styles popular in those halcyon years.

1 Victorian house. 1441 Grand St. This large late-Victorian house has a Queen-Anne-style corner turret and an unusual, rounded porch across the front. c. 1895—1900.

2 Anthony House. 1630 Central. Unquestionably, this house is Alameda's finest remaining Bracketed Italianate structure. The delicate refinement of the incised decorative motif on the porch columns and the brackets is unexcelled anywhere in the East Bay. John Anthony was a prosperous railroad official. 1876.

*ALAM A-3*

3    Tudor Revival mansion. Paru at Central, southeast corner. This unique mansion has not only fearsome, winged gargoyles crouching beside the main entry, but also two beautifully textured, molded-glass windows flanking the door. These windows, depicting scenes of Venice, Italy, were commissioned by the original owners to commemorate their honeymoon. The original shingled section was built in 1898; the later, stuccoed wing was added around 1930.

4    Queen Anne house. 1135 Morton. This house has Stick—Eastlake trim, and the palm trees that flank it are the original ones. c. 1893.

5    Queen Anne house. 1117 Morton. Designed by Charles Shaner, this house shows a restrained design and a good restoration. 1891.

6    Colonial Revival house. 1421 San Antonio. Fine, leaded windows augment a design that was popular in its day. 1898—1899.

7    Queen Anne house. 1023 Morton. c. 1890—1895.

8    Queen Anne house. 1015 Morton. This house has fine porch detailing. c. 1890.

*ALAM A-13*

9    Queen Anne house. 1007 Morton. This recently shingled house added a period-style porch and stained-glass windows. c. 1890.

10    Queen Anne house. 1001 Morton. This house has intricate sawn-decoration and stickwork. c. 1885—1895.

11    Queen Anne house. 1400 San Jose. Details are in the Colonial Revival style. c. 1890—1895.

12    Queen Anne house. 1000 Paru. This huge home has lots of stickwork. c. 1890.

13    Colonial Revival house. 1004 Paru. This very fancy house has an unusually ornate Palladian-window design (note the eagle). c. 1900—1905.

14    Stick—Eastlake house. 1018 Paru. The porch has carved, Moorish pointed arches. 1890.

15    Stick—Eastlake house. 1602 San Antonio. This house was done in a dignified, San Francisco style, with superb detail. 1889.

16      Tudor Revival house. 1100 Grand. There is a good rusticated-stone porch. c. 1915–1925.

17      Miller House. 1012 Grand. Designed by the Alameda firm of Gilbert and Brown, this house is in the Stick style but the roof and porch were remodeled in Craftsman style around 1917. E. H. Miller was the secretary–treasurer of the Central Pacific Railroad. 1881–1882.

18      Colonial Revival house. 1011 Grand. This house has a Queen Anne tower. c. 1900.

19      Colonial Revival house. 1007 Grand. Note the good detail. c. 1900.

20      Stick–Eastlake house. 1001 Grand. Designed by Charles Shaner, this immense home has solid Eastlake ornament. 1891.

21      Colonial Revival house. 1000 Grand. There is an interesting curved porch. 1901.

22      Colonial Revival house. 921 Grand. The array of ornaments is charming, and the paint job is cheery. c. 1900–1910.

23      Hansel and Gretel half-timbered house. 912 Grand. c. 1920–1930.

24      Moffitt House. 911 Grand. Originally a Stick-style cottage (carriage house with its Gothic-style gable still intact), this was remodeled in French Provincial. 1870; remodeled c. 1930s.

25      Bracketed Italianate house. 900 Grand. This magnificent house was built around 1878. A Queen Anne tower was added to the back corner around the 1890s.

26      Stick-style house. 903 Grand. c. 1880–1890.

27      Queen Anne house. 815 Grand. The chimney is ornate, and the volutes on the porch steps are massive. c. 1885–1890.

28      Hjul House. 701 Grand. This superb, rambling Craftsman bungalow was designed by its owner, a Danish immigrant. The setting, with its large lot, moon-gate porch, and lavish garden plantings, creates a truly Romantic atmosphere. c. 1905–1920.

*ALAM A-20*

*ALAM A-25*

# Alameda Tour B

## Gold Coast

### Tour Notes

No other neighborhood in the East Bay contains so many outstanding examples of Victorian residential architecture as Alameda's so-called Gold Coast. Lying along the old southern shoreline near the middle of the island, this area derived its nickname from the fact that many well-to-do business and professional people from San Francisco and elsewhere chose to settle in the district in the 1880s and '90s, and that, according to the custom of the day, they displayed their opulence by building large, lavishly decorated homes. A number of tract developments occurred during this period, which led to the creation of varied lot sizes and street widths in this section.

Some of the "men of substance" who arrived in Alameda during the late nineteenth century and influenced its development were Alfred A. Cohen, J. W. Dwinelle, J. J. Kellog, and E. B. Mastick. Local architects Charles Shaner and Charles Foster were among the most prolific in the Gold Coast region, and their work represents some of the finest Victorian domestic designs to be found in the Bay Area. Anyone who appreciates such architecture will find numerous examples of every major style popular during the later part of the Victorian Era. Undeniably, the large Queen Anne tower houses are the most impressive homes in the Gold Coast, and no more delightful samples of these can be found than the two incredible concoctions that straddle the intersection of Willow and San Jose (see cover photo).

*ALAM B-1*

1    Greenlease House. 1724 Santa Clara Ave. Attributed to Ernest Coxhead, this exceptional Brown Shingle house blends a variety of elements — medieval overhang, hipped roof, dormer windows, wide turret, neo-Classic volutes, and curved portico — that were characteristic of the early work of the English-born Coxhead. 1892–1894.

2    Georgian Colonial Revival house. 1428 Union St. at Santa Clara. This charming house has a klinker-brick foundation line and a tall portico that creates an aura of serenity. c. 1900–1906.

3    Stick cottage. 1419 Union St. Note the Italianate-style windows and angled bay. c. 1870–1880.

4    Queen Anne house. 1209 Union St. The towers are large. 1893.

5    Queen Anne cottage. 1117 Union St. The Gothic porch has horseshoe arches, and there are paired, Gothic, attic windows. c. 1890–1895.

6    Queen Anne house. 1021 Union St. This subtly elegant house has a curved porch, and its refined detailing is enhanced by a tasteful color scheme. c. 1890–1895.

7    Early Colonial Revival house. 900 Union St. at Clinton. This substantial house was enlarged after the turn of the century. It has very lovely stained-glass windows and is now a boarding house. c. 1893; enlarged 1906.

8    Queen Anne house. 893 Union St. This elegant, towered house has a superb radiating-spindlework design on the porch. c. 1890–1895.

9    Hatch House. 891 Union St. Designed by Joseph Leonard, this immense, brown-shingled, late-Victorian mansion can only be described as "breathtaking." The flanking turrets have an almost Romanesque quality, and the rusticated stonework along the first floor gives a feeling of solidity. This lot originally looked out over the open Bay before the land fill was created after World War II, and a third tower once graced the center of the back of the house. 1896.

10    Queen Anne cottage. 1828 Clinton Ave. This fine cottage has robust sunburst panels. It recently was restored by its owners. c. 1890–1895.

*ALAM B-2*

ALAM B-9

11      Stick–Eastlake/Queen Anne house. 912 Lafayette St. c. 1894.

12      Queen Anne house. Lafayette St. at San Jose, southwest corner. Note the wave-pattern shingling. c. 1890–1895.

13      Spanish Colonial Revival house. 942 Chestnut St. at San Jose. Exemplifying the Spanish Colonial Revival style, this house also has a Monterey-style balcony near the back and a Mission-style arched entry. The original owner designed it. 1932.

14      St. Joseph's Basilica. Chestnut St. at San Antonio. This beautifully designed Spanish-Baroque-style church handles decorative detailing with great sophistication, especially on the tower. c. 1920–1930.

15      Queen Anne house. 2025 San Antonio Ave. This house has a deep corner porch and heavy stickwork. c. 1890–1895.

16      Queen Anne house. 2019 San Antonio Ave. This large house has a striking scrollwork frieze below the main gable. c. 1890.

17      Queen Anne house. 2105 San Antonio Ave. Designed by Charles Foster, this truly phenomenal house has a rounded "bowler-hat" dome on the tower. The rich ornamentation has been made all the more vivid by the sublime color scheme that recently was applied. 1893.

ALAM B-14

*ALAM B-24*

18    Raised-basement, false-front Victorian cottage. 2156 San Antonio Ave. This cottage absolutely defies stylistic categorization. c. 1870s.

19    Stick–Eastlake, raised-basement cottage. 2165 San Jose Ave. Note the squared corner porch on this very good example of this style. c. 1890–1895.

20    Queen Anne house. 2122 San Jose Ave. c. 1890–1895.

21    Queen Anne house. 2103 San Jose Ave. at Willow. Designed by Charles Shaner, this house is a superb example of an ornately decorated Queen Anne. Its perfect, rounded corner turret is topped by a witch's hat spire and an iron finial. 1891.

22    Queen Anne house. 2070 San Jose Ave. at Willow. This incredible house, also designed by Charles Shaner, used absolutely every ornamental motif popular at that time on its multitextured facade. It's easy to see why the Queen Anne style is often referred to as the "final flowering" of Victorian architecture. 1893.

*ALAM B-17*

23    Siegfried House. 2044 Alameda Ave. This subdivided "San Francisco Stick" style house grew from an original cottage. Seigfried was an Alameda tea dealer. c. 1870–1880.

24    First Congregational Church. Central Ave. at Chestnut, northwest corner. Designed by Daniel F. Oliver, this basically Romanesque Revival design has an unusual admixture of Gothic arched windows and brown-shingle and sandstone surfacing. 1904.

25    Immanuel Lutheran Church, 1420 Lafayette St. Designed by Joseph Craft, this church is a modest yet well-rendered example of a late-Victorian, wooden Gothic Revival church. 1891.

# Alameda Tour C

## Downtown Area

### Tour Notes

Alameda's central business district and civic center are concentrated along Park Avenue and the wide boulevards northwest of it. A number of fine Romanesque Revival and neo-Classic civic and commercial buildings may be found; City Hall's red sandstone Romanesque facade dominates the area. Many Victorian homes, including several early "Pioneer" cottages just off Park Street, are scattered in small enclaves throughout these streets. And raising its sweeping, streamlined, concrete outline above Central Avenue is the Alameda Theater, one of the East Bay's best renditions of Zigzag Art Deco architecture.

*ALAM C-15*

1    Bracketed Italianate house. 2225 San Antonio Ave. This house with its fine quoining on the corners, resembles the Anthony House at 1630 Central. c. 1875–1880.

2    Late-Queen-Anne house. 2249 San Antonio Ave. This house has Colonial Revival details. c. 1895.

3.    Miniature Stick-style villa. 2253 San Antonio Ave. This villa comes complete with a diminutive, squared corner tower. c. 1880s.

4    Late-Queen-Anne/Stick–Eastlake cottage. 2250 San Antonio Ave. An interesting sawn-wood pattern decorates the frieze above the porch. See also the full sunburst panel on the second floor. c. 1890.

5    Late-Victorian house. 2254 San Antonio Ave. This odd house has stickwork, a squared corner bay, and heavy-set, stubby turret. c. 1890–1895.

*ALAM C-14*

6    Queen Anne house. 2258 San Antonio Ave. This large, pleasantly designed house has a tower that dovetails into the gable, Colonial Revival latticing on the windows, and a horseshoe "Islamic" arch around the porch. Notice the superb wrought-iron gate with a stenciled-out four-leaf-clover motif and neo-Classic, turned-baluster-style gateposts. c. 1891.

7    Streamlined Moderne gas station. Oak at Encinal Sts., southeast corner. This gas station, crammed into a small corner lot, exemplifies the late Streamlined Moderne style. c. 1940s.

8    Raised-basement Italianate cottage. 1214 Oak St. Note the miniature dentils along its bay and porch. c. 1875–1880.

9    "Pioneer classic box." 1218 Oak St. This house has latticed windows and a dentil-and-frieze lined gable. c. 1870–1875.

10    Raised-basement Italianate cottage. 2306 Alameda Ave. A porthole window looks out from the bracketed pediment. c. 1870s.

*ALAM C-16*

11    Raised-basement Italianate cottage. 2310 Alameda Ave. The Classical Revival storefront was added in the early 1900s. c. 1870s.

12    "New" Masonic Lodge. 2324 Alameda Ave. Built when the Masons moved from their Park Street building, the hall a fine rendering of the Spanish Baroque Revival style, with good detailing. c. 1920s

13    Old Masonic Hall. Park St. and Alameda Ave., southwest corner. Designed by C. F. Mau, this brick-and-sandstone Romanesque Revival commercial block has a meeting hall upstairs. The solid-looking squared tower gives the building an almost midwestern, Main-Street appearance. c. 1891.

14    Old U.S. Post Office. Central Ave. at Park Ct. John Knox Taylor designed this concise example of government Roman/Renaissance Revival. But it is no longer a post office; plans are being made to reopen the building to serve a new community function. 1912.

*ALAM C-17*

*ALAM C-20*

15     Alameda Theater. 2315 Central Ave. This concrete Zigzag Moderne form of an Art Deco movie theater was designed by the same firm that did the Paramount Theater in Oakland. The interior has been subdivided into three sections, and the original furnishings and decor have been retained. 1932.

16     Twin Towers United Methodist Church. 2265 Central Ave. at Oak St. This impressive, Italian-Romanesque-style church has open-arched towers and neo-Classic, Roman-Composite-style attached columns on the rounded apsidal entry. Several very nice stained-glass windows grace the walls facing the streets. 1908–1909.

17     Alameda High School. 2200 block of Central Ave., even side. This supremely dignified late-Beaux-Arts design has the longest neo-Classic facade in the East Bay. The Ionic collonade on the central pavilion and the allegorical bas-relief panels in columned niches above large urns are handled with great sophistication. 1926.

18     Stick house. 2221 Central Ave. A formal elegance exudes from this very vertical, two-story house. c. 1880–1890.

19     Alameda Free Library. 2264 Santa Clara Ave. at Oak St. This yellow-brick Roman Renaissance design has Corinthian columns on a tall, shallow portico and a traditional symbolic "open book" motif in the medallion set into the pediment. Inside is a barrel-vaulted, coffered atrium, supported by paired Corinthian columns and lit by five stained-glass windows in the rear wall. 1902.

20     Alameda City Hall. Santa Clara Ave. at Oak St., northeast corner. Designed by Percy and Hamilton, this large, dignified, brick-and-sandstone Romanesque Revival civic building has a wide, sweeping central staircase. The original central clocktower, damaged slightly in the 1906 earthquake, was finally removed around 1937, when the building was remodeled. 1896.

## Tour Notes

The east end of Alameda was the first part of the island to be settled after William Chipman and Gideon Auginbaugh bought the entire peninsula from Antonio Peralta in 1851. A townsite was located in the east end after the two men subdivided the island, and at least one house remains from those early years — the ancient Gothic Revival cottage at 1238 Versailles (built about 1852 or shortly thereafter). As in the rest of Alameda, settlement was sparse in the east end until the 1870s, when the railroad lines were completed and several substantial "capitalists" (as they then preferred to be called) began to take advantage of the area's development possibilities. A number of tract developments were laid out in the 1880s and '90s, and a fair percentage of interesting Victorian residential architecture has survived from this period. The two pleasantly shaded blocks of homes along the grassy island between Park Avenue West and Park Avenue East constitute not only the best-preserved enclave of Victoriana in this neighborhood, but also a good place to begin a walking tour of the east end.

1    Stick house. 1237 Park Ave. W. An odd combination — this house blends a rounded corner, topped by a diminutive spire and a Colonial Revival portico on the opposite side. c. 1890.

2    Stick house. 1215 Park Ave. W. Note the mansarded corner-turret and the heavy stickwork. c. 1885–1895.

3    Stick–Eastlake house. 1193 Park Ave. W. The house has fine, solid, sawn-wood details. c. 1880–1890.

*ALAM D-2*

4    Colonial Revival house. 1181 Park Ave. W. This small house could be everyone's "grandma's cottage." c. 1906.

5    Queen Anne house. 1222 Park Ave. E. This house has an unusual turret. c. 1890–1895.

6    Stick/Queen Anne house. 1224 Park Ave. E. Both styles are represented in a delicate and lacy mix of ornament. c. 1885–1895.

7    Queen Anne house. 1226 Park Ave. E. The richly textured, shingled surface resembles a purple wedding cake. c. 1890.

8    Raised-basement, Bracketed Italianate cottage. 1220 Regent St. Notice the ornate porthole in the pediment. c. 1875–1880.

9    Stick house. 1203 Regent St. The pyramidal roof is set back pleasantly in its slot, and the brown shingles (probably added about 1910) give it an East Coast quality. c. 1885–1895.

10    Eastlake/Queen Anne house. 1206 Broadway. This formidable design is made even more so by its black-and-white paint job and its finely carved Eastlake doors. c. 1885–1895.

11    Queen Anne house. 1240 Broadway. c. 1890.

12    Queen Anne house. 1244 Broadway. c. 1890.

13    Stick–Eastlake house. 1354 Broadway. Note the lavish sawn-wood friezes and the pediment detail. c. 1885–1895.

14    Queen Anne house. 1412 Broadway. This house has a unique finial on the tower and some of the finest plaster scrollwork panels in town. c. 1890.

*ALAM D-9*

*ALAM D-10*

15    Stick–Eastlake house. 1416 Broadway. The Eastlake trim around the porch and windows is tastefully concise. c. 1880–1890.

16    Neo-Classic Victorian house. 1420 Broadway. This Victorian has heavy bracketing, stickwork around the windows, and a triple-columned portico. c. 1880–1890.

17    Colonial Revival house. 1512 Broadway. A wide porch, angled bays, and Italianate curved windows adorn this unusual house. c. 1890–1895.

18    Queen Anne house. 2071 Santa Clara Ave. c. 1890–1895.

19    Queen Anne house. 2700 Central Ave. This large house has some interesting details. c. 1890.

20    Italianate-style "Pioneer box." 1318 Versailles Ave. One of the earlier homes in the area, this has a double-wide, latticed dormer window. c. 1870.

21    Gothic Revival cottage. 1238 Versailles Ave. This one was probably prefabricated in the East and brought around Cape Horn by ship during the Gold Rush. Features typical of this style are the high-peaked gables lined with "icicle" bargeboards and the split pilasters connected by pointed-arch tracery along the porch. The brown shingles were added later. This is almost certainly the oldest remaining structure in Alameda. c. 1852.

22    Stick house. 1202 Versailles Ave. There is an ornate, two-level porch on the side, as well as a fanciful bargeboard. c. 1880–1890.

*ALAM D-8*

# Alameda Tour E

## West End

### Tour Notes

The west end usually is ignored by any architectural survey of Alameda, but it does contain several fine Victorian houses, many nineteenth- and early-twentieth-century workingman's cottages, and a number of historic commercial buildings. Croll's Bar, at Webster and Central streets, is by far the most historic structure in the area, and one of Alameda's most interesting buildings. Not only is it a rare example of a mansard-roofed commercial structure, but the saloon downstairs contains memorabilia of the many lightweight and heavyweight boxers who once lived upstairs and trained at the Neptune Beach Amusement Park (which, at the turn of the century, stood across the street).

The side streets west of Webster are lined with many fine Victorian cottages as well as with a number of stately homes from the 1880s and 1890s. In addition to the buildings listed in the following tour, a stroll through these pleasant, shaded thoroughfares will reveal many small, unlisted gems.

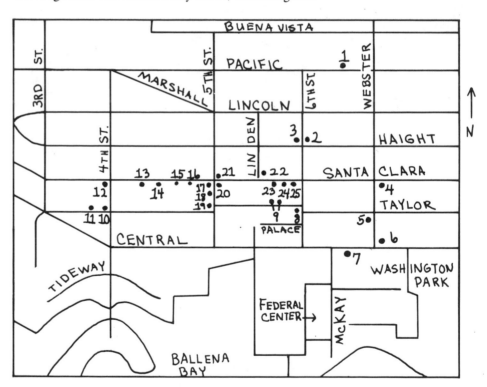

1    Alameda Fire Station. 635 Pacific St. This rarified Spanish-Colonial-style building has a wide, scalloped arch over the truck entrance, massive lintels above the window, and paired, curved brackets below the split-planed gable. 1926.

2    Mediterranean-style bungalow. 607 Haight St. The "punched-out," false-front. squiggle motif across the facade achieves a humorous effect. c. 1925–1935.

3    Queen Anne house with Eastlake trim. 529 6th St. at Haight. This large house has a hipped roof, Colonial Revival latticed windows on the second floor, and some fine stained glass. c. 1890–1895.

4    Wells Fargo Bank. 1442 Webster at Santa Clara. This Beaux Arts, neo-Classic building has volutes on the keystones and cornice, and banded

*ALAM E-1*

columns on the entrance — above which is the inspiring inscription, "Dedicated to Industry and Thrift." 1917.

5       Victorian commercial building. 1431 Webster St. at Taylor. The building has a Queen Anne corner turret, stickwork on the windows, and a false front lined with scrollwork brackets. c. 1885–1895.

6       Croll's Bar. 1400 Webster St. at Central. This mansard-roofed, neo-Classic commercial building has shelf molding above the upper windows and a fascinating history. Originally containing a curved, columned veranda around it, the building first was used as a real estate office. The Croll family then converted the ground floor into a saloon in 1883, of which the original bar, brass railings, beveled mirrors, and wood paneling remain intact. Around 1900, electric lights and cash registers were installed. At that time the upstairs was used as a rooming house by several boxers who were training across the street at Croll's Neptune Gardens, in the amusement park called Neptune Beach. These boxers included heavyweight champion James Corbett, and lightweights "Little" Jim Corbett and Joe Gans (the first black lightweight champion). Just before Prohibition, the leaded- and stained-glass windows were put in. The current owners of the saloon, the second since the Croll family, are planning to restore the building fully to its turn-of-the-century appearance. The bar inside was made by the Brunswick Calendar Company of Boston and brought around Cape Horn; the beveled mirrors were made in Belgium and brought by sailing ship. Original building, 1879; rear wing added c. 1889.

*ALAM E-6*

*ALAM E-7*

7       Neptune Court Apartments. 600 Central, on the site of the old Neptune Beach Amusement Park. These Spanish-Colonial-style, one-story, attached apartments have ornately trimmed, arched windows, bas-relief garlands on the facade, and an open courtyard behind the central arched gateway. In the middle of the gateway is a small, Baroque-style fountain. c. 1925–1935.

8       St. Barnabas Catholic Church. 1431 6th St. at Taylor. This unpretentious Mission Revival church comes complete with bell tower and pilastered and arched doorway. c. 1930–1940.

9       Two Queen Anne cottages. 543 and 547 Taylor St. These supremely rich, ornamented cottages have a fairly uncommon arrangement of machine-cut patterns. Similar to the ones on Santa Clara, they may be by the same builder. c. 1890.

10       Queen Anne house. 345 Taylor St. at 4th. The setting is attractive, and the decoration on the porch and windows is subtle. A modern "neo-Victorian" turret is being added on the back. c. 1890–1895.

11       Brown-shingled Colonial Revival house. 337 Taylor St. Both high-peaked and gambreled gables are found here, as well as a fine carriage-house behind the main house. c. 1900–1910.

*ALAM E-12*

12       Queen Anne/Stick–Eastlake house. 342 Santa Clara Ave. at 4th. The arrangement of Eastlake decorations and Queen Anne spindles and shingling is rather bizarre. c. 1885–1895.

13       Stick-style cottage. 424 Santa Clara Ave. Note the fine iron cresting along the roof. 1895.

14       "Cape Cod"-style Colonial Revival house. 432 Santa Clara Ave. This refined, New-England-design house has its original, rich brown shingles in place. There is a superb beveled-glass oval window in front. 1908.

15       Late-Italianate-style house. 452 Santa Clara Ave. This house has an unusual combination of late Italianate style with such Colonial Revival details as the dormer in the roof and the leaded window behind the portico. c. 1890.

16       Stick-style house. 462 Santa Clara Ave. c. 1880–1890.

*ALAM E-14*

*ALAM E-20*

17 Stick–Eastlake cottage. 1411 5th St. at Santa Clara. The shingles are diamond-shaped. c. 1890–1895.

18 Stick house. 1439 5th St. This very vertical house has board-and-battening and delicate saw-tooth trim above the window in the squared bay. c. 1880–1890.

19 Raised-basement Stick house. 1437 5th St. The main gable has a small bargeboard and fish-scale shingles. c. 1885.

20 Colonial Revival house. 502 Santa Clara Ave. at 5th. This house has an "East-Coast"-style, wide, pedimented gable and a recessed attic window on the side. There are also fine, leaded windows. c. 1900–1910.

21 Late-Victorian rooming house. 503 Santa Clara Ave. at 5th. This eclectic building has heavy stickwork, an odd, flat roof, and fish-scale shingles. Overall, it has a "New Orleans" look. c. 1890–1895.

22 Queen Anne cottage. 529 Santa Clara Ave. at Linden. An Islamic-arch motif appears around the left corner window, and there's a cake-icing of curved shingles in the gables. c. 1890–1895.

23 Queen Anne/Eastlake cottage. 540 Santa Clara Ave. Note the stenciled and machine-cut woodwork across the facade. c. 1890–1895.

24 Queen Anne cottage. 546 Santa Clara Ave. There is a bargeboard and a porthole window in the gable. c. 1890–1895.

25 Queen Anne/Eastlake cottage. 548 Santa Clara Ave. Gothic arched attic windows look out onto the street, and a horseshoe arch decorates the porch. This cottage and numbers 546 and 540 are all very likely by the same builder. c. 1890–1895.

*ALAM E-21*

# Albany

Population: 16,000. First settled: About 1900, near San Pablo Avenue. Incorporated: 1908. Area: 1.71 square miles. Architectural characteristics: The flatlands between the eastern city limits and Albany Hill are almost entirely filled with modest bungalows in variations of the Mediterranean, Tudor, and Craftsman modes. Albany Hill has a number of larger tract and architect-designed homes, mostly from the Post World War Two Era.

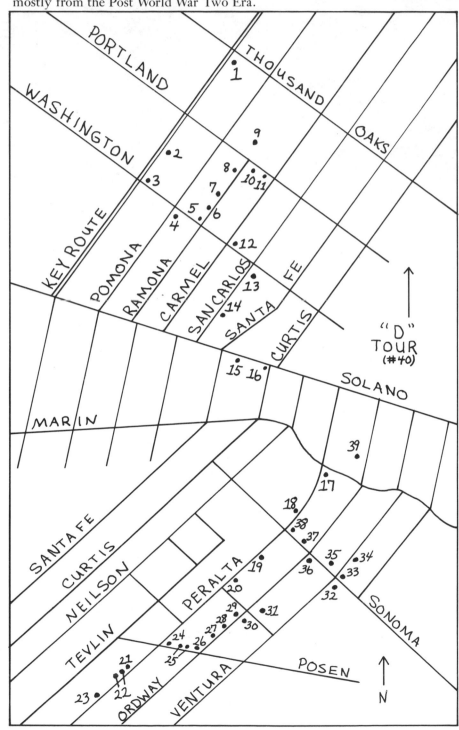

# Albany Tour

## Tour Notes

With the laying of the stagecoach line along San Pablo Avenue in the 1850s the first indication of the advance of "civilization" came to what is now Albany. Before then, Albany was an undeveloped part of the Peralta Rancho. The scattered commercial and residential development that grew up in the flatlands east and west of San Pablo Avenue around 1900 constituted the first significant settlement. In 1908, the fledgling community of 200 citizens was incorporated under the name "Ocean View." The following year, it was rechristened "Albany," and five years later it had grown to a population of about 1,500.

Residential development mushroomed throughout Albany in the 1920s and '30s. During those years, most of the characteristic stucco and wood bungalows that still cover the city's flatlands were erected in tracts. The major developer of quality bungalow tracts in Albany was a man who came to be known by the now-famous epithet of "One-Nail MacGregor" (implying that he used one nail *more* than all his competitors did). MacGregor, for many years a bungalow builder in Oakland, came to Albany in the late 1920s to settle and begin his most extensive projects in the new and growing community. During the next several years, up until the start of World War II, MacGregor built literally hundreds upon hundreds of one- and two-story bungalows in every conceivable stylistic mode, always using the highest quality of craftsmanship available. Today, Albany celebrates the contribution of its most renowned former citizen by holding an official "MacGregor Day."

Although MacGregor and other builders continued to erect a smattering of new homes in the late '40s and the '50s, the bulk of residential construction had been completed before World War II began. The surprising variety, originality, and often whimsical charm of Albany's many sturdy bungalows make them well worth a detailed examination. Try strolling along the neatly landscaped residential streets to the north and south of Solano Avenue, and see for yourself.

1    Albany High School. Key Route Rd. between Portland and Thousand Oaks Blvd. This concrete, two-block-long, late W.P.A. Moderne building is painted institutional yellow. The auditorium, at the southwest corner of Thousand Oaks and Pomona Street, is the most original part of the design. 1941.

2    Small bungalow. 713 Key Route Rd. The geometric slab motifs along its false-front roofline and flanking porch are enhanced by a very esthetic color scheme. c. 1925–1935.

3    Norman Revival bungalow. 1315 Washington St. at Key Route Rd. The chateau-style turret is topped by an unusual decorative weather vane. c. 1925–1935.

4    Georgian Revival house. 1330 Washington St. at Pomona. This tidy, small-scale Georgian has an extra-wide dormer and "New England"-style shuttered and latticed windows. c. 1930s.

5    Tudor Revival house. 732 Ramona St. Note the finely finished brickwork on the ground floor and the stone quoins at the corners. c. 1930.

6    Monterey-style bungalow. 728 Ramona St. It has an ornamental false balcony. c. 1930–1940.

7    High-peaked bungalow. 712 Ramona St. One side of the gable extends down into a three-part, stepped arcade that can only be described as funky. (The same motif can be seen on other bungalows in Albany.) c. 1930s.

*ALB-5*

*ALB-9*

8    Small bungalow. 704 Ramona St. There is a punched-out facade and a good cartouche above the entry arch. c. 1925–1935.

9    Veteran's Memorial Building. 1325 Portland Ave. at Ramona. This Mission Revival building has a Moorish arched- window in the west wing, a Spanish-style arcade across the entrance, nice tilework along the lower front walls, and a very unique Churriqueresque niche in the middle of the main gable. From the niche, a bust of a World War I doughboy gazes at passersby. 1932.

10    High-peaked bungalow. 1332 Portland Ave. The curves in the gables above the porch are emphasized sharply, and the fanlight front window is latticed delicately. c. 1930s.

11    Mediterranean Revival bungalow. 1336 Portland Ave. and Carmel. The bungalow is typical for this style, but the Conestoga wagon wheels worked into the front fence are rare. c. 1930–1940.

12    Mediterranean Revival bungalow. 1427 Washington at Carmel. This pleasingly rendered bungalow has a Gothic arched front window and entry, a belfry-like chimney, and neat awnings over every window. Note the rare street furniture nearby at Ramona and Washington streets: a "Slow Chidren" sign with a running child on it. c. 1930s.

13    Low-roofed bungalow. 801 San Carlos at Washington. This rambling building has interesting geometric configurations on the porch. c. 1925–1935.

14    Mediterranean-style bungalow. 837 San Carlos. There are diminutive, Mission-style turrets, as well as bas-relief garlands above the windows and door. c. 1925–1935.

15    Craftsman bungalow. 1496 Solano Ave. at Curtis. Although this solid structure, one of the oldest buildings left on Solano, has been converted into an antique shop, none of the original shingling, brickwork, or the elongated dormer has been eliminated. c. 1915.

16    Medical building. 1498 Solano Ave. at Curtis. This Mediterranean Revival building is connected to 902 Curtis by a low-walled garden patio. Note the tilework around the doorway and arched window. c. 1925–1935.

17    Craftsman bungalow. 937 Peralta. This fine building has klinker-brick porch pillars, and the porch shingling has an interesting, wave-like pattern. Attractive fieldstone steps traverse the finely landscaped, raised lot. c. 1915.

18    Craftsman bungalow. 990 Peralta. This house has stucco pillars, red-stained shingles, and an unusually wide, cutely trimmed dormer window. c. 1915–1920.

*ALB-16*

*ALB-25 and 26*

19      Mediterranean-style bungalow. 1019 Peralta. Built on a raised lot, this building pleasantly integrates a neo-Classic portico, flanked by urns on pedestals, with traditional Mediterranean red-clay tiles and iron grillwork along the roofline. c. 1920–1930.

20      Craftsman-like house. 1033 Peralta. This solid, two-story structure has rustic clapboarding covering its entire surface. c. 1910–1920.

21      Norman Revival bungalow. 1090 Peralta. This delicate version has a half-timbered, hipped roof, with a touch of geometric detailing on the small, enclosed corner porch. c. 1925–1935.

22      Two bungalows. 1092 and 1094 Peralta at Posen. Arranged unusually, these have bracketed, square corner towers above their ground-floor garages. Number 1094 has a miniature "false" balustrade below the tower, just wide enough for a cat to walk across. (And if you wait long enough, one will!) c. 1920s.

23      Bungalow. 1096 Peralta. This small, stucco bungalow has a superb color scheme. c. 1915–1925.

24      Mediterranean Revival bungalow. 1491 Posen at Peralta. Built on a nicely shaded lot, this bungalow has a touch of California Mission in the corner "tower." c. 1920–1930.

25      Two "Alamo Revival" bungalows. 1495 and 1497 Posen. False-front curves, españade gables, and fitted-stone false arches around the doorways decorate these homes. c. 1925–1935.

26      Bungalow. 1499 Posen at Ordway. This truly whimsical bungalow has Mediterranean-style detailing along the main floor. A projecting, built-in garage, with its exaggerated motifs projecting from the sides like ears and its two porthole windows on the doors, resembles a cartoon character's face. c. 1915–1925.

27      Stucco bungalow. 1070 Ordway. Craftsman touches are evident in the bracketed roofline and klinker-brick chimney. c. 1910–1920.

28      Craftsman bungalow. 1044 Ordway. The porch is wide and deep-set, and the landscaping is good. c. 1915–1920.

29      Stucco bungalow. 1036 Ordway. The general form is common, but its five banded windows across a wide bay and raised geometric motif on the chimney show the influence of the Prairie School, particularly the influence of John Hudson Thomas. c. 1915–1925.

30      Tudor Revival bungalow. 1041 Ordway. There is rough-textured stuccoing between the mock half-timbers, a false gable below the main gable, and an intricate curved and gracketed bargeboard. c. 1925–1935.

31      Large, two-story house. 1031 Ordway. The pilastered dormer is lined with a bracketed bargeboard. c. 1915–1925.

32      Large bungalow. 1614 Sonoma at Ventura. A fine, beveled-glass design is set in the front door. c. 1915.

33      Two-story house. 975 Ventura at Sonoma. The clean, horizontal lines and raised, geometric motifs on its surface give this impressive house, very possibly designed by John Hudson Thomas, a heavy Prairie School flavor. c. 1915–1920.

34      Mediterranean Revival bungalow. 973 Ventura. This small bungalow has an unusual arrangement of stepped, false-front designs, punctuated by arches along the roof and porch. c. 1925–1935.

*ALB-35*

35      Small, whitewashed-stucco bungalow. 1607 Sonoma. There is a unique, almost Deco flavor to the boldly rendered geometric lines that march across the arched porch and balustraded roofline. c. 1930s.

36      Monterey-Revival-style house. 1602 Sonoma. Note the triple-arched front windows. c. 1930s.

37      Mediterranean-style bungalow. 1553 Sonoma. Its stepped-arched porch and corner turrets have a truly funky design. c. 1925–1935.

38      Large, clapboarded wooden bungalow. 1555 Sonoma at Peralta. A deep, Doric-columned portico is topped by projecting brackets that provide trellises for climbing rosebushes. This design for wooden bungalows was once common throughout California. c. 1915–1925.

39      Stucco bungalow. 916 Ordway. This immaculate, cheerfully painted place has bracketed gables, a glass-enclosed porch, urns flanking the entry steps, and very pleasant landscaping. c. 1920–1930.

## Detour — Worth a Side Trip

40      Grace Lutheran Church. Santa Fe and Ward, southwest corner. This Mission-Revival-style church looks as neat as a pin and is very late for this style. 1950.

*ALB-29*

# Benicia

Population: 12,500. First settled: 1847 (state capital from 1853 to 1854). Incorporated: 1850. Area: 4.6 square miles. Architectural characteristics: The primarily wooden Victorian buildings range from late Greek Revival through Queen Anne styles. An exceptional number of "Pioneer Era" homes and prefabricated wooden houses came from the East during the Gold Rush. The military reservation at the east end of town contains many brick and stone buildings in various nineteenth-century styles.

**Area Covered in the Walking Tour**

The "Old Town" Historic District

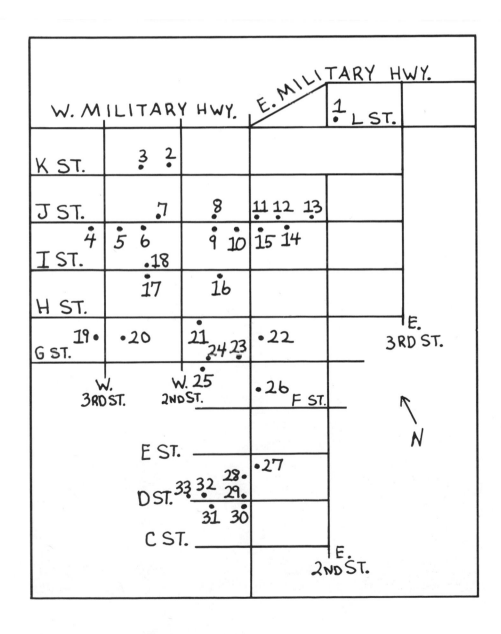

# Benicia Tour

## Tour Notes

Of all Bay Area towns, only Benicia can create the feeling of a mid-1800s Mississippi River town. The predominant architecture of the "Old Town" district is decidedly rustic mid-Victorian. With the solid Greek Revival facade of the Old State Capitol Building dominating its main street, Benicia preserves an air of nineteenth-century-village tranquility, though its past has not always been totally peaceful.

Named after General Mariano Vallejo's eldest daughter, the town was first settled by easterners in 1847, after the Bear Flag Revolt, and two years before the Gold Rush began. By 1853, the new town had become sufficiently important as a deep-water port to become the state capital — a position it enjoyed for only one year. During the 1850s and '60s, the area at the lower end of 1st Street was a haven for bordellos and gambling houses, of which the Washington Hotel (still standing) is the most famous. At this time, many prefabricated homes were brought from back East and erected along the residential side streets. A fair number of the clapboarded "Pioneer boxes" remain.

Benicia was also the site of several private academies and prep schools in the nineteenth century, among them the original Mills College campus. In 1847, the U.S. Army established the Benicia Barracks at the east end of town, which remained an important military base until the 1920s and housed such famous military figures as Ulysses S. Grant and William Tecumseh Sherman.

After the turn of the century, Benicia's growth and development slackened. The "red light" area at the foot of 1st Street remained active until 1954, when it was closed down by a major crackdown that indicted the police chief. Today,

*BEN-1*

much of the nineteenth-century building stock of this unique Bay Area hamlet is being restored carefully, and Benicia is emerging as a popular spot for lovers of Victorian architecture.

1    Walch Cottage. 235 E. L St. This Gothic Revival house originally was prefabricated in Boston and then shipped here. The lacy, carved-pendant bargeboards along the gables, the finials above the roof peaks, and the Gothic arched window facing the street demonstrate the salient features of the Gothic cottage quite perfectly. This is one of the earliest houses erected in Benicia. 1849.

2    Brown Shingle Craftsman bungalow. 1121 W. 2nd St. This is a solid example of this mode. c. 1910.

3    Queen Anne house. 245 W. K St. This stunningly impressive house has one of the lushest settings in town, including three of the original palm trees. The fence retains its original wrought-iron, Gothic tracery design. 1891.

4    Stick house. 304 W. J St. Note the intricate jigsaw-cut latticework along the porch. This is a fine restoration. c. 1880s.

5    Queen Anne cottage. 288 W. J St. This humble cottage has delicate spindlework on the porch. c. 1890–1895.

*BEN-3*

6    "Pioneer" classic box. 280 W. J St. This clapboarded house has a pedimented roof that lends a hint of Greek Revival. c. 1865–1875.

7    Stick house. 261 W. J. St. Perfectly framed by two enormous palms and the original cement steps, this house also has unusually lacy, machine-cut, Eastlake-style decoration on its squared bay. c. 1880–1890.

8    Wooden Gothic Revival church. 135 W. J St. The tower is bulky. c. 1870s.

9    Mission Revival wood-front meeting hall. 120 W. J St. The corners have neo-Classic trim c. 1915–1925.

10    Masonic Hall. 110 W. J St. This simple "midwestern" version of a wooden Greek Revival building, the first Masonic Temple built in California, has the original hand-split clapboards, square-latticed windows, and pilasters at each corner. 1850.

11    Colonial Revival house. 1st and E. J sts., northwest corner. The house has a fine setting, a deep-set corner portico, and a very vertical emphasis to its design. c. 1900.

12    Eastlake cottage. 121 E. J St. Note the stepped roofline and the uncommon array of wood trim. c. 1885–1890.

13    Stick cottage. 145 E. J St. The Gothic gable comes complete with a narrow bargeboard, and the long corner porch is lined with spindles. c. 1875–1885.

*BEN-14*

14    Reverend McAllister House. 120 E. J St. Here stands an extremely rare example of an eighteenth-century New England saltbox, transplanted to California. The house was originally erected in 1790 in Torrington, Connecticut. Its typical period-design shows in the long slope of the roofline toward the rear, the wood-latticed windows, and the clapboarded facade. In 1865, Julian McAllister bought the house. Then he had it disassembled and shipped around Cape Horn to its present site. In 1865, a master bedroom and kitchen were added to the rear in "lean-to" fashion. If this house's true age is the original date of construction, then it can be considered the oldest standing building in the East Bay. Now it's the Rectory of St. Paul's Church.

15    St. Paul's Episcopal Church. 1st and E. J sts., southeast corner. This redwood Gothic Revival church is a clean, finely rendered example of "Carpenter Gothic." The tower, with its crisp, vertical lines and hollow wooden "buttresses," is especially nice. The stained-glass windows in the nave are superb. (Ask at McAllister House for permission to see them.) The congregation was formed in 1854, and the church was erected between 1858 and 1859.

16    Stick house. 140 W. I St. Exceptionally refined sawn-wood floral friezes are enhanced by the tasteful color scheme. The original wrought-iron fence is still in place. c. 1880–1890.

17    Late-Victorian Colonial Revival cottage. 224 W. I St. In addition to the two palm trees in front, there is also an elongated portico. c. 1895.

18    Stick-style house. 281 W. I St. c. 1880–1890.

19    Stick–Eastlake house. 715 W. 3rd St. Note the unusual patterns of sawn-wood decorations on the porch and main gable. c. 1880–1890.

20    Stick–Eastlake house. 124 W. H St. This huge house has an ample, farmhouse-like setting. The subdued color scheme pleasantly offsets the delicate stickwork and sunbursts in the gables. A small carriage house in the front yard, a white picket fence, and several large trees scattered about the spacious lot lend a country air to the entire setting. c. 1876.

21    False-front Italianate house. 166 W. H St. c. 1870s.

22    Classic Revival commercial building. 718 1st St. This stone structure has an indented pediment and a portico motif. c. 1890s.

23    Old State Capitol Building. 1st and W. G sts., northwest corner. About the best example of Greek Revival architecture remaining in California, this building resembles many of its eastern counterparts. The massive Doric columns (actually made of stuccoed-over brick) and wide, dentiled pediment with a bull's-eye window are quite impressive. The building was the state capitol for only one year. After that it served various municipal functions — most recently (several years ago), it was converted into a state historic monument and was opened to the public for tours.

24    Fischer House. 137 W. G St. This Gold-Rush-Era hotel was built about 1848 at another location. Bought by Joseph Fischer in 1856, moved to its present site, and greatly remodeled, this house blends the Greek Revival style (its split-pilastered and dentil-lined portico) with the East Coast Federal style (hipped roof; tall, rectangular chimneys; and shuttered and square-latticed windows). It is now open to the public as a state monument. (Ask at the State Capitol about hours.)

25    "Pioneer classic box." 150 W. G St. Note the spindled porch. c. 1870s.

26    Brick Italianate commercial storefront building. 636 1st St. Note the detailed cornice. c. 1880s.

27    False-front commercial building. 440 1st St. The gable is in Mission Revival style. c. 1900–1910.

28    Old City Hotel. 415 and 411 1st St. These two "classic Pioneer box"-type buildings moved to their present site from the waterfront in 1910. Once they served as a workingman's hotel, where rooms were 25 cents a night and a hot bath (a luxury in those days) was 50 cents. The sign on the transom is a recent restoration, and the brackets were taken from another building. c. 1870–1875.

29    Classic Revival wood-front commerical building. 401 1st St. The Colonial Revival trim on the ground floor probably was added later. c. 1880s.

BEN-20

30      Washington House Hotel. 1st and W. D sts., southwest corner. A true remnant of the raucous and sometimes raunchy Gold-Rush-Era lifestyle, this Pioneer-box-style "house" was built by shipwrights between about 1846 and 1850 and probably was moved to its present location from a waterfront pier that was sinking. In its early days it was an inexpensive hotel, but in 1895 it reopened as the first-class Washington House Hotel, on its current site. At various times in its checkered past, the building has been used as a residence for state legislators, a Chinese lottery, a brothel, a speakeasy, and a gambling house (which finally was closed after the police chief was indicted in a pay-off scandal in 1954). The structure currently houses an antique shop.

31      "Pioneer box"-style house. 120 W. D St. c. 1870.

32      Pioneer saltbox. 123 W. D St. Prefabricated in the East, this house was assembled on its current site. c. 1848.

33      Saltbox house. 145 W. D St. This one is situated attractively near the water's edge. c. 1850s.

## Detour — Worth a Side Trip

34      Benicia Industrial Park. (Go north on 1st St. to E. Military Highway; turn right; follow it all the way to the end.) Ulysses S. Grant and the famous southern commander of the Civil War, General Johnston, were young officers in this military installation, formerly the U.S. Army Benicia Arsenal, established in 1847. Matthew Perry also visited here in 1854, after a trip around the world. A large number of the original buildings still stand, and many remain in good condition or have been restored. Walk around the grounds and visit. Guard House (1872); Clock Tower (1859 — one of the oldest and finest stone buildings in the state); Commandant's House (1860 — open to the public as a restaurant); Powder Magazine (1857); Camel Barns (1853–1854); and the Corinthian-colonnaded Enlisted Men's Barracks (c. 1870).

35      John Muir House. 4 Alhambra Rd., Martinez. (Go south across the Martinez Toll Bridge to Highway 580; turn right off the freeway at the Martinez exit; then follow the signs.) This excellent Italianate villa, set in lush surroundings, was for many years the home of John Muir, the great conservationist who founded the Sierra Club. The 1848 Martinez Adobe, a two-story Mexican adobe with a Monterey-style balcony, is also on the grounds, at the rear. The Muir House is a California state landmark and is open to the public as a museum, including on Saturdays. c. 1884.

# Berkeley

Population: 120,000. First U.S. settlement: 1852, along the Bay (first called Oceanview). Incorporated: 1878. Area: 18.07 square miles. Architectural characteristics: Several hundred Victorian homes and churches still exist throughout the city, of which several dozen are noteworthy. Mainly known for its Brown Shingles of the First Bay traditionists by resident architects such as Maybeck, Morgan, Coxhead, and others. U.C. campus spans various styles from mansarded, Italianate to Brutalist, preponderance of buildings in Beaux-Arts neo-Classical tradition by John Galen Howard. The city also has numerous fine Colonial Revival, Prairie-influence, and Moderne and Art Deco buildings, as well as a heavy complement of Period Revival homes in the residential hills and Claremont district.

## Areas Covered by Walking Tours
Tour A: Victorian North Berkeley
Tour B: North Berkeley Foothills
Tour C: Northgate
Tour D: "Nut Hill"
Tour E: University of California Campus
Tour F: Downtown
Tour G: South Campus
Tour H: College Homestead Area
Tour I: Claremont Area
Tour J: Ocean View
Tour K: Southwest Berkeley

It often surprises many non-Californians that Berkeley is an established city of gracious old homes, wide, tree-lined streets, and winding hillside paths reminscent of Alpine settlements. But an enduring fabric of late-nineteenth- and early-twentieth-century architecture has remained behind the scenes, lending a note of stability to this avant-garde community throughout all the social and political upheavals that have characterized recent Berkeley history. Berkeley architecture itself was once revolutionary in its own way; at the turn of the century, the First Bay Tradition designs of the city's great architects were considered provocative. But what now remains of historic architecture in Berkeley — much of it painstakingly protected by a strong preservation movement — is, in its almost infinite variety and charming character, truly delightful to behold.

Berkeley began as dozens of other Bay Area towns had — as a small community of squatters setting up homesteads on a Spanish land grant during the Gold Rush. Oceanview, the first Yankee settlement, occurred in 1852 along the Bay. By the time the stagecoach line came through along San Pablo Avenue in the 1860s, Oceanview was a fair-sized town whose working-class citizens worked for the various light industries that began to locate there.

Meanwhile, a very different type of community slowly took root in the gentle, rolling foothills surrounding the newly established University of California campus. The community began with a few scattered farms in the 1860s, and after the university was chartered in 1868, the settlement that was to become Berkeley grew steadily. In 1876, the Central Pacific Railroad branch line connected Berkeley with Oakland and led to a real estate boom: several large tracts of land in the south campus area that had been owned by such prominent city fathers as Francis Shattuck and George Blake were subdivided and sold off in lots to new residents. In the 1870s, the San Francisco–Berkeley ferry line carried

*BERK F-15*

increasing numbers of people to Berkeley who came to settle in the rapidly growing areas around the university. In 1878, the campus community and Oceanview were finally joined together and incorporated as the city of Berkeley. The name was derived from England's Lord Berkeley, who made the now-famous statement, "Westward the course of empire takes its way."

Berkeley continued to grow throughout the 1880s. During that decade, steps were taken to ensure the development of a dignified community, one that would properly reflect its status as the seat of a great institution of learning. The following passage, from Joseph E. Baker's *History of Alameda County* (1914), demonstrates this aspiration well:

> *War against selling liquor within one mile of the university broke out in 1885 and involved all the best citizens against the saloon owners. The law had gone into effect April 3, 1876, but there were constant violations regardless of numerous prosecutions which seldom secured convictions — juries decided for the saloon keepers. Finally the regents agreed to unite to pay the costs of such vigorous prosecutions as would establish the supremacy of the law and the best businessmen agreed to stand back of them. Under the first attack there were ten acquittals to one conviction; this condition of affairs caused the citizens' committee to extend their line of attack and to arm for permanent results. In the end they succeeded.*

Mostly between the years 1890 and 1930, the flatlands between Grove Street and San Pablo Avenue were filled in. During those years, the local community of architects who created the movement that came to be known as the First Bay Tradition helped transform the largely rural Berkeley townscape into an urban setting of unique architectural quality and character.

Increasingly conscious of their fine architectural heritage, Berkeleyans have taken major steps to ensure its survival: a city-wide preservation movement concentrates on preserving the historic and esthetic character of the city's various neighborhoods. As a result, Berkeley has managed to retain a special architectural quality in each of its major districts. This gives the city an unusual variety of human environments, considering the size of its community. That is why so many walking tours are included in this section. Berkeley is still, as old real estate brochures used to proclaim, truly "the city of homes," and the diversity to be explored is practically endless.

# Berkeley Tour A

## Victorian North Berkeley

### Tour Notes

The North Berkeley flatlands between Oxford and McGee streets have a rich history of early settlement in the late nineteenth century and of large-scale development in the early twentieth century. An interesting variety of Victorian homes and commercial buildings can be seen here, ranging from the Bracketed Italianate houses to late Queen Anne cottages. A number of seafaring men chose to settle in this neighborhood, and one of them, Captain Joseph Boudrow, built an imposing Queen Anne towered house at 1536 Oxford Street — unquestionably the largest and finest Victorian remaining in Berkeley. Another retired seaman, a ship's carpenter named John Paul Moran, left two of the best Eastlake-Villa-style homes in Berkeley, including his own residence at 1712 Lincoln Street (c. 1880s). The area was subdivided around 1900, and several tract developments were created. After the turn of the century, the North Berkeley flatlands attracted hundreds of residents who built homes in these developments. Thus, the streets of this area contain not only scattered pockets of Victoriana, but also many fine Colonial Revival houses, most of them with intact facades. Amid their pleasantly landscaped settings, these homes give a good idea of what life in an upper-middle-class residential community was like three generations ago.

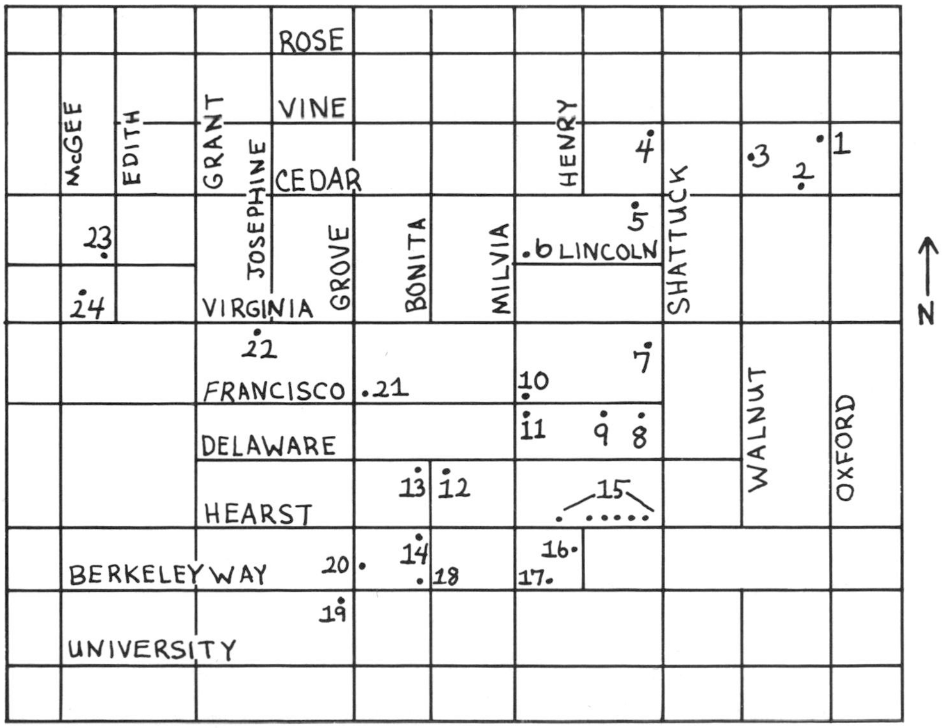

1     Captain Boudrow House. 1536 Oxford St. Recently declared a city landmark, this imposing Queen Anne Revival home was built by a retired sea captain who owned a fleet of merchant ships. The four-story tower, balustraded front stairway, cast-iron fence, and stained-glass window (depicting Boudrow's flagship) set into an intricately carved redwood door all create an aura of elegance that is fast vanishing from the urban scene. 1889.

2    Cast-iron railings. Cedar between Oxford and Walnut. These railings, which run the entire length of Boudrow's original property along Cedar and halfway up Walnut, include a section that winds up a double-curved flight of concrete steps to a landscaped landing. c. 1890.

3    Hanscom House. 1525 Walnut. One of the earliest homes in North Berkeley and the oldest house on Walnut, this double-bayed Italianate was shingled around the turn of the century. 1875.

4    Queen Anne wood-front store. Shattuck and Vine. Probably the oldest commercial building still standing along Shattuck Avenue, this store has a small, porticoed side-entrance for second-floor residences. 1895.

5    Colonial Revival apartments. 2022–2028 Cedar St. With an attractive Doric-columned portico and a frieze and cornice line above each bay, this four-unit building is one of the earliest apartment houses in Berkeley. c. 1900.

6    Queen Anne/Eastlake house. Lincoln and Milvia Sts. Large machine-cut, Eastlake-style sunburst panels are set into each gable. c. 1892.

*BERK A-10*

7    Stick–Eastlake/Queen Anne cottage. 1708 Shattuck Ave. This attractively restored, raised-basement cottage mixes Eastlake-style sunbursts, stickwork, and Queen Anne fish-scale shingles; and, since it recently was converted into small shops and offices, it is an excellent example of adaptive reuse. c. 1885–1890.

8    Queen Anne/Colonial Revival house. 2028 Francisco St. This very original color scheme emphasizes the Colonial Revival details (garlands above the tower windows, dentils along the cornice). c. 1895–1900.

9    Queen Anne house. 2026 Francisco St. Together with number 2028, these two late-Victorian homes provide a good idea of the nineteenth-century urban residential environment. c. 1890–1895.

10    Flagg–Wright House. Milvia and Francisco sts., northeast corner. An absolutely magnificent example of an "individualized" Stick–Eastlake villa, this impressive home was built by an English ships' carpenter named John Paul Moran for Isaac Flagg, a professor of Greek at U.C. Later, a Mr. Wright, owner of the Golden Sheaf Bakery, bought the house, and the Colonial Revival porch was probably added at that time (1901). Note especially Moran's "signature" below each corner of the rear-gable bargeboard: twin sets of carved anchors. 1880.

11    Colonial Revival house. 1729 Milvia St. This high-peaked house has a curved, overhanging bay window along the side, fine, narrow clapboarding, and leaded windows. It was moved to its present site from Shattuck Avenue around the time of the 1906 earthquake. c. 1900.

*BERK A-17*

12    Italianate house. 1930 Delaware St. The cupola and tall, narrow, curved windows are original features of what was probably an early farmhouse. The klinker-brick chimney, dormer windows, and pillared porch were added shortly after 1900. c. 1880–1885.

13    Colonial Revival house. 1802 Bonita St. This early-Colonial-Revival design has a sloping "lean-to" roofline, an outsized dormer window with pilastered corners, and a large Palladian window in front. c. 1895–1900.

14    Italianate house. 1942 Hearst. This small, hipped-roof house has delicately cut brackets along its cornice. c. 1875–1885.

15     Six late-Victorian houses. 2009, 2019, 2027, 2029, 2033, and 2035 Hearst, between Shattuck and Henry Sts. These small homes display all the popular stylistic motifs of their day in a typically late-Victorian mixture. Note especially numbers 2035 (recently restored) and 2019, with their combination of Queen Anne, Stick–Eastlake, and Colonial Revival details. This block presents an unusually large and well-maintained remnant of nineteenth-century Berkeley. c. 1890–1895.

16     Italianate house. 1912 Henry. A broken pediment on the main gable and pipe-stem columns in the angled bay embellish this small "workingman's" Victorian. c. 1875–1885.

17     Stick/Gothic cottage. 2009 Berkeley Way. No pure examples of the Gothic Revival house remain in Berkeley, but this weather-beaten Stick cottage, with its high-peaked gables decorated by bargeboards, pendants, and board-and-battening, manages to create a distinctly Gothic mood. c. 1875–1880.

18     Bay Commons. Berkeley Way and Bonita St., southeast corner. This Colonial Revival commercial building was originally a stable built by the City of Berkeley. The fine Georgian-style motifs (shutters, pedimented gable, scrollwork above the Bonita entrance, and prominent cupola) have remained intact, although the building itself has been used for a variety of purposes. 1905.

19     Stick–Eastlake villa. 1830 Berkeley Way. Still owned by the daughter of its builder, this house's perpendicular facade and odd-shaped tower have a wealth of Eastlake details, including stylized sunbursts, upright curved brackets, and geometric, stained-glass windows. c. 1888.

20     Colonial Revival house. 1905 Grove St. The common Colonial Revival details, such as half-round portico, oval windows, and scrollwork above the balcony, are rendered quite inventively on this exceptionally graceful building. The two flanking palm trees provide a handsome framework. c. 1900–1905.

21     Colonial Revival house. Francisco and Grove Sts., northeast corner. This early example has a corner turret, a vestige of the previous Queen Anne style. c. 1895–1905.

22     Schmidt House. 1816 Virginia. Built by a prosperous cabinetmaker, this unique, raised-basement "cottage" is embellished elaborately — fish-scale shingles, Ionic columns, Gothic arch, and fine latticework along the porch; molded scrollwork and cut-out floral panel in the gable; and a mysterious figurehead (perhaps of Ludwig von Beethoven) above the attic window. A superb restoration. c. 1885–1890.

23     Italianate house. 1612 Edith. This house has a double-angled bay, and uses a tall, narrow, rowhouse-type design, which was then common in San Francisco and parts of Oakland but rare in relatively rural Berkeley. c. 1880.

24     Moran House. 1712 Lincoln St. Visible only from the driveway that leads to its site in the middle of the block, John Paul Moran's own house, a Stick–Eastlake villa, looks like an inverted ship's hull, topped by a catty-corner captain's bridge. From this bridge, Moran looked out through his spy glass at the Bay — in all, a fitting home for an old seafaring man. The rich ornamentation, much of it Moran's own design, includes his anchor signature; three- and four-leaf clovers cut out of the flower box; stickwork; an Eastlake sunburst panel; and an American Indian "God's-eye" motif along the porch above the entrance. c. 1880–1890.

## Tour Notes

The area of Berkeley that lies north of the U.C. campus, between Arch and Walnut streets and up to Glen Avenue, is a region of gently rolling foothills. Once this region was divided into nine separate tract developments, and the romantic-sounding names of some of these subdivisions give some idea of the neighborhood's Alpine character around the turn of the century: Grandview Terrace, Berkeley Villa, Antisel Villa, and Highlands. The first American settlement in North Berkeley occurred in this area, when Napoleon Byrne arrived from Missouri and, in 1868, built a house that still stands at 1301 Oxford Street. Not much development occurred until the 1880s and '90s, when tracts of homes on Arch and Vine Streets were built.

After 1900, many professional people, including a number of families connected with the university, moved into this neighborhood and commissioned some of the best architects of the day to design their homes. In 1923, a fire damaged the area greatly, but fortunately most of the section north of Cedar was spared. Anyone exploring these pleasant streets has a most rewarding experience in store. A fine selection of late-Victorian, First Bay Tradition and Period Revival houses are to be enjoyed.

# North Berkeley Foothills

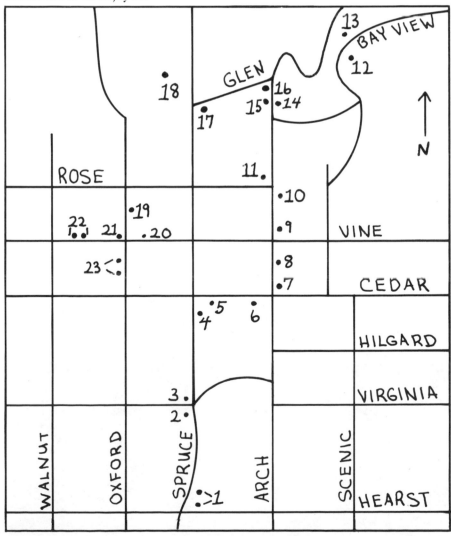

*BERK B-2*

1       Thornberg Village. 1817–1839 and 1781–1783 Spruce St. Sometimes called Normandy Village, this whimsical collection of apartment houses in Hansel and Gretel style was designed by one of the masters of the genre, William R. Yelland. Yelland designed the complex for Thornberg, a personal friend who had been an ace in the Lafayette Escadrille in France in World War I. The crazily exaggerated gables and humorously carved gargoyles on beam ends mask a meticulous craftsmanship and use of historically correct materials that give these structures an authentic, if somewhat "Disneyesque," character. 1927–1928.

2       Loring House. 1730 Spruce St. Designed by John Hudson Thomas, this is one of the best examples of the Prairie Style in the Bay Area. Indeed, it almost could have come directly from some of Frank Lloyd Wright's prototype designs published in the *Ladies Home Journal*. 1914.

3       William Acheson House. 1650 Spruce St. This Mediterranean, stuccoed house with Prairie-style influence was designed by James W. Plachek, the man who later designed the Berkeley Public Library. c. 1923.

4       Georgian Revival house. 1609 Spruce St. Here is a good example of a gambrel-roofed house with "Williamsburg" flavor. c. 1925–1935.

5       Georgian Revival house. 2274 Cedar St. This small, whitewashed brick house has a charming, formal, boxwood garden, enclosed by an attractive picket fence. c. 1935.

6       Hillside Club. 2286 Cedar St. The brown-shingled walls of this sophisticated, First Bay Tradition building blend in beautifully with their surroundings. The original building was designed by Bernard Maybeck to house a private club of esthetically minded Berkeley citizens dedicated to spreading their high ideals of art and beauty. (Maybeck himself was one of their founders.) After the 1923 fire, the club was rebuilt along similar lines by Maybeck's brother-in-law, Mark White. Original design c. 1914; rebuilt 1924.

7       Queen Anne house. 1515 Arch St. This sizeable house has a wide corner-turret, a Colonial Revival porch, and brown shingling (probably added at a later date). c. 1890–1895.

8       Captain Marston House. 1511 Arch St. This impressive Georgian Colonial Revival house has a fine Palladian window in its pedimented gable. Kidder and McCullough designed it for one of several sea captains who settled in North Berkeley. 1905.

*BERK B-6*

*BERK B-17*

9      Gough House. 1431 Arch St. An uncommon Queen Anne house, this has an interesting, hexagonal tower above its spindle-lined porch. Attributed to Ira Boynton, a highly successful Victorian-Era Berkeley architect, this is the oldest recorded house on Arch Street. 1886.

10     Late-Victorian house. 1415 Arch St. Transitional character is evident in the square corner turret, stickwork trim, clapboarding, and Colonial Revival detailing. 1897.

11     Fred Wallace House. 1340 Arch St. at Rose. Here is an excellent First Bay Tradition house that blends Craftsman and Swiss Chalet elements, and is set into a beautifully wooded lot. 1905.

12     Senger House. 1321 Bayview Pl. Bernard Maybeck designed this uniquely arranged First Bay Tradition house, which has a fake ceremonial entrance and a floorplan oriented toward a large private garden off the street. 1907.

13     Swiss-Chalet-style house. 1322 Bayview Pl. Henry Gutterson designed this charming house, which has colorful, folk-style stenciled patterns. c. 1924.

14     Schneider–Kroeber House. 1325 Arch St. This magnificent Swiss chalet, set high up on a terraced lot, was designed by Bernard Maybeck and appears to have been transported directly from a Swiss mountainside. Professor Kroeber, who occupied the house for many of its early years, was one of the founders of the School of Anthropology at the University of California, and his wife Theodora later chronicled his experiences with a native California Indian in the book *Ishi*. 1907.

15     Cutter House. 1314 Arch St. Richard Swaesey designed this large, whitewashed, Tudor Revival house. 1910–1912.

16     Hitching post. In front of 1300 Arch St. The post is a rare survivor of horse-and-buggy days, complete with tether ring. c. 1890s.

17     Dempstor House. 2204 Glen Ave. at Spruce. This impressive, owner-designed Brown Shingle house has a witch's hat corner turret and massive, Craftsman-style beaming along the porch. This porch was designed to allow the house to withstand earthquake shocks — an important consideration, since the house stands almost directly over a major fault line. 1908.

18     Napoleon Byrne House. 1301 Oxford St. at Berryman Path. This substantial Italianate villa has a midwestern-style, balustraded veranda across the front. The generous, lushly landscaped lot in which the house now sits is only a small part of the original Byrne estate. The iron gateway at the front entrance was added arond 1910, when Oxford Street was cut through. Byrne was an ex-slave-owner from Missouri who brought several freedmen with him as hired hands. Those freedmen thus became the first black residents of Berkeley. This is the oldest documented building remaining in the city. 1868.

19     Late-Victorian house. 1425 Oxford St. This house has an uncommon blend of Italianate and Stick-style elements and a rather awkward handling of the porch and bays. c. 1890.

20     Large Queen Anne house. 2213 Vine St. The enclosed, lattice-windowed sun porch probably was added later. c. 1892.

21     Andrew Weir House. 2163 Vine St. at Oxford. This raised-basement, Stick–Eastlake cottage has a spindled front porch, as well as an elongated exposure along Oxford that displays all the hallmarks of this style (squared bays, stickwork, geometric friezes, and sunburst panels). Weir was an early trustee of the Berkeley School District. c. 1885–1895.

22     Two eclectic Victorian houses. 2155 and 2157 Vine St. Elements of both Queen Anne and Stick–Eastlake styles are visible. c. 1890–1895.

23     Captain McCleave Houses. 1510 and 1512 Oxford St. Designed by George Embry, these two Queen Anne houses were built speculatively. 1891.

*BERK B-21*

## Tour Notes

The neighborhood commonly referred to as Northgate was first settled in the 1890s, when U.C. professors and other professional people began building homes in the area. One of the first was the Frank Wilson House, an early (1894) brown-shingled structure that stood at Ridge Road and Le Conte until it was demolished in 1976. Wilson, a businessman and developer, helped plot many of the subdivisions in the area and planted the row of feather-duster palm trees that still line Ridge Road above Euclid.

In the early years of the twentieth century, Northgate was the site of many fine, architect-designed homes, all of which blended well with their usually woodsy sites. The 1923 fire swept through much of the neighborhood, destroying or damaging many of the wooden houses. After the fire, large-scale apartment house development began, mostly in the Mediterranean mode. The area between Arch and Euclid known as "Holy Hill" housed a number of theological seminaries during the 1920s and '30s. Now these are joined together under the Graduate Theological Union, and several impressive Gothic Revival buildings in brick and stone currently crown the hillside. A stroll through this esthetically pleasing neighborhood reveals excellent work by nearly every major architect active in Berkeley during the early twentieth century, as well as fine representatives of most of the Period Revival styles popular at that time.

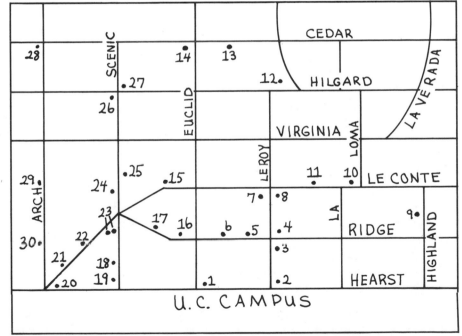

1    Euclid Apartments. 1865 Euclid Ave. at Hearst. John Galen Howard designed this sophisticated, neo-Classic building. c. 1912.

2    Beta Theta Pi House. 2607 Hearst Ave. at LeRoy. Coxhead and Coxhead did the original design, and Bakewell and Brown did the later additions. This is a superb, English-Tudor style complex of connected wings. The half-timbered section paralleling LeRoy has been resurfaced. Now the building is used as the Graduate School of Public Policy, and the rich, oak, Elizabethan-style "curtain-fold" paneling inside can be seen (make a request at the front desk). 1893; later additions 1909.

*BERK C-2*

3     Cloyne Court. 2600 Ridge Rd. at LeRoy. Designed by John Galen Howard, this relatively straightforward, brown-shingled, four-story block has shallow balconies facing the street and an interesting, three-sided court in back, enhanced by short turrets along the roofline. 1904.

4     "Allenoke," Freeman house. 1765–1769 LeRoy Ave. at Ridge. Coxhead and Coxhead designed this klinker-brick-surfaced mansion in a cross between the Georgian and Dutch Colonial modes, with a high-peaked gable, quoining, and gambreled dormers. The gardens along Ridge Road are especially beautiful, with their high, brick, enclosing wall; formal boxwood landscaping; sundial; and wood-lath, gazebo-like garden house at the rear. 1904–1906.

5     "Allenoke" carriage house and gates. 2533 Ridge Rd. Behind these fabulous wrought-iron entry gates with basket-of-fruit finials atop their pillars is the old Freeman Mansion's carriage house, also designed by Coxhead and Coxhead, with ornate metal hanging light fixtures projecting from its brick facade. The tree in the middle of LeRoy Avenue once stood on the grounds of Allenoke, between the mansion and the carriage house. 1904.

6     Late-Victorian house. 2531 Ridge Rd. One of the few Victorian homes in this neighborhood, this one has a Queen-Anne-like squared corner tower. c. 1890–1895.

7     Oscar Mauer Studio. 1772 Le Roy Ave. Bernard Maybeck designed this small, rambling photographic studio that integrates harmoniously with the bank of the stream it sits along. 1907.

8     "Weltevreden," Moody House. 1755 LeRoy Ave. A. C. Schweinfurth originally designed this klinker-brick, Dutch-Colonial-style house with a stepped gable, but in the 1950s U.C. architect Michael Goodman completely remodeled the upper portion. Only the surfacing along the lower wall and the bridge over the stream are original. This was one of the first uses of klinker brick in the East Bay. 1896.

9     Keeler House and Studio. 1770–1790 Highland Pl. This was Bernard Maybeck's first design in the Bay Area and a prototype of the First Bay Tradition. Built for the head of the U.C. Engineering Department, who had placed Maybeck n his faculty the year before, this highly personal building contains a variety of steeply pitched gables and integrates them sensitively into its heavily

wooded site. When Maybeck remodeled the house after the 1923 fire, the original shingles were removed and stucco surfacing was added. Notice the original wooden fence around the property with its carved-out four-leaf-clover designs along the pitched railing. 1895; addition at rear 1902; remodeling 1925.

10    Hatfield House. 2695 LeConte Ave. at La Loma. This white stucco house shows Julia Morgan's characteristic blend of Mediterranean details (around the arched door) and Craftsman beaming (above a recessed corner portico). The generous site is landscaped exquisitely. c. 1912.

11    Brown-Shingle-style house. 2609 LeConte Ave. Several high-peaked gables and banded, latticed windows adorn this huge house, as well as an odd corner-turret with an Islamic-style gilded mosaic dome that was added recently. c. 1905–1915.

12    Spanish Colonial house. 1636 LeRoy Ave. at Hilgard. Alfred Henry Jacobs designed this unusual, octagonal-shaped house. 1925.

13    "Pueblo Revival"-style house. 2532 Cedar St. A bit of the old Southwest in Berkeley, this fascinating house has Prairie School overtones in its horizontal massing. c. 1920–1930.

14    Foulds House. 1600 Euclid Ave. at Cedar. This First Bay Tradition house was designed in architect Henry Gutterson's own blend of adobe and Swiss Chalet styles. Note the bench at the corner; it was included in the overall plan. 1928.

15    Graduate Theological Union. 2465 LeConte Ave. An immense, hipped-roof, klinker-brick, Georgian Revival building, this handles the dormer windows, coach porch, and pedimented portico with great refinement. c. 1925.

16    Church Divinity School of the Pacific. 2449 Ridge Rd. Walter Ratcliff, Jr., designed this brick, Gothic Revival chapel and hall, which are connected by a short, Gothic-arched, covered walkway. 1929.

17    Dominican School of Philosophy and Religion. 2401 Ridge Rd. Stafford Jory rendered an English Tudor Revival design somewhat rigidly and precisely. 1923.

18    Benjamin Ide Wheeler House. 1820 Scenic Ave. This wide, neo-Classic-style house with black-stained shingling and a latticed, glass-enclosed porch was built for the flamboyant, horseback-riding president of the university. 1900.

BERK C-4

19    Pergola for the Edgar Bradley House. Hearst at Scenic, northwest corner. Walk up the stairs on the Scenic Avenue side to see this romantic, vine-covered neo-Classic-style ruin that was designed by Lewis P. Hobart and left over from the 1923 Berkeley fire. A finely carved marble garden-seat, adorned with flanking griffins, completes this feeling of timeless mystery about the place. 1911.

20    Anthony House. Le Conte at Hearst Ave. John B. Anthony's own house provides an excellent example of Streamlined Moderne; it projects upward from its gothic "V"-shaped lot like the captain's bridge of an ocean liner. 1939.

21    Modified Norman-style apartment house. 2317 Le Conte Ave. There is a touch of half-timber trim on this stuccoed building, attributed to Julia Morgan. c. 1924.

22    Kofoid Hall. 2369 Le Conte Ave. Reminscent of early seventeenth-century Parisian apartment houses, this hipped-roof, Louis-XIII-style residence hall comes complete with slate roofing. c. 1925.

23    Phoebe Apperson Hearst House. 2368 Le Conte Ave. Ernest Coxhead designed this Mediterranean Revival house, which has Ionic columns and a broken scrollwork pediment around the doorway. The wood-trimmed reception hall, fronting at 1816 Scenic Avenue, is a more characteristic Coxhead design. Inside the main house is a fine, balustraded stairway and a Spanish-style enclosed patio with an Art Nouveau metal hanging lamp, lush tropical plants, and a cracked tile floor. Built for Phoebe Hearst, the "patron saint" of the university, this house was saved from the 1923 fire by students who diligently kept the roof wet. It is now used as a library by theology students. Ask at the Le Conte entrance for permission to visit. 1900; reception hall, 1902.

24    Holbrook Hall, Pacific School of Religion. 1798 Scenic Ave. at Le Conte. Designed by Walter H. Ratcliff, Jr., and serving as the library and administration building for the Pacific School of Religion, this fine, English Academic Gothic design has rusticated-stone walls, clasping buttresses, and ornate finials. Inside the library wing are a huge chandelier, massive roof beams, and a large Tudor fireplace. 1924.

25    University Christian Church. Scenic Ave. between Le Conte and Virginia. Walter J. Ratcliff, Jr., also designed this English Parish Gothic church, with its imposing tower. The largest redwood beams in Berkeley support the roof of the nave. 1931.

26    Mediterranean Revival house. 1600 Scenic Ave. at Hilgard. Mixing modes, this unusual house has a Monterey Revival balcony on Scenic. An arcaded, covered stairway runs along Hilgard. c. 1925–1935.

27    Spanish Colonial Revival house. 1645 Scenic Ave. at Hilgard. There is a round turret above the entrance. c. 1925–1935.

28    New-England-saltbox-type house. 1650 Arch St. at Cedar. Julia Morgan designed this unpretentious place, and its simple beauty is achieved by the well-balanced use of brown-stained shakes and white-trimmed, latticed windows. The attractive picket fence and gate were added recently. 1920.

29    Spanish-style house. 1750 Arch St. With its Moorish pointed-arch windows and wide, sloping corbels on the main floor, and its Islamic-style glazed-tile insets on the second- and ground-floor levels, this is quite a magnificent place. Currently, the Conimicut Foundation uses it for chamber music concerts. c. 1925–1935.

30    Modified Tudor Revival apartment houses. 1810–1836 Arch St. This complex of buildings is set on a U-shaped courtyard. The high-peaked gables are shingled and filled with half-timber trim, while the white stucco walls and arched doorways lend a Mediterranean flavor. c. 1930s.

*BERK C-24*

## Tour Notes

# "Nut Hill"

Various fascinating stories about how this area got its rather unusual nickname abound, but most likely the phrase came from the eccentric character of many of its early residents. Bernard Maybeck was the most prominant (but certainly not the most outlandish) of the many "artistic" souls who lived here during the first few decades of the twentieth century. Other inhabitants included the acclaimed photographer Dorothea Lange, the artist Worth Ryder, the author George Stuart, the painter Lillian Bridgeman, and the dance instructor Boynton. Mark Twain, Jack London, and Isadora Duncan were among those who visited the area.

Many fine First Bay Tradition homes were built including some of Maybeck's best residential designs. But in addition, there are some truly unique, eclectic houses that just delight the senses. Hume Castle and Temple of the Wings are the most outstanding, but many other homes will vie for your attention. Bring a pair of hiking boots and a good walking stick along on this tour — it's strictly uphill all the way!

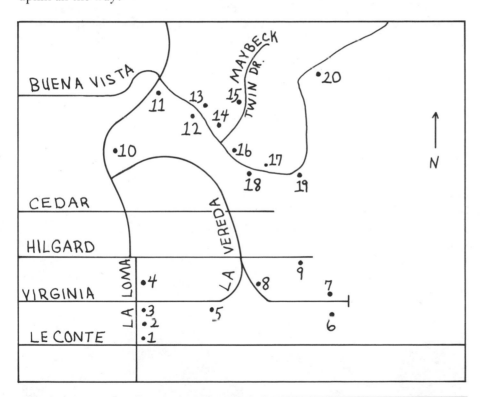

This tour was prepared with some information provided by Jane and Chris Adams of the Berkeley Architectural Heritage Association.

1    Lillian Bridgeman House and Studio. 1715 La Loma Ave. The artist herself designed this to suit her special needs. 1899, 1908.

2    E. C. Priber House. 1709 La Loma Ave. This stucco house, designed by Bernard Maybeck, has wide, overhanging, wood-beamed eaves and neo-Classic balustraded balcony above the side wing. 1910.

*BERK D-3*

3    Reese House. 1705 La Loma at Virginia. Here is a First Bay Tradition version of a Swiss chalet, with dummy log-ends projecting from the corners. It was designed by E. A. Hargreaves, an architect who worked for several years in Maybeck's office. 1905.

4    Jensen House. 1675 La Loma Ave. This late-Victorian home (one of the few Victorian houses in the area) was stripped of its ornament and brown-shingled sometime shortly after 1900. 1894.

5    Bray House. 2708 Virginia St. This builder-designed Brown Shingle house was remodeled by John Hudson Thomas about ten years after it was built. The stucco and half-timbering on the facing and the wide Prairie lines show Thomas' contribution. Mrs. Bray was Thomas' sister. 1912; remodeled c. 1922.

6    Lezinsky House. 1730 La Verada Rd. This charming Victorian homestead combines a Dutch Colonial Revival gambrel roof and "hex sign" in the gable with stickwork around the windows and spindles on the front porch. 1894.

7    Brown-Shingle house. 1731 La Verada Rd. The columned porch of this brown-shingled, steeply gabled house shows its Colonial Revival influence. This house was said by its owners to have been built for a German-immigrant dairy farmer who provided milk for much of the U.C. campus community at the turn of the century. c. 1890–1900.

8    Peterson House. 1631 La Verada Rd. Its builder, a Danish interior decorator, used this California "coaching inn"-style residence as a boardinghouse. 1895.

9    Worth Ryder House. 2772 Hilgard Ave. This is a Mediterranean Revival house, with Spanish-Colonial- and Italian-Renaissance-style elements. Worth Ryder painted early California landscapes and entertained such prominent guests as Bernard Maybeck, Jack London, and Isadora Duncan. The original house was begun about the turn of the century, but when it was later damaged by a mild earthquake, Ryder rebuilt most of the present house himself. c. 1930s.

10    Lawson House. 1515 La Loma Ave. The horizontal lines of this concrete "Pompeii villa"-style house have a Prairie School influence. Bernard Maybeck designed Lawson House (one of the first two prestressed concrete houses to be built in California) as an earthquake-proof building. Lawson, Maybeck's client, discovered the San Andreas Fault. 1907.

*BERK D-10*

*BERK D-11*

11 Mathewson "Studio"-House. 2704 Buena Vista Rd. at La Loma. Architect Bernard Maybeck combined a Prairie School horizontality with First Bay Tradition woodcraftsmanship. 1916.

12 Spanish Colonial Revival house. 2718 Buena Vista Rd. Note the Swiss-Chalet-style roofline. c. 1925.

13 Maybeck "Sack" House. 1711 Buena Vista Rd. This was Bernard Maybeck's own residence for many years. His innovative "bubblestone" siding was created by dipping gunny sacks in concrete. 1924.

14 Tufts House. 1733 Buena Vista Rd. One of Maybeck's later designs, this house combines fire-resistant materials (the concrete walls) with natural wood-craftsmanship (the steeply pitched, shingled gables). The brightly colored, stenciled patterns on the garage door facing Maybeck Twin Drive are a delightful touch. 1931.

15 First Bay Tradition house. 1 Maybeck Twin Dr. Bernard Maybeck used the same bubblestone siding on his own home, nearby, as he did on this small house. c. 1925–1935.

*BERK D-16*

16 Wallen Maybeck House. 2751 Buena Vista Rd. at Maybeck Twin Dr. Bernard Maybeck originally designed this steeply gabled house for his son, and it displays all the hallmarks of the elder Maybeck's highly personal blend of modern and traditional materials and design elements. Damaged by fire a few years after it was built, the house was restored lovingly by Maybeck. Its original design was retained, and so — by sanding away its charred surface — was most of the original wood. 1933; restored c. 1940.

17 Thomas Brown House. 2753 Buena Vista Rd. William C. Hays designed this unique, First Bay Tradition house for a minister. The design is essentially a Renaissance Florentine palazzo, in wood and stucco. The arcaded balcony on the upper floor provides a sweeping vista of the Bay and the hills below. 1914.

18 Gannon House. 2780 Buena Vista Rd. Here is a shingled, late-First-Bay-Tradition-design house by Bernard Maybeck. 1924.

*BERK D-19*

*BERK D-20*

19    "Temple of the Wings," Boynton House. 2800 Vista Rd. This stunning Beaux Arts neo-Classic building could not be more aptly named. The curved Corinthian colonnade joins the two main wings of the house, which was designed by A. Randolph Monroe to provide an area for dance instruction as well as for living in. The central section has an open-air stage for dance performances, which Mrs. Boynton's daughter still gives. Originally, Bernard Maybeck was asked to draw up plans for the house, but Mrs. Boynton pronounced his design unacceptable and found a younger architect, who followed her specifications to the letter. The house was badly burned in the 1923 fire (only the columns were left standing), and the present home was rebuilt in a more fire-resistant manner. 1914; rebuilt 1924.

20    Hume Castle. 2900 Buena Vista Rd. Truly the crowning achievement of "Nut Hill" architecture, this breathtaking mansion, designed by John Hudson Thomas, is a concrete replica of a thirteenth-century-type southern French monastery. Elements of both Romanesque and Gothic styles can be seen in its turreted walls. A crouching lion guards the entrance stairway, and two superbly detailed, wrought-iron Gothic lamp-holders from Italy are at the door. Inside is a perfect replica of a French Gothic cloister, with an ornate, iron-grillwork shroud over a genuine thirteenth-century well in the center. Mrs. Hume has donated the house to the university to be used as an ecclesiastic law library, and once it undergoes some minor remodeling it should be open to the public in 1980. This house is well worth the climb! 1928.

## Tour Notes

Just a little over a hundred years ago, the U.C. Berkeley campus was set in a sylvan, tree-covered grassland traversed by the two branches of Strawberry Creek, which ran down gently from the rolling hillside. Today, the roughly two-mile-square main campus boasts of several dozen structures, whose style ranges from high Victorian elegance (South Hall) to the frankly stark, late-twentieth-century Concrete Brutalism.

As the inscription on Founder's Rock above Gayley Road at Hearst shows, the decision to locate the university at Berkeley was made in 1860. However, construction of the first building, South Hall, was not completed until 1873. In 1865, the regents invited Frederick Law Olmstead, the great landscape architect, to come from New York to lay out the plan for the new college grounds. Although most of his designs for the arrangement of buildings were never used, his plan to retain both branches of Strawberry Creek, with their tree-shaded banks, was; and it is largely to his foresight that we owe the survival of these natural wonders.

When the university was chartered in 1868, David Farquharson was appointed the first campus architect. His idea was to provide a sweeping, uninterrupted view of the Bay by orienting the campus on an east–west axis, running down from the high ground around the Campanile. The regents accepted Farquharson's designs for the first six campus buildings, but all but South Hall have since been torn down.

A handful of other late-Victorian structures were added to the campus over the next generation, without any overriding architectural concept. Then, in 1897, Mrs. Phoebe Apperson Hearst took Bernard Maybeck's suggestion and sponsored an international competition to develop a master architectural plan for the university. In 1902, after much deliberation, John Galen Howard, a New Yorker who had run fourth in the competition, was appointed as university architect, to

# University of California Campus

*BERK E-8*

*BERK E-4 and 8*

*BERK E-7*

interpret and carry out the winning design. Howard revised that plan several times, making it into virtually a new one of his own. Restrained Beaux-Arts neo-Classic buildings in white stone, with red clay-tile roofs, were used as the unifying theme. Howard remained the university architect for a quarter of a century (until 1927), during which time he designed such campus landmarks as Sather Gate, the Campanile, and Doe Library. George Kelham followed as supervising architect until 1936, and most of the last major monumental structures were erected under his tenure, until the Depression slowed construction. The final university architect, Arthur Brown, Jr., resigned in 1948. Since the 1950s, new development has occurred in a "design-by-committee" fashion. To this trend we owe such symbols of the modern age as Evans Hall and Wurster Hall. A stroll through the still park-like setting of the U.C. campus, however, will reveal the enduring esthetic quality of the university's fine historic buildings.

1    Sproul Hall. Arthur Brown designed this heavy, compact version of late-neo-Classic architecture — the last building in this style built on campus. 1940.

2    Sather Gate. Designed by John Galen Howard, this formal, Beaux-Arts-style arched gateway marks the original entrance to the campus (before Sproul Plaza was laid out in 1960). The blank panels that now decorate the stone pillars originally had bas-relief sculptures of nude male and female figures. The still-visible inscription beneath one of the male figures, honoring the woman who donated the gate to the university, reads, "Erected by Jane K. Sather." When Mrs. Sather saw a photograph of the nude figure with the inscription directly below it, she ordered all the panels to be removed posthaste. 1908–1910.

3    Old university heating plant. John Galen Howard designed this brick, Romanesque Revival building with a large skylight, which served as the University Art Museum for many years. The east wall shows large, neo-Byzantine-style mosaics that were done in 1937 by W.P.A.-sponsored artists. 1904.

4    Wheeler Hall. John Galen Howard was responsible for this well-proportioned, Beaux Arts building with a raised colonnade across the upper floors. Above the Palladian window at both ends of the main facade are keystones, adorned with imperious, Napoleon-like faces. 1916–1918.

5    Durant Hall. Another John Galen Howard design (and one of his earliest to be completed), this small, clean-lined, neo-Classic building originally housed the School of Law. The Roman-style hanging lamps in the marble lobby and the rich, original decor in the library upstairs are worth noting. 1912.

6    California Hall. This building, also by John Galen Howard, is a relatively unadorned neo-Classic design, with a row of Roman-like bronze finials across the top. 1905.

7    The University Library (Doe Graduate Library). John Galen Howard created a truly monumental Beaux Arts design in Roman-temple form. The deeply dentiled cornice, massive Corinthian colonnade, and huge, arched windows set below the pediments clearly show Howard's mastery of the Beaux Arts tradition. Above the main entrance on the north face is a bronze head of Athena, the Greek goddess of wisdom. Inside, the most impressive features are the reading room, with its high, barrel-vaulted ceiling and arched windows that provide sweeping vistas; and the incredibly ornate, Renaissance-style coffered bronze ceiling in the reserve room of the main stacks. Main wing 1907–1911; additions until 1917.

*BERK E-9*

8    Sather Tower, "The Campanile." John Galen Howard designed this 315-foot-tall Italian Renaissance bell tower as the symbol of the university. It pierces the sky with graceful dignity. The limestone sheathing its steel skeleton was quarried in New York. The magnificent bells in the carillon were cast in England and brought across the Atlantic by convoy in the perilous days of World War I. The 10 cents elevator ride to the top, with the spectacular view of the Bay Area, is the best bargain in the East Bay. 1913–1917.

9    South Hall. David Farquharson designed this elegant example of a French Second-Empire, mansard-roofed college hall. The first building erected on campus, South Hall's red-brick, ivy-covered walls give it an air of venerable antiquity. On the upper walls of the north and south facades are bas-relief panels depicting the various fruits, vegetables, and grains produced in California at that time. At the top of the rain spouts on each corner, just underneath the cornice, are devil's-head gargoyles. They glare ominously at mortal passersby. Begun 1870; finished 1873.

10    Moses Hall (Philosophy Department). With this building, architect George Kelham gave the campus a bit of olde English Tudor architecture. 1931.

11    Stephens Hall (the Academic Senate, etc.). Here is John Galen Howard's relatively unadorned example of late-Tudor-Revival style. An arcade leads through the building and down a staircase to the faculty glade. 1923.

12    Le Conte Hall. The original Beaux Arts wing, on the east side, has an unusual, stylized Ionic colonnade and fine, solid-oak doors. The new wing, on the west, opens on the glorious esplanade at the base of the Campanile. Landscaped by John Galen Howard in 1917; original wing 1924; addition by Miller and Warnecke 1950.

13    Gilman Hall. Together with the original wing of Le Conte Hall, Gilman Hall (also designed by John Galen Howard) forms a symmetrically balanced neo-Classic corridor running north from Strawberry Creek to Hearst Mining Circle. 1917.

14    "Men's" Faculty Club. Nestled comfortably into its setting in the Faculty Glade, this building (designed by Bernard Maybeck *et al.*) is a mix of several stylistic elements that harmonize quite well. Maybeck's original wing has a concrete, Mission Revival arcade on the exterior and a rustic, beamed hall with a stone fireplace at one end. The later additions were primarily in keeping with the Brown-Shingle First Bay Tradition. In recent years, the club has been sexually integrated, and now it is open to the public during working hours. Original wing 1902–1903; additions by Warren Perry (1914 and 1925) and George Downs and Henry Lagorio (1959).

15    Senior Men's Hall. John Galen Howard's design for this genuine log cabin, built of massive redwood logs set in a small grove of redwood trees, proves that even Beaux Arts classicists can design for the fun of it. 1906.

16    "Women's" Faculty Club. John Galen Howard was responsible for this dignified, brown-shingled, neo-Classic structure with attractive grounds. 1923.

17    Girton Hall. This woodsy, low-lying, clapboarded, First Bay Tradition structure was designed by one of the greatest First Bay practitioners, Julia Morgan. 1911.

18    Bowles Hall. George Kelham designed this impressively scaled, Tudor Revival concrete "castle" — the first men's undergraduate dormitory built on campus. 1929.

19    Hearst Greek Theater. John Galen Howard, assisted by Julia Morgan, designed this Classical-Greek-style open-air amphitheater. Tiered concrete seats set into the hillside can accommodate several thousand spectators. This was one of the first projects Morgan assisted Howard with, after she returned from the École des Beaux Arts in Paris. 1903.

20    Hearst Mining Building. Also by John Galen Howard, assisted by Julia Morgan, this generally is considered Howard's master interpretation of the Beaux Arts mode. The main pavilion sports elegantly designed, arched entryways and busts of working men and women in the form of stone corbels below the wood-beamed cornice. Inside, the entrance hall sweeps upward from brick walls lined with metal, arched stairways, toward the umbrella-like skylights set into the ceiling. 1902–1907.

21    Naval Architecture Building. John Galen Howard did this superb rendering of the Brown-Shingle First Bay Tradition, with a touch of neo-Classic trim. The step arrangement of the windows on the south facade is an especially pleasing touch. In 1977, the building was narrowly saved from demolition to make way for the site of the new Engineering Department building. 1914.

*BERK E-20*

*BERK E-28*

22    North Gate Hall. John Galen Howard *et al.* designed this brown-shingled structure that was built in stages. Its interior staircase allows visitors to literally climb the hillside inside the building. First wing 1906; additions by Walter Stileberg (1936) and Howard Moisel (1952 and 1955).

23    Leuschner Observatory. Once the home of the student observatory where undergraduates could gaze at the stars, this rambling, one-story, brown-shingled structure was damaged seriously by a fire several years ago. Now it is a fascinating, vine-covered ruin. Original wing by Clinton Day, 1885; addition by John Galen Howard, 1904.

24    Haviland Hall. The west entrance to this late-Beaux-Arts building that John Galen Howard designed is quite grand, with its long, sloping stairway and finely ornamented portico. 1924.

25    University House. Designed by Albert Pissis, this was the first of the buildings to be completed in the white-stone, red-tile-roof, Beaux Arts mode that was to be the unifying theme for the university's architecture for the next generation. The formally landscaped grounds are immaculately kept. Once the university president's house, it is now the home of the chancellor. 1902.

26    Giannini Hall. William C. Hays blended a cleaned-up, late-Beaux-Arts style  with an Art Deco, portico-like pavilion in front. The main lobby has a splendid Egyptian Deco ornamental decor. 1930.

27    Wellman Hall. A curved, rotunda-like projection distinguishes the front of this otherwise-straightforward Beaux Arts building, designed by John Galen Howard. It forms the centerpiece of a U-shaped grouping of structures; the "arms" of the horseshoe are Giannini Hall and Hilgard Hall. 1912.

28    Hilgard Hall. Also by John Galen Howard, this hall has a superb colonnaded facade on the west side, adorned with bas-relief bulls' heads symbolizing fertility and with arabesque panels depicting various farmyard animals. Across the upper frieze a paen to agriculture is carved: "To rescue for human society the native values of rural life." 1916–1918.

*BERK E-32*

29      Life Sciences Building. At the time of its construction, this was the largest academic building in the nation. Designed by George Kelham, this mammoth edifice is a unique blend of neo-Egyptian Art Deco projecting slabs and bas-relief details in front, with neo-Classic columns and pilasters along the north and south sides. 1930.

30      Harmon Gymnasium. Also by George Kelham, this is an early Stream-lined Moderne building, with bas-relief panels of robust male figures between the slabs on the central pavilion. 1933.

31      First Unitarian Church. In the days when Dana Street ran through to the creek, this was not originally part of the campus. This First Bay Tradition, Brown Shingle church was exceptionally well designed by A. C. Schweinfurth. The layered shingling above the round, latticed window on the west end, and the unpeeled redwood log used for the corner porch are especially interesting. The university now uses the building for the Dramatic Arts Department. 1898.

32      Hearst Memorial Gymnasium. Designed by Julia Morgan, assisted by Bernard Maybeck, this building is a masterpiece of modestly scaled Beaux Arts design. The lion-faced urns ringing the exterior may be the nicest touch of all. Around the open-air pool enclosed in the back wing are an assortment of delightful sculptures of united womanhood clad in Grecian gowns, and of female cherubs clutching pigskins. 1925.

33      Two late-Victorian cottages. 2241 and 2243 College Ave. Tucked away behind the monumental concrete block of Wurster Hall, these two cottages were built by Warren Cheney and are the only buildings remaining from what was once a residential block of College Avenue. Number 2241 has a mix of Queen Anne and Eastlake details; 2243 is done in Swiss Chalet style with stickwork trim, and was once the home of James Turney Allen, professor of Greek. Now the university uses them as offices for the "English as a Second Language" program. c. 1895 and c. 1901, respectively.

*BERK E-33*

## Tour Notes

## Downtown

Berkeley's central business district differs from that of most other large Bay Area cities: the unusual width of its main thoroughfare, Shattuck Avenue, resembles Canal Street in New Orleans, for example, more than it does the built-up urban corridors of San Francisco or Oakland. This phenomenon has its historic roots in the laying of the Berkeley Branch Railway of the Central Pacific Company in 1876. The Berkeley Branch Railway was a steam train system that ran from the Oakland Ferry docks through Emeryville and down Shattuck Avenue to a terminal and freight yards that occupied the triangular strip of land running from Center Street to University Avenue. (An electric line was introduced in 1903, and the last streetcars were removed in 1958.) By the 1890s, downtown Berkeley still looked like a western frontier town, with one- and two-story wood-front stores and wood-plank sidewalks. Today, only the Yellow House Restaurant remains to remind us of those primitive times.

*BERK F-2*

Shortly after 1900, downtown Berkeley experienced a business boom that led to the erection of a number of "modern" brick and stone commercial structures. The first "high-rise" steel-frame buildings (for example, the Studio Building at Addison Street) went up around 1905. By the end of World War I, most of the brick buildings that now line Shattuck Avenue were completed. The 1920s saw another building boom, and such structures as the twelve-story Wells Fargo Building at Center Street and the picturesque Tupper and Reed Music Store further south along Shattuck were built during that time. In the Depression decade of the 1930s, the last major architectural projects were completed in the downtown corridor, which included the main library, the United Artists Theater, the Farm Credit Building, and the Grove Street wing of Berkeley High School.

Except for a handful of utilitarian bank and office buildings, little significant architectural development has gone on in downtown Berkeley since World War II. Some business leaders plan to carry out a large-scale "revitalization" of this area, including major new construction, and this plan is being discussed. But at present, the central business district retains its early-twentieth-century character, offering a wide variety of modestly scaled commercial structures that mix historic and Moderne styles. The side streets west of Shattuck Avenue contain a number of Victorian homes in pleasant settings and are just as rewarding as the downtown area itself.

These tour notes were prepared with information obtained from Louis Stein and Anthony Bruce of the Berkeley Architectural Heritage Association.

1    Auto garage. Milvia St. at Addison, northeast corner. This ancient, vine-covered, whitewashed-brick garage originally was used as a livery stable, then as a planing mill. It's one of the oldest remaining commercial structures in downtown Berkeley. c. 1885–1890.

2    Golden Sheaf Bakery. 2071 Addison St. Clinton Day designed this dignified, red-brick, neo-Classic building with Romanesque arching on the second story. The building's original use as a bakery is clearly symbolized in the carved shaft of wheat that adorns the middle of the false-front scrollwork pediment. 1905.

3    S. H. Kress and Co. Shattuck Ave. at Addison, northwest corner. This restrained Art Deco commercial building uses yellow brick with glazed-tile zigzag detailing. 1933.

4    Italian Renaissance building. 2014 Shattuck Ave. Look up above the modern storefront to see an Italian-Renaissance-style second story in glazed terra-cotta tile, complete with cable molding and Venetian Gothic tracery above the arched windows. It was designed by James W. Plachek. 1918.

5    Acheson Physician's Building. 2131 University at Shattuck. This large neo-Classic commercial structure has decorative lintels and a fine, voluted arch flanked by pilasters at the entrance. 1908.

6    Studio Building. Addison St. at Terminal, northeast corner. A rare example of a mansard-roofed commercial building with clay tiles and round metal bays, this, one of Berkeley's finest metal-frame high-rise structures, was designed by Clinton Day. The upper rooms once housed a number of photographic and art studios, including the original classrooms of the College of Arts and Crafts. Mason–McDuffie Realty Company occupied a major portion of the building

until about 1927, and until the occurrence of a fire in 1970, a hotel operated in the building. The current owner is lovingly restoring the exterior and renovating the interior for use as office space. 1905–1906.

7    Old Mason–McDuffie Building. 2101 Shattuck Ave. at Addison. Walter H. Ratcliff, Jr., designed this Mediterranean, tile-roofed, commercial building with tall, plate-glass windows and neo-Classic columns. The column capitals show humorous animal and human figures. 1928.

8    Victorian Inn. 2109 Shattuck Ave. William H. Wharff designed this five-story apartment house, one of the earliest and oldest remaining multiunit apartment buildings in Berkeley. The angled bays reveal a Georgian Revival design. 1909.

9    Mission-Revival-style commercial building. 2124 Center St. This amusing building has curved española false front, leaded-glass windows in its second-floor bays, and an iron-grillwork balcony between them. c. 1910–1920.

10    Sutch Building (now Oxford Hall). Allston Way at Oxford, northwest corner. Built by the man who ran the Sutch Dairy in the Berkeley hills, this very attractive, neo-Classic commercial block has an exaggerated klinker-brick facing, a wide, voluted cornice, and a sophisticated, voluted arch of soft yellow sandstone above the Allston Way entrance. Note the many beam anchors visible on the off-street facades. 1908.

11    Hink's Building. Shattuck Ave. between Allston and Kittridge, east side. Benjamin McDougall designed this massive, Mediterranean-style business block, which has vigas lining its wide, overhanging eaves, as well as Moorish arching and tilework above the entrance to the Shattuck Hotel on Allston Way. 1909–1913.

12    Berekeley Main Post Office. 2000 Allston Way at Milvia. A superb example of government Roman Renaissance Revival, this Oscar-Wederoth-designed building has a magnificent loggia and a recently redone color scheme that is sheer perfection. 1914.

13    Y.M.C.A. 2001 Allston Way at Milvia. Another building by Benjamin McDougall, this one is a solid Georgian neo-Classic design in red brick and white stone. 1910.

*BERK F-12*

14 Farm Credit Building. 2180 Milvia St. James W. Plachek used the late-Streamlined-Moderne style on this high-rise office building. Now it houses most departments of the Berkeley city government. 1938.

15 Berkeley City Hall. 2134 Grove St. Using a Beaux Arts design, this building has massive, attached Doric columns and a soaring spire intended to support clocks (which have yet to be purchased and put in place). It was designed by Blackwell and Brown, the same firm that designed the San Francisco City Hall. 1908.

16 Berkeley High School, Grove Street Buildings and Auditorium. Grove St. and Milvia. All designed by Gutterson and Corlett, the buildings facing Grove Street are excellent examples of the Streamlined Modern Style. (Note the "Truth Shall Make You Free" W.P.A. relief sculpture on the north end.) The Florence Schwimley Auditorium is very late W.P.A. Moderne, with bas-relief panels depicting the various performing arts. (Its construction was interrupted by World War II.) The older "A Building," designed in 1920 by William C. Hays, is worth noting — its Mediterranean, neo-Classic facade is adorned with ornate, glazed-tile decorations and supported by bizarre-looking steel buttresses (added recently as an earthquake-safety measure). Go up the stairs through the Grove Street entrance and to the right. Grove Street Buildings 1938; Auditorium 1940–1946.

17 Armstrong College. 2222 Harold Way at Kittredge. Walter H. Ratcliff, Jr., blended the Spanish Colonial style in the tile roof and decorative trim with neo-Classic radiating arched windows on the upper level. 1924.

18 Berkeley Library. Kittredge St. and Shattuck, southwest corner. James W. Plachek used the Zigzag Art Deco mode on an institutional building in a highly original and somewhat playful manner. The zigzagging at the top of the windows, punctuated by evenly placed slabs running across the facade, is characteristic Art Deco design; what is unusual are the scrollwork and ram's-head sculpture around the entrance and on top of the corner slabs, and the concrete "scarfillio" paneling depicting ancient Middle Eastern figures. The current color scheme is not the original one, but it enhances the overall effect greatly. 1930.

*BERK F-26*

19    United Artists Theater. 2274 Shattuck Ave. Although it has been stripped of its original marquee and divided into four theaters, this Art Deco movie house still has an interesting, incised decorative design on the upper facade, as well as some fine Deco furnishings in the lobby. c. 1930.

20    Tupper and Reed Music Store. 2277 Shattuck Ave. William R. Yelland designed this absolutely captivating Hansel and Gretel-style gem, which has an Elizabethan flavor to its steep, vine-covered gable and piper weather vane. Note the gargoyles in the courtyard to the right. Currently a restaurant. 1926.

21    Masonic Temple. Shattuck at Bancroft, southeast corner. For this fraternal order, architect William H. Wharff created this typical turn-of-the-century neo-Classic design. Note the stained-glass transom, hanging light fixtures, and blind balcony above the Bancroft Street entrance. 1905.

*BERK F-27*

22    Boone Academy. 2035 Durant Ave. A part Stick-, part Italianate-style three-story Victorian structure, this originally housed a private academy for students preparing to enter the university, and was run by an educational pioneer named Phillip Riley Boone. Begun 1884; finished 1890.

23    Yellow House Restaurant. 2377 Shattuck Ave. This false-front wooden Victorian commercial building with stickwork trim is the last survivor of many such buildings that sprang up along Shattuck Avenue in the late nineteenth century. 1886.

24    Colonial Revival apartment house. 2035 Channing Way. This elegant building has rounded bays and a fine garland frieze. c. 1902.

25    Late-Victorian house. 2014 Channing way. This large, tree-sheltered home blends Stick–Eastlake and Colonial Revival styles. c. 1895.

26    Morrill Apartments. Shattuck Ave. at Haste, northeast corner. This large, brick, Mediterranean-style apartment block has balconies with window seats that originally functioned as storage space for rollaway Murphy beds. The "gilded bird cage" elevator is worth a ride. 1910.

27    Barker Building. Shattuck Ave. at Dwight, northwest corner. A. W. Smith achieved a beautifully integrated mixture of Romanesque arched windows with a Mission Revival roofline on a brick commercial block. Barker was an early pioneer and Berkeley booster who helped create the city government, the first newspaper, and civic and real estate development along Shattuck Avenue. 1904–1905.

28    Queen Anne cottage. 2022 Dwight Way. A richly deocrated cottage with an unusual, purple-toned color scheme, it still has its original palm tree and cast-iron fence in front. c. 1890–1895.

29    Three late-Victorian houses. 2020–2012 Dwight Way. These homes have varying degrees of Stick–Eastlake trim, as well as verdant settings. c. 1895–1900.

30    Queen Anne house. Haste and Milvia, northeast corner. This attractive house has some Colonial Revival details. c. 1892.

31    Queen Anne cottage. 1940 Channing Way. Newsom and Newsom designed this robust cottage — the only known example of their work remaining in Berkeley. It sports a steeply spired corner turret and lush ornamentation. c. 1892–1895.

32    Colonial Revival house. Channing and Grove, southeast corner. Here is a fine, gambrel-roofed house that has been painted handsomely. c. 1900–1910.

# Berkeley Tour G

## South Campus

### Tour Notes

The South Campus area, known across the nation as the setting of dozens of student demonstrations and riots in the 1960s and early '70s, may be hard to envision as tranquil. But a walk through the residential side streets east of frenetic Telegraph Avenue will give some idea of the more serene lifestyle of the campus community around the turn of the century.

A scattering of Victorian homes remain in the South Campus area, left from the years when its earliest settlers came to take advantage of living near the new university. But not until the late 1890s and early 1900s did the neighborhood really begin to develop in earnest. From this period came many of the finest designs of such First Bay Tradition masters as Bernard Maybeck and Julia Morgan. The best place to begin this edifying tour is with Maybeck's most famous work — the Christian Science Church on Dwight at Bowditch.

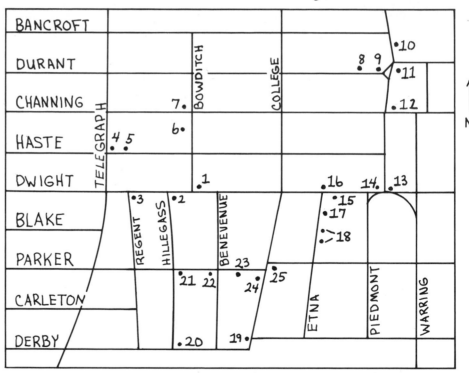

1      First Church of Christian Science. Dwight Way at Bowditch. Unequivocally Bernard Maybeck's greatest masterpiece, this church has to be seen to be fully appreciated. The six stylistic elements (Gothic, Renaissance, neo-Classic, Japanese, Mediterranean, and Modern Industrial) harmonize so perfectly that the total effect is one of transcendent beauty. One fine example of Maybeck's ability to integrate such disparate components is the asbestos paneling on the upper walls. Maybeck disguised the paneling with red, diamond-shaped ornaments that blend in perfectly with the esthetic character of the overall design. This church is now a registered national landmark. Guided tours are given every Sunday at 12:30 (walk in). 1910; Sunday school addition by Henry Gutterson, 1927.

2      Hobart Hall. 2600 Dwight Way at Bowditch. Julia Morgan designed this dignified, red-brick, Tudor Revival administrative building for the American Baptist Seminary of the West. 1918—1920.

*BERK G-2*

3    Stewart House. 2524 Dwight Way. This Queen Anne house with a Colonial Revival portico was designed by Albert Pissis, the man who later designed the president's house on the U.C. campus. 1891.

4    Berkeley Inn. Haste St. at Telegraph, northeast corner. J. Cather Newsom designed this red-brick, neo-Classic-style hotel, which has an unusual pattern in the cornice line. 1911.

5    Wooley House. 2509 Haste St. This raised-basement Italianate cottage, one of the first houses in the South Campus area, was built for a boilermaker from Oakland. 1876.

6    Anna Head School. Bowditch between Haste and Channing. Edgar S. Fisher and Walter J. Ratcliff, Jr., designed this magnificent collection of Brown-Shingle-style buildings. The original section at Channing and Bowditch is one of the first uses of the Brown Shingle mode in the Bay Area, with its gambrel roof and Colonial Revival detailing. The later additions along Haste match the quality and stylistic character of the original design. Now owned by the university, these buildings house a variety of special services, including, a child-care center. Original section by Edgar S. Fisher, 1892; auditorium addition by Walter J. Ratcliff, Jr., 1923.

7    Davis House. Channing and Bowditch, northwest corner. This attractive transitional Colonial Revival house, with its rounded corner and sophisticated use of natural materials such as brown shingles and rusticated stone, was designed by William Mooser. 1899.

8    Atkinson House. 2735 Durant Ave. This is by Bernard Maybeck — a First Bay Tradition, Brown Shingle house with a sun porch on the front. Before the monolithic student dormitories were erected, the porch gave a sweeping view of the entire Bay. 1909.

*BERK G-7*

*BERK G-12*

9    Professor Charles M. Bayley House. Piedmont at Durant, northwest corner. One of Julia Morgan's first domestic designs, this house has been considerably remodeled on the exterior. Now it functions as a fraternity house. 1905.

10    International Student's House. Piedmont at Bancroft. George Kelham blended Mediterranean elements, Mission Revival elements, and an Indian "Stupa-shaped" tower. 1928.

11    Thorsen House. 2307 Piedmont Ave. This forms the only example of the work of the highly renowned Pasadena firm, Greene and Greene, in the East Bay. Essentially it is an outsized Craftsman bungalow. The entranceway displays the Greene brothers' characteristic use of Japanese elements in its Torrigate-arch motif. The heavy beams are sanded and rounded to a smooth surface — another Greene brothers hallmark. The brick entrance-stairs have an interesting, recessed Gothic arch pattern, and the landscaping is gorgeous. 1908.

12    Sigma Pi Delta Fraternity House. Piedmont at Channing, northeast corner. Frederick Reimers designed this Italian-Renaissance-Revival-style building, which has a klinker-brick facade and a double-esplanade stairway. c. 1925.

13    Stuccoed, Mediterranean-style house. 2499 Piedmont Ave. This house with neo-Classic elements, now a fraternity house, was originally designed by Walter J. Ratcliff, Jr. as a private residence. c. 1910.

14    Brown-shingled Colonial Revival house. 2498 Piedmont at Dwight. Note the massive gambrel roof. c. 1895.

15    Wilkinson House. 2730 Dwight Way. A solid Stick-style house designed by Clinton Day and remodeled on the front sometime after 1900, this is one of the two or three oldest remaining homes in the neighborhood. 1876.

16    Paget-Gorill House. 2727 Dwight Way at Etna. Willis Polk designed this brown-shingled house. Tudor Revival half-timbering was added in a later remodeling. 1891.

*BERK G-10*

*BERK G-11*

17      Cedric Wright House. 2515 Etna. Bernard Maybeck created this small late-First-Bay-Tradition design, which uses his favorite red and blue stenciling on the facade. 1921.

18      Two modest Brown Shingle homes. 2531 and 2535 Etna St. Designed by Julia Morgan, these were built as speculative housing. c. 1910.

19      St. John's Presbyterian Church. College Ave. at Derby. This superbly designed building, Julia Morgan's greatest essay in the Brown Shingle First Bay Tradition mode, integrates so well with its surroundings that at first glance it appears to be a large house rather than a church. Red-stained clapboards, tinted-glass Gothic arched windows in the clerestory, and wide, overhanging eaves harmonize in a manner resembling Maybeck's later Christian Science Church (with which it is often compared). Now a registered national historic landmark and owned by the Epic West Association, St. John's is open to the public upon request. Monday to Friday, 9 to 5 — ask at the office inside. 1908.

20      Gifford–McGrew House. 2601 Derby at Hillegass. The steeply pitched gable of this fine, brown-shingled house reveals the medieval woodcraftsman influence common in many of Bernard Maybeck's early residential designs. 1900.

21      Lindblom House. 2601 Hillegass Ave. Marshall designed this excellent example of a Colonial Revival house, with a deep-columned veranda, ornate pilasters, and oval windows. 1898.

22      Apartment house. 2600 Benvenue at Parker. George Anderson blended Mediterranean and neo-Classic elements in this very unusual apartment house that was built for Eric Lindblom. 1911.

24      Colonel Greenleaf House. 2610 College Ave. Albert Dodge Coplin created an interesting design, using primarily the Colonial Revival style but also adding Craftsman touches. Note the crouching lions guarding the entry. 1902.

25      Professor Merrill House. 2609 College Ave. Edward B. Seely designed this attractive Colonial Revival house with brown shingles. 1902.

*BERK G-21*

# Berkeley Tour H

## Homestead Area

### Tour Notes

The area near the U.C. campus commonly referred to as "below Telegraph" was one of the first neighborhoods settled south of the university. The College Homestead Tract, centered around Dana and Channing Streets and laid out in 1879, is one of the oldest tract developments in the city. During the late 1860s and 1870s, this area experienced other scattered settlements; some of the lots along Blake Street, for example, were subdivided from the original Luis Peralta land grant. A number of really fine Victorian homes can be found in this neighborhood, including the circa-1868 raised-basement cottage at Parker and Dana, the oldest home in the south end of Berkeley.

After 1900, the various Colonial and Period Revival modes dominated building design in the College Homestead area. The superb Colonial Revival McReary House on Durant and the First Congregational Church on Dana, for example, reveal the eclectic character of early-twentieth-century architecture in this neighborhood. Bernard Maybeck and Julia Morgan both graced the area with masterpieces of their own personal architectural idioms — the Town and Gown Club and the City Club, respectively.

There has been much cracker-box apartment house construction in the College Homestead area over the last two decades, although the 1974 Neighborhood Preservation Ordinanace halted it temporarily. Nevertheless, what remains of the area's earlier architectural heritage is significant and worth seeing.

*BERK H-1*

1    St. Mark's Episcopal Church. 2300 Bancroft Way at Ellsworth. William Curlett created this beautifully designed Mission Revival church, which has flanking bell towers and a curved espáñada gable. The stained-glass windows in the nave are magnificent; a number of them were made by the famous Tiffany and Company. 1901.

*BERK H-3*

2    Berkeley City Club. 2315 Durant Ave. Julia Morgan's second-largest commission after San Simeon, this concrete, Italian-Renaissance-style palazzo has some of the feeling of a castle, itself. The trefoil tracery and ornate pilasters around the massive metal-and-glass doors create an air of sumptuous grandeur. Now it's a national historic landmark. Completed 1929.

3    Maria Marsh House. 2308 Durant Ave. The broad, sweeping lines of the corner tower and enclosed, columned porch mark this house as a fin de siècle Victorian with Queen Anne and Colonial Revival elements. It was designed by Charles F. Mau. 1891.

*BERK H-7*

4    McReary House. 2318 Durant Ave. This magnificent colonial Revival house is certainly one of the best examples of this style in the East Bay. The curved, balustraded portico and stained-glass Palladian window in front are exquisite. In the back of the lot stands the original carriage house, complete with finialed turret. 1904.

5    Stick—Eastlake villa. 2421 Durant Ave. This home, which has almost abstract sunburst patterns and a solid, squared tower, was illustrated in an 1889 real estate booklet called *Homes of Berkeley*. c. 1880–1889.

6    Carlton Hotel. Telegraph and Durant, northwest corner. This dignified, red-brick, neo-Classic structure was used to help house victims of the 1906 San Francisco earthquake. 1906.

7    First Congregational Church. Dana St. between Durant and Channing. Horace Simpson designed this excellent example of an impressively scaled Colonial Revival church. The landscaping is pleasant. 1924.

8    J. A. Squire House. Channing and Dana, northwest corner. This exuberant Queen Anne cottage was designed by George Embry. Its delightful confection of sawn-wood ornamentation is brought out by a tasteful color scheme. The house had a brush with fame in 1968 when it was used as a setting for scenes in the film, *The Graduate*. 1892.

9 Captain Luttrell House. 2328 Channing Way. This charming Queen Anne house, with its bold stickwork and hexagonal sloping tower, resembles the one on 1431 Arch Street by the same architect, Ira A. Boynton. (See Berkeley Tour B.) 1889.

10 Lizzie Hume House. 243 Ellsworth St. Designed by Fred Esty, this attractive Stick–Eastlake house recently had a good "facelift." 1892.

11 Nelson Trowbridge House. 2239 Dwight Way. George Embry designed this large Queen Anne house, which has Colonial Revival dormer windows set into its tower. 1892.

12 Stick-style house. 2244 Dwight Way. Note the split-level porch. c. 1885–1895.

13 Boxy Italianate house. 2248 Dwight Way. This is one of the oldest homes in the neighborhood. c. 1880-1890.

14 Two Queen Anne cottages. 2336 and 2338 Dwight Way. These very nice cottages have been expertly restored. c. 1890–1895.

15 Seneca Gale House. 2446 Dana St. at Dwight. A. W. S. Smith designed this multiturreted, transitional Queen Anne/Colonial Revival house, with stucco added later. c. 1895.

16 Town and Gown Club. 2401 Dwight Way at Dana. Bernard Maybeck's second-oldest design in the East Bay is a registered city historic landmark. This early-Brown-Shingle, First Bay Tradition masterpiece has a projecting hipped roof that is supported by extended "outrigger" bracketing similar to that used in many homes recently built in the Berkeley hills. 1899.

17 George Wilson House. 2415 Blake St. This small, Italianate cottage has shelf molding and a bracketed cornice. M. J. Welch designed it for Wilson, a banker from San Francisco who bought this lot for 300 dollars in gold coin to build a summer house. Not long after its construction, Wilson's wife complained of the "many howling coyotes" that roamed the neighborhood at night. 1885.

*BERK H-17*

*BERK H-19*

18    Queen Anne cottage. 2412 Parker St. This cheerful cottage has excellent Eastlake stenciled designs on the front bay. c. 1885—1895.

19    Hillegass House. 2601 Dana St. at Parker. This finely preserved, raised-basement Italianate cottage has a balustraded veranda and a false-front bracketed pediment above its arched entryway. An intact cast-iron railing with Gothic gateposts encloses the lot. This is undoubtedly the oldest building in the South Campus area, and evidence indicates that it was moved from Telegraph Avenue. c. 1868.

20    Stick—Eastlake cottage. 2320 Blake St. Note the unusual, three-banded window in front. c. 1885—1889.

21    Transitional Colonial Revival house. 2239 Blake St. at Ellsworth. The high-peaked gable is filled with fish-scale shingles and underlined with a garland frieze. c. 1900.

22    Queen Anne house. 2211 Blake St. This large house has wide arching across its split-level corner porch, and huge, sweeping brackets under the gables. c. 1885—1895.

23    Queen Anne cottage. 2205 Blake St. This was built as a wedding present for a daughter of the Bartlett family, next door. c. 1890—1895.

24    Alfred Bartlett House. 2201 Blake St. at Fulton. This elegant Bracketed Italianate house has angled bays, tall double doors, an etched vase-pattern in the transom, and a porthole window in the side gable. The house is set back on a heavily wooded, raised lot. Both the carriage house and servant's quarters remain in the rear. When Bartlett moved into the home with his new bride, he planted the two pine trees in the front yard so that the couple could watch them "grow up" with the family — a typically romantic Victorian custom. 1877.

25    Captain Whiteham House. 2198 Blake St. at Fulton. A. W. Pattiani and Co. designed this large, towerless Queen Anne house for one of Berkeley's many retired sea captains. Much of the original landscaping is intact; so is the entire cast-iron fence. 1889.

*BERK H-9*

# Berkeley Tour I

## Claremont Area

### Tour Notes

The Claremont area is Berkeley's most elegant community. Centering around Ashby and Claremont Avenues, this neighborhood has more substantial homes designed by famous architects than does any other section of the city. The graceful beauty of these streets dates back to 1905, when the Mason–McDuffie Realty Company initiated a major development of the area. Many prominent residents came in response, bought one of the spacious lots being sold, and commissioned the best architects of the day to plan their homes. The list of architects associated with this neighborhood is quite impressive: Bernard Maybeck, Julia Morgan, John Hudson Thomas, Ernest Coxhead, John Galen Howard, Willis Polk, Henry Gutterson, and William Wurster, to name only the most renowned.

Many superbly rendered Period Revival styles are the predominant residential designs found in the Claremont area. Brown-shingled, First-Bay Tradition homes appear in significant numbers, nestled among the hilly roads that wind around the Uplands district above Claremont Avenue. A scattering of more whimsical creations exist as well, lending an occasional note of humor to the otherwise refined dignity that characterizes the splendid architecture of this neighborhood.

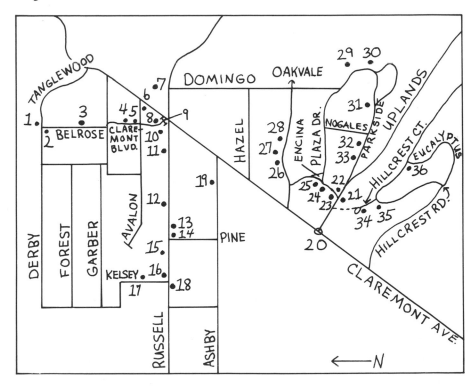

1    California School for the Blind, auditorium. Derby St. at Belrose. Designed by Geroge B. McDougall, this Mission Revival academic building has Art Deco touches in the projecting slabs along its facade. The style of the present campus, now also used as a school for deaf students, is entirely Mediterranean (this mode replaced the Victorian structures that were built in the 1860s and '70s). The original iron fence still runs along Warring Street. The university currently is considering plans for the purchase and adaptive reuse of the buildings. 1930.

*BERK I-5*

2    Randolph School. 2700 Belrose Ave. at Derby. This collection of steeply gabled, brown-shingled pavilions, designed by Bernard Maybeck, is now a private residence. 1911.

3    Tudor Revival house. 2721 Belrose Ave. This imposing structure has stuccoed walls and a fine, pilastered brick chimney. c. 1910–1920.

4    Campbell House. 2815 Claremont Blvd. One of the few examples of a Jacobean Revival manor house in the East Bay, this house, designed by T. Patterson Ross, resembles the seventeenth-century Bacon's Castle in tidewater Virginia, especially with its brick facade, end chimney, and curved, stepped gable. 1909.

5    Seldon Williams House. 2821 Claremont Blvd. at Avalon. One of Julia Morgan's best residential designs, this Mediterranean Revival house has elements of both Italian Renaissance and Gothic detailing. Below the iron-grillwork balcony over the front entrance is an excellent frescoed inset around a richly coffered door, and the windows behind the Venetian Gothic tracery along Avalon are deftly disguised sliding-glass panels. The university now owns the building, which serves as the vice chancellor's residence. 1928.

6    McDuffie House. 3016 Avalon Ave. at Claremont. Henry Gutterson's design blends the Prairie, Craftsman, and Mediterranean elements that characterized his personal style. 1915.

7    Claremont Hotel. Russell St. at Domingo. Frank Lloyd Wright described this building, designed by Charles W. Dickey, as one of the few hotels in America with true grace and charm — and, looking up at its magnificent countenance, you can easily see why. Its unusual design combines French Chateau form with an impressive Spanish-Renaissance-style tower. Before it was whitewashed, the facade's half-timber trim was emphasized. c. 1906–1915.

8    St. Clement's Episcopal Church. 2837 Claremont Blvd. at Russell. Willis Polk created this grey-shingled, high-gabled, New England meetinghouse design. The nave has excellent stained-glass windows. 1908.

*BERK I-4*

*BERK I-8 and 9*

9    Claremont Court Gates. Claremont Blvd. at Russell. John Galen Howard thought up this neo-Classic, Palladian, arched motif in brick, stone, and iron, which formally delineated the boundaries of Mason–McDuffie's Claremont Court tract. 1907.

10    Paul Tietzen House. 2840 Claremont Blvd. at Russell. This massive, whitewashed, neo-Classic, Mediterranean-style block, designed by Hodges and Mitchell, is so large that its occupants can jog around the living room! 1912.

11    Mereen House. 2959 Russell Ave. Hodges and Mitchell also designed this stunning, southern ante-bellum-style Colonial Revival mansion, set imperiously on a steep, terraced lot. 1914.

12    Burke House. 2911 Russell Ave. D. J. Patterson designed this huge, neo-Tudor house in klinker brick. The spacious lot was landscaped by John McLaren, for whom McLaren Lodge in San Francisco's Golden Gate Park was named. It is now the Judah L. Magnes Museum of Jewish Art. 1914.

13    Large Craftsman bungalow. 2908 Russell Ave. Note the ornate bargeboards. c. 1911.

14    Craftsman bungalow. 2900 Russell Ave. It has fine, leaded windows. c. 1910.

15    Tudor Revival house. 2851 Russell Ave. This substantial house has a glorious, pilastered chimney. c. 1910–1920.

16    E. M. Marquis House. 2827 Russell Ave. at Kelsey. This unusually big Mission Revival "bungalow" has a curved española gable and a coach porch on the east side. This house was taken from a popular design in the *Wilson Bungalow Book*. The current owners have repaired the foundation painstakingly and restored the plaster facade. The row of original palms sets the house off nicely. 1909.

17    Kelsey House. 2815 Kelsey St. This is a late-Victorian house with stickwork trim and rare gumwood beams. The oldest house in the neighborhood, Kelsey Street was named for its builder. 1899.

18    Smith House. 2812 Russell Ave. at Kelsey. William Wurster designed this diminutive, Regency-style manor house in whitewashed redwood. The landscaping is authentic. 1927.

*BERK I-22*

*BERK I-34*

19    Stucco house. 2955 Ashby Ave. Stucco houses aren't ordinarily unusual, but this one is — it has a Mission-style arched porch and exaggerated, voluted brackets on its wide, overhanging eaves. 1910–1915.

20    Claremont Park Company Gates and Pavilions. Claremont Ave. at The Uplands. William C. Hays was responsible for this impressive, cast-iron Art Nouveau scrollwork gateway, which is flanked by rusticated stone pavilions with clay-tile hoods. 1905.

21    Walter Chowen House. 94 The Uplands. This relatively rare essay by John Hudson Thomas in the Brown-Shingle, First Bay Tradition mode commands its hillside lot impressively. 1908.

22    Douglas House. 35 Parkside Ave. This charming Tudor Revival house by Albert Farr has twin half-timbered gables and asymmetrical fenestration. 1910.

23    Eitel House. 9 The Uplands. N. W. Shaw created this pristine-white Colonial Revival house with a beautiful garden. 1915.

24    Brackenridge House. 10 Encina Pl. Here's a stuccoed, First Bay Tradition design by Ernest Coxhead. 1906.

25    Van Sant House. 6 Encina Pl. Another Ernest Coxhead design, this solid, Brown Shingle, First Bay Tradition house is set into a spacious, lavishly landscaped lot through which a creek runs. 1906.

26    Sellander House. 35 Oakvale Ave. Only John Hudson Thomas could have created this lighthearted blend of a Tudor-Revival-gabled form with Prairie-style detailing. 1914.

27    Dungan House. 41 Oakvale Ave. A joint effort between architect John Hudson Thomas and owner H. L. Dungan produced this handsomely executed, First Bay Tradition house with neo-Tudor timbered gables. 1911.

*BERK I-33*

28      Hall House. 51 Oakvale Ave. This was one of John Hudson Thomas' earliest designs. 1908.

29      Kidd House. 95 The Plaza Dr. This house displays elements of the Prairie Style, à la John Hudson Thomas. 1913.

30      Gertrude White House. 99 The Plaza Dr. Taken together with number 95, this house creates an interesting architectural balance. Harris Allen was the architect. 1913.

31      Dubrow House. 123 Parkside Dr. Yet another John Hudson Thomas home; it almost seems like John Hudson Thomas designed the entire Claremont tract singlehandedly. 1909.

32      Cole House. 81 Parkside Dr. This comfortable Brown-Shingle-style house, designed by Leola Hall, has affinities with much of Julia Morgan's earlier work. 1907.

33      Landregan House. 77 Parkside Dr. Also by Leola Hall, this fine Craftsman bungalow has unpeeled redwood logs as porch columns. 1907.

34      Merrill House. 10 Hillcrest Ct. This is John Hudson Thomas' personalized version of the stucco California Bungalow, with Prairie-style horizontal emphasis added. 1911.

35      Johnson House. 2 Hillcrest Ct. By John Hudson Thomas (Again!) 1912.

36      Elliott House. 1 Eucalyptus Rd. at Hillcrest. In its nearly pure historicism, this letter-perfect example of a large-scale Georgian Revival house is somewhat uncharacteristic for architect Julia Morgan. 1919.

*BERK I-36*

# Berkeley Tour J

## Tour Notes

## Oceanview

Since Oceanview is one of Berkeley's oldest neighborhoods, it really deserves the careful attention it has been getting from students of nineteenth-century architectural history. And even for the more casual observer, this area contains literally scores of mid- and late-Victorian structures that are worth exploring.

The original community was first settled in 1852 at the height of the Gold Rush Era, and its heart was the area west of San Pablo Avenue, between Hearst and Jones Streets. The streets of this new town were laid out in a traditional grid pattern, and by the late 1860s Oceanview was important enough to have its own stagecoach stop along the San Pablo line. It also was home to dozens of pioneer working-class families, many of whom were employed by the several heavy and light industries that had begun to locate in the area.

Residential and commercial development of Oceanview increased in the 1870s and '80s, made possible (as elsewhere) by the arrival of railroad lines. Once the community was incorporated into the city of Berkeley in 1878, settlement accelerated; and by the end of the 1890s, Oceanview was almost all built up. The Victorian buildings that remain in Oceanview today were built largely between 1870 and 1895. Most of them can be described as "workingman's cottages," exhibiting varying degrees of decorative trim according to the styles of their day. Many of the earliest homes truly can be called pioneer stock, and several may date from the 1860s. This highly historic neighborhood contains two of the finest Gothic Revival churches in the East Bay (on Hearst Street), as well as a number of real surprises for the first-time visitor.

At the time of this writing, Oceanview's future is uncertain: the City of Berkeley is considering a number of alternative proposals for salvaging part or all of the nineteenth-century housing stock, while at the same time exploring the

113

*BERK J-5*

possibility of converting much of the district into an industrial park. With luck, some accommodation will be reached that will allow most of the structurally sound historic buildings to be restored and used as part of a rejuvenated community. In any case, so far Oceanview remains one of the East Bay's best untapped historic resources.

---

The following walking tour was prepared with historic information provided by Stephanie Manning of the Oceanview Neighborhood Preservation Association.

1    Finn Hall. 1819 19th St. Now on the National Register of Historic Places, this uniquely designed wooden meeting hall has a recessed, columned portico, latticed balconies, wide, overhanging eaves, with scalloped brackets, and an odd-shaped roof that projects like the bow of a ship. 1908.

2    Queen Anne cottage. 10th St. and Hearst, northwest corner. Nice detailing enhances this beautifully preserved, raised-basement cottage. The cast-iron fence and gateway around it provide superb street furniture. c. 1893.

3    Charles Schnelle House. 1924 19th St. Schnelle, a farmer who was one of the area's earliest pioneers, built this raised-basement, hipped-roof "Pioneer box." 1878.

4    Church of the Good Shepherd. 1823 9th St. at Hearst. Designed by Charles Bugbee, this is certainly one of the finest Victorian "Carpenter Gothic" Revival churches in the East Bay. The hollow, wooden buttresses on the gracefully tapering spire are completely superfluous on this wood-frame building. 1878.

5    Westminster Presbyterian Church. 8th St. at Hearst, southeast corner. Designed by Charles Geddes, Westminster Presbyterian is the only wooden Gothic Revival church remaining in Berkeley, other than the Church of the Good Shepherd. 1879.

6    Three Queen Anne cottages. 931, 933, and 935 Hearst. Attributed to the prominent Berkeley carpenter C. W. Davis, these attractive, raised-basement cottages have been restored recently. c. 1890.

*BERK J-2*

*BERK J-14*

7    Cooley House. 914 Hearst. The decorative trim on this small, Italianate cottage is still intact. c. 1875–1880.

8    Two-story Victorian house. 913 Hearst. A cottage with stickwork around the windows, this house has hood molding above the door, and a pleasant pastel color scheme (due to a recent restoration). c. 1880.

9    Seventh Street School. 1814 7th St. A. H. Broad designed this large, Stick-style early schoolhouse with a pent eave. 1887.

10   Store. 834 Delaware St. Originally, this was an early pioneer store, with a pedimented roof and latticed windows. This is the oldest store in Berkeley; and judging by its design, it could well be the oldest building remaining in the city. c. 1855–1865.

11   George Wilkes House. 835 Delaware St. This modest, late-Victorian home has Queen Anne trim in the gable and Italianate windows. 1891.

12   Frederick Wilkes House, 831 Delaware St. A raised basement Queen Anne cottage with an arched entrance. 1891.

13   Plaza. Delaware between 5th and 6th Sts. This space is to be used as a central location for several transplanted Victorian homes and commercial buildings in the neighborhood, which will be restored as a group. The Alphonso House of 1878, which currently sits at 1731 5th Street, will be the centerpiece of this complex. With its high-peaked pedimented roofline and shelf molding above the windows, it is one of the finest homes remaining in Oceanview.

14   Jose Joaquin de Silva House. 1824 5th St. This is an excellent example of a raised-basement, false-front, Victorian "workingman's cottage," with Italianate-style shelf molding. Mr. Alphonso built it as speculative housing. 1878.

15   Charles W. Heywood House. 1808 5th St. This raised-basement cottage, with its Italianate-style curved windows and door and Stick-style trim, was built for Charles Heywood, a member of the prominent West Berkeley Heywood

*BERK J-18*

family. Charles' brother was mayor of Berkeley in 1886, and his nephew became mayor in 1913; but Charles himself had no claim to distinction except for a scandalous affair. 1878.

16      Chego House. 1809 4th St. The Heywoods built this two-story, hipped-roof, neo-Classic box. Note the shelf molding. 1877.

17      Conestoga wagon wheels. Empty lot on 4th Street between Virginia and Cedar. Embedded in the trunk of an old tree is a set of wooden, spoked wagon wheels from about the 1890s. In the back of the lot is a 200-year-old cypress that is undoubtedly the oldest standing structure in Oceanview!

18      Neo-Classic "Pioneer box." 749 Cedar St. The house, which has unusual, deeply curved brackets under its shelf molding, was moved from 4th Street when Spenger's Restaurant built its parking lot there in 1910. c. 1880s.

19      Farallones Institute. 1516 5th St. Originally built for the French-immigrant Ehret family, this raised-basement Italianate cottage with an angled bay is currently an "integral urban ecology" house. Tours are given on Saturdays to show how ecological conservation and urban living can go hand in hand. 1886.

20      Late-Victorian house. 1504 5th St. This strange-looking house has twin angled bays that extend to the false-fronted roofline. c. 1875–1885.

21      Queen Anne cottage. 1517 5th St. Note the diminutive spindles on the porch and the Italianate, arched windows. c. 1890.

22      Queen Anne cottage. 1521 5th St. This raised-basement cottage has a beveled, oval window in the door behind a tiny, recessed entry porch. c. 1890.

23      Three "Pioneer boxes." 1607, 1609, and 1613 5th St. These pediment-roofed houses may be the oldest homes left in Berkeley. 1607 has a wide, pillared porch, and the small, pedimented portico gives 1613 a hint of Greek Revival flavor. (Compare these with 1777 and 1781 West 8th Street in West Oakland, Tour D.) Currently boarded up and in disrepair, they nonetheless evoke a vivid image of life on the frontier. c. 1865–1875.

24      Borchard House. 1610 6th St. This is an intricately ornamented, Queen-Anne-style "workingman's cottage." 1891.

25      Charles Brown House. 1614 6th St. Another ornate, Victorian "work-ingman's cottage," this one blends Queen Anne and Stick–Eastlake detail. Both this and number 1610 were built by a local builder named Gimbal. 1889.

26      Water tower. 6th St. between Cedar and Virginia. This striking remnant of Berkeley's rural past is still in perfect working order. c. 1890s.

27      Paschold House. 1647 6th St. at Virginia. Paschold, a German tailor, built this refined, neo-Classic, raised-basement Victorian house with a hipped roof. It was once part of a two-acre homestead with stables, barns, and a willow grove. One surviving willow still shades the front of the house. 1886.

28      O'Keefe Saloon. 1723 6th St. An early Stick-style, false-front commercial building, this structure perhaps best epitomizes the pioneer character of late-nineteenth-century Oceanview. A saloon at night, the building doubled as a grammar school during the day. 1878.

*BERK J-26*

## Tour Notes

The community of Southwest Berkeley greatly resembles the neighboring district of Oceanview; indeed, it was considered a part of Oceanview for many years. The area began to be settled in the 1860s. During the last three decades of the nineteenth century, hundreds of homes went up in the neighborhood. These spanned the architectural spectrum from raised-basement "workingman's cottages" to several impressive, large houses in the fashionable styles of the times. The most noteworthy building in Southwest Berkeley is the Niehaus Villa, an imposing Stick–Eastlake concoction at 7th and Channing that the owner of the nearby West Berkeley Planing Mills built with materials from his own stock. Southwest Berkeley also houses Berkeley's first official (if temporary) city hall — a rustic, whitewashed, wooden meeting hall at 7th and University. The town board of directors used the building as a meeting place for six months; then they chose a more permanent location. Many of the homes in this area are now being researched historically, and private owners have already restored a number

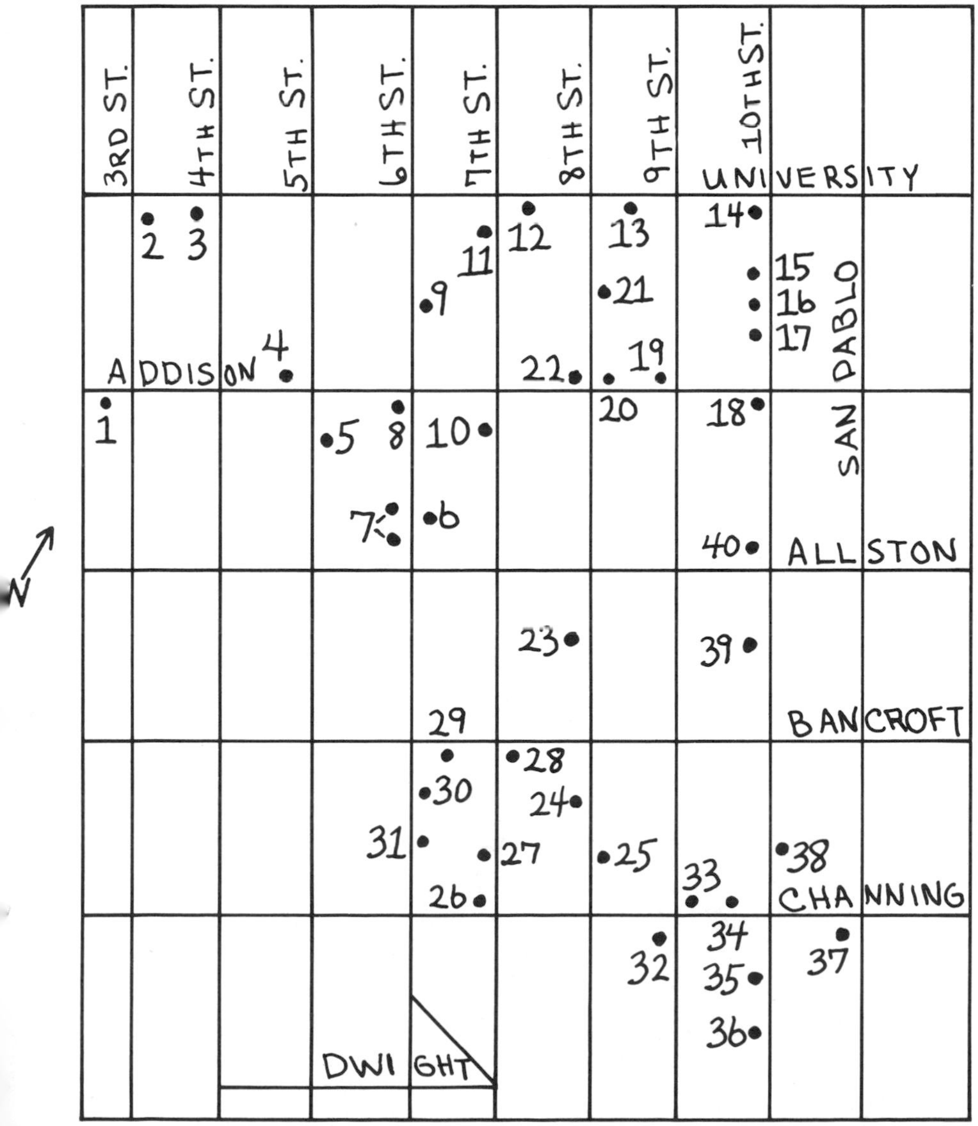

# Southwest Berkeley

3RD ST. 4TH ST. 5TH ST. 6TH ST. 7TH ST. 8TH ST. 9TH ST. 10TH ST.

UNIVERSITY

2 3

11 12 13 14

9

15 16 17 SAN PABLO

22 19 21

ADDISON 4

1 5 8 10 20 18

7 6 40 ALLSTON

23 39

BANCROFT

29

30 28

24

31 27 25 33 38 CHANNING

26

32 34 35 36 37

DWIGHT

*BERK K-11*

of them, with others to follow. These historic, if somewhat modest, buildings have a pleasant Victorian character that makes them well worth a walk through the neighborhood.

1     Feeney's Wire Rope Factory. 600 Addison at 3rd St. This small, wooden factory building is wholly functional but very funky (note the hand-painted signs around the entry). Originally built by Captain R. P. Thomas as part of the Standard Soap Company, this is the oldest operating commercial building in Berkeley. c. 1875.

2     China Station Restaurant. 3rd St. at University. This was the old Southern Pacific Railroad Depot, designed by company architects in the then-popular Mission Revival style but without a bell tower. When it was converted into a restaurant, the Mission arcade was carefully preserved and the interior was paneled with woodwork from the Alaska Building of the 1915 Golden Gate Exposition. 1913.

3     Golden Bear Leasing. 2000 5th St. at University. This is a one-story, Streamlined moderne, commercial building. c. 1945–1950.

4     Victorian cottage. 743 Addison at 5th St. This is a very vertical, raised-basement cottage, with an extensive, bracketed false front and wide-angled bay. c. 1875–1885.

5     Velasca House. 2109 5th St. This bracketed, pedimented, raised-basement Italianate cottage still has its original retaining wall around the raised lot. (Note the "avocado revival" paint job.) Velasca was a Portuguese tanner from San Francisco. 1878.

6     Stick–Eastlake cottage. 2115 6th St. This one is uncommonly "decked out" in machine-cut decorations. c. 1885–1895.

7     Two Stick-style, raised-basement cottages. 2112 and 2110 6th St. The gables have Queen Anne decor. These cottages probably were built by the same contractor, as speculative housing. c. 1890s.

8     Late-Victorian cottage. 2100 6th St. at Addison. This raised-basement cottage has a wide, nicely decorated porch and gable. c. 1890s.

9     Berkeley Day Nursery. 2031 6th St. Walter Ratcliff, Jr., designed this Norman-Revival-style preschool building, with a Hansel and Gretel flavor in its

heavily decorated, Gothic front porch. The slate roof, small-paned latticed windows, ornate rainspouts in green-patinaed copper, and intricate half-timber trim all create an air of late-medieval authenticity. 1927.

10    Queen Anne cottage. 2110 7th St. This fine cottage has an attractively bracketed corner porch and picket fence railing. c. 1890.

11    Christ Chapel Church, Inc. 2016 7th St. This is a beautifully simple, late-Victorian meeting hall with touches of stickwork around the windows and on the double entry-doors toward the back. Its spacious, grassy lot, square-latticed windows, and whitewashed walls give the place a distinct New England meeting-house flavor. Recent historical evidence indicates that this was very likely the original Workingman's Library, built by the Workingman's Club (one of the first political groups in Berkeley), and used by the town board of trustees as a meeting hall, until they moved six months later to a more permanent city hall at Sacramento and University. 1879.

12    Walter Mork Metal Works Co. 844 University at 7th St. This false-front commercial building has tall, pleasantly proportioned, latticed windows across the facade. c. 1880–1890.

13    Neo-Classic Victorian commerical building. 892 University. Note the excellent shelf molding above the second-floor windows and the Italianate-style bracketing on the cornice. c. 1875–1885.

14    U.C. Hotel. University at 10th St., southwest corner. This brick, neo-Classic building has Renaissance-style glazed-tile trim around the second-floor windows and the arched entry. The original stamped-metal decorative marquee is still in place, and a superb Art Nouveau stained-glass window with hand-painted swans graces the stairway landing inside. 1926.

15    Italianate cottage. 2010 10th St. A delicate bargeboard made up of stenciled "eyelet" needlepoint motifs decorates this attractive cottage, which is one of the oldest homes in the area. c. 1870–1880.

16    Colonial Revival house. 2012 10th St. Built as a split level, this has a columned porch on the upper level. c. 1900–1910.

*BERK K-26*

17    Late-Queen-Anne cottage. 2016 10th St. The enclosed porch has square-latticed windows. The remains of a water tower can be seen in the back of the lot. c. 1895–1900.

18    One-story, whitewashed Victorian "box." 1020 Addison at 10th St. Note the stickwork trim. c. 1880–1890.

19    Large Stick house. 2028 9th St. This was converted into a corner market on the ground floor. Notice the intricate bracketing along the cornice and the fancy spindlework in the gable protruding from the hipped roof. c. 1885–1895.

20    Small, raised-basement Italianate cottage. 939 Addison St. Stick-style decor embellishes the gable, as well as two finely corbeled chimneys. c. 1880–1890.

21    Queen Anne cottage. 2017 8th St. This is a wide, horizontal version of a Queen Anne cottage. The wealth of spindlework and machine-cut decorative paneling probably came from Niehaus' local planing mill. c. 1885–1895.

22    Large, Stick-style house. 2028 8th St. at Addison. This is the original setting. The house has fine, oak double doors and many finials gracing its numerous gables. c. 1885–1895.

23    Stick–Eastlake-style early duplex. 2230 & 32 8th St. Note the separate entrances and diamond-shaped shingles. c. 1890.

24      Colonial Revival cottage. 2320 8th St. An excellent example of this mode, this high-peaked cottage has diamond-paned windows and a projecting corner portico. c. 1895–1905.

25      Victorian cottage. 2317 8th St. This hipped-roof, raised-basement Victorian cottage has stickwork and spindles across the porch. c. 1880s.

26      Niehaus Villa. 7th St. and Channing, northwest corner. This is one of the most outstanding examples of the Stick–Eastlake villa remaining in the East Bay. The massive, curved, Eastlake brackets, intricately carved capitals on the porch columns, and machine-cut sunflower panels on the second floor were all made in Niehaus' own local planing mill (it was Oscar Wilde who popularized sunflowers as decorative motifs, on his U.S. lecture tours in the 1880s). The fancy wrought-iron fence set into the concrete retaining wall remains along 7th Street. 1889.

27      Stick–Eastlake house. 2320 7th St. This two-story house has a stenciled, curved bargeboard. The slanted bay window below the gable is a recent addition. c. 1880s.

28      Mount Emory Baptist Church. Bancroft Way at 7th, southeast corner. This false-front Victorian commercial building was converted into a "storefront" church. c. 1880–1890.

*BERK K-40*

29      "California Connection." 832 Bancroft. This raised-basement cottage with Stick–Eastlake decor was restored lovingly. c. 1890.

30      Stick–Eastlake house. 2321 6th St. Good geometric-patterned trim decorates this modest house. 1885–1895.

31      "English country cottage"-version of a Stick–Eastlake house. 2329 6th St. This well-rendered house has a finely stenciled, curved bargeboard and carved bracketing around the entrance. c. 1880–1890.

*BERK K-41*

32      Colonial Revival house. 2410 9th St. This fine, raised-basement house has a curved corner portico. c. 1900–1910.

33      False-front Victorian store. 1001 Channing St. at 9th. Note the stickwork trim and the barn at the rear. c. 1885–1895.

34      Ornate Queen Anne Cottage. 1007 Channing St. This has been excellently restored. c. 1885–1895.

35      Late-Victorian raised-basement house. 2436 10th St. Note the stickwork and twin gables. 1895.

36      Raised-basement Queen Ane cottage. 2448 10th St. There are intricate decorations around the porch and windows. c. 1890–1895.

37      Italianate commercial building. Channing at San Pablo, southwest corner. This store has a squared projecting second-floor corner bay. c. 1880–1890.

38      Early Victorian split-level duplex. 2407 10th St. This wide building has neo-Classic shelf moldings above the windows and an added porch. c. 1880.

39      Late-Victorian cottage. 2238 10th St. This home has stickwork, coffered paneling in the gable, and a gambrel roof on the back half. c. 1890s.

40      Victorian house. 1019 Addison at 10th St. This unusual, large house has a combination of Eastlake stenciling in the front gable, a wide, angled double bay, spindles on the porch, and a porthole window in the side gable. c. 1880–1890.

*BERK K-42*

## Detour — Worth a Side Trip

41      Two-story Italianate house. 2120 Sacramento St., just south of the University. This is a large, recently restored house with diminutive bracketing on the cornice, windows, and pedimented portico. c. 1880s.

42      Enclave of fine Victorian buildings. California St. Between Fairview and 63rd Sts. At 3200 is Harvel's Grocery, a boxy, Stick-style commercial building with projecting squared bays on the second floor (c. 1880–1890). Number 3342 is a fine, raised-basement Queen Anne cottage with oodles of ornament, recently restored (c. 1885–1895). And number 3338 is a large Queen Anne house with a corner turret, a squared bay, multipatterned shingling, and an imposing water tower in the back that is now used for living quarters (c. 1890).

# Emeryville

## Tour Notes

Population: 4,500. First settled: Late 1800s, near San Pablo Avenue. Incorporated: 1896. Area: 1.20 square miles. Architectural characteristics: Heavily commercial near the railroad tracks, with several interesting Period Revival designs on industrial buildings, as well as a few good examples of Streamlined Moderne commercial structures. Modest Victorian and Colonial Revival houses line the streets between Doyle Street and San Pablo Avenue. A small enclave of these structures may also be found in the southeast corner of the city, just east of San Pablo.

Most travelers passing through the town as they drive along the Eastshore Freeway see Emeryville as little more than an island of luxury high-rise residential buildings near the Bay, contrasted by a cluster of nondescript factories and commercial structures to the east. But if you look closer at the industrial area east of the railroad line, you'll see several attractively designed commercial buildings in various Period Revival styles, a number of fine Streamlined Moderne structures, and many well-built "workingman's" Victorian homes.

Originally called Klinkerville, Emeryville began as a smattering of small residential and commercial structures that grew up around the early stagecoach line along what is now San Pablo Avenue. In the 1870s, when the railroad line was complete along the Bay, industrial development along its route began in earnest. By the mid '90s the community had grown sufficiently to be considered a separate town, independent of neighboring Berkeley and Oakland, and in 1896 it was incorporated as a city. By 1910 it had over 2,600 residents, an electric lighting system, two grammar schools, stockyards, and a race track.

Emeryville's population grew very slowly over the next several decades, but the industrial area continued to boom — new factories and commercial structures were built continually. In the last decade or so, the peninsula on the Bay

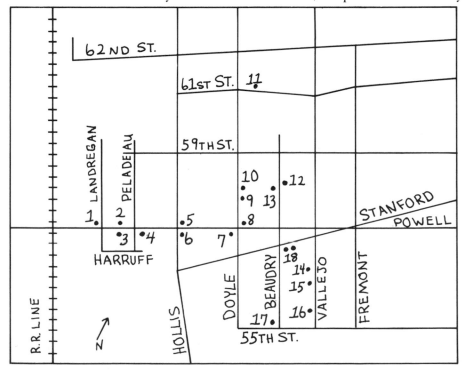

shore has been developed into an area of luxury apartments and hotels, while the old residential and industrial section has retained most of its pre-World War II appearance. Thus Emeryville appears to be two distinct communities. The following walking tour will let you explore the historic character of the "old" Emeryville's industrial and residential areas.

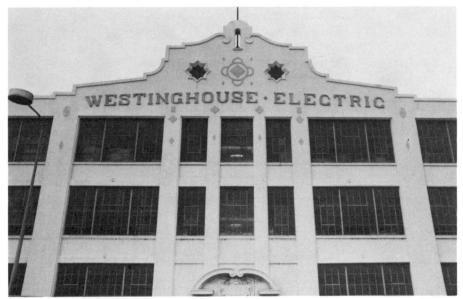

EMER-2

1    Brick commercial building. 1520 Powell St. This has a Dutch stepped-gable in front and brick dentils along the cornice. c. 1915–1925.

2    Westinghouse Electric Building. Powell at Peladeau St., northwest corner. A loosely Mission-Revival-style design was used on this large, industrial building. Moorish pointed-star windows stand out below a Spanish Baroque curved gable. Above each of the main doors are fancy scrollwork pediments and bas-relief cartouches bearing the date of construction. 1924.

3    Brick office building. 1475 Powell St. Using a modest, early-Georgian-Revival design, this building has a U-shaped floor plan that's reminiscent of tidewater Virginia manor houses. Brick quoining adorns the second-story corners, and above the arched, stone entry is a paired-arch window, topped by a voluted keystone. In all, the feeling is one of restrained elegance. c. 1920–1930.

4    "Bavarian Village." 1411 Powell St. The original trim is still visible on the west facade of this Italianate Victorian house. In recent years, it has been converted into a European "olde world" beer hall by adding stucco and imitation half-timbering to the outside. c. 1880–1890.

5    Balaam Brothers Welding Supplies. Powell St. at Hollis, northeast corner. This is a Stremalined Moderne version of a stuccoed-over "radio set." The current sign matches the style of the building. 1940.

6    Streamlined Moderne commercial building. Hollis at Powell, southeast corner. The decor in the entry lobby is original. c. 1935–1940.

7    Solid-brick commercial building. Powell at Doyle St., southwest corner. The metal beam anchors are still visible along the street side, and on the west facade the original arched windows have been bricked in. c. 1900–1910.

EMER-3

8    California Syrup and Extract Co. 1290 Powell. Now the California Omega Food Company, this refined, yellow-brick commercial building has inlaid glazed tiles in geometric patterns above the windows and a square tower similar to Italian Renaissance palazzos. c. 1920–1930.

9    "Vernetti's Town House." 5862 Doyle St. When this wooden Victorian house was converted into a bar, a new false front was added. Note the front end of a buckboard wagon above the entrance. c. 1885–1895.

10    Late-Victorian house. 5874 Doyle St. A touch of neo-Classic trim stands out on the ground-floor facade. c. 1895–1900.

11    Large Italianate house. 1270 61st St. The largest Victorian in Emeryville, this house has a bargeboard and a stenciled geometric design in the gable peak. It recently received a striking color scheme. 1894.

12    Late-Victorian house. 5894 Beaudry. Note the stickwork trim and the sunburst and fish-scale shingles in its gable. c. 1890–1895.

13    Queen Anne cottage. 5885 Beaudry. The large, lushly planted lot is like those of most modest homes in Victorian times. c. 1890–1895.

14    Queen Anne cottage. 5561 Vallejo St. Note the tasteful designs in machine-cut trim around the gable. c. 1890–1895.

15    Late-Victorian house. 5553 Vallejo St. Two carved garlands adorn the bay, and there's a swag motif on the door. c. 1895–1900.

*EMER-5*

16    Late-Victorian house. 5521 Vallejo St. The lattice-paned, enclosed porch is flanked by engaged columns. c. 1895–1900.

17    Queen Anne cottage. 1300 55th St. at Beaudry. This modestly decorated cottage has a white picket fence enclosing its tree-shrouded lot. c. 1895.

18    Two shingled bungalows. 1249 and 1253 Stanford St. at Beaudry. These homes, with their lead-latticed windows and decorative shutters, are typical of the inexpensive yet charming planning-book designs of the period — designs that many working-class families in industrial communities like Emeryville could afford to purchase. c. 1905–1915.

*EMER-8*

# Fremont

Population: 127,000. First settled: About 1846, by Mormons, in the Alvarado district. Incorporated: 1956. Area: 96 square miles. Architectural characteristics: Predominantly post-World War II tract housing in the newer, expanding neighborhoods. There are many Victorian homes and commercial buildings and two pre-Gold Rush, Spanish-Colonial-design adobe structures in the old districts of Niles and Mission San Jose.

## Areas Covered by Walking Tours
A: Niles District
B: Mission San Jose District

Only as recently as 1956 Fremont, which previously was five separate, unincorporated communities, was incorporated into a city. Primarily an area of recent tract housing, Fremont spreads across the southern end of Alameda County. Within its ninety-six square miles (the largest land area of any East Bay city) are the nuclei of five formerly independent towns that grew up along the Southern Pacific Railroad tracks laid in the 1860s: Irvington, Centerville, Niles, Mission San Jose, and Warm Springs. Before the 1840s, most of this area was the Mission San Jose's grazing land. Later, it was divided up into three large Mexican land-grant ranches, which inevitably gave way to the pernicious Yankee squatters who came during the Gold Rush Era.

Niles and Mission San Jose are the most historic districts within Fremont, as well as the most interesting architecturally. Mission San Jose contains the only mission in the East Bay and is the oldest European settlement in the region. Niles still looks like a turn-of-the-century town and holds a special interest for early-movie-industry buffs, since it was the site of the West's first movie studio. Together, the following two tours provide a pleasant day's exploration by car and foot.

## Tour Notes

Niles, home of the earliest movie studio in the western United States, was first settled by Europeans in 1842 as part of the Rancho Alameda granted to Jose de Jesus Vallejo (General Vallejo's brother). Before that, the area was used as grazing lands for the Mission San Jose cattle herds. An adobe erected on J. J. Vallejo's property to help secure his land grant still stands, on what today are the grounds of the California Nursery.

Yankee settlers began arriving during the late 1840s and the 1850s, following the Gold Rush. As elsewhere, they squatted on the rancho lands and seized them for their own use, legally or otherwise. One of the first squatters was James Shinn, whose old cottage (and another farmhouse) is now a city historic park. When Chinese laborers built the Southern Pacific Railroad line through Niles Canyon in the late 1860s, the area developed steadily along the route of its tracks. In the late 1800s, modest residences and small-scale commercial establishments were built on the streets along Niles Boulevard. The community was called Vallejo Mills until 1888, when it was renamed Niles after Judge Niles, an official of the Southern Pacific Railway. By the early years of the twentieth century, the town included most of the current row of commercial buildings lining Niles Boulevard and a majority of the residences to the west of it. Its later incorporation into the city of Fremont (in 1956) had little impact on its architectural character.

By far the most fascinating period in Niles' history was the one between 1909 and 1914: at that time, Niles was the location of the Essanay Studios, which filmed some of the earliest western and comedy movies made in the United States. (*The Great Train Robbery*, the first "western," had actually been filmed in

## Niles District

1903 in the wilds of New Jersey.) Literally hundreds of single-reel comedy and western shorts were filmed by the Chicago-based company in those five busy years. The wilderness of Niles Canyon and the storefronts along Niles Boulevard provided perfect settings for these films, since they were still basically part of the Wild West. Essanay Studios hired several famous stars of the silent screen to appear in those early films, including Charlie Chaplin, Ben Turpin, Wallace Beery, Chester Conklin, "Mustang Pete," and "Bronco Billie" Anderson. Bronco Billie, who had a part-ownership in the studio and starred in most of the westerns, was one of the most prolific actors of his time.

In 1914, Essanay closed down its Niles studios and moved to the backwater Los Angeles suburb of Hollywood, which offered a warmer climate and plenty of clean air and open space in which to film. Today, historic markers along Niles Boulevard indicate the location of some of the original buildings in which the early films were made. Walking along the old storefronts, it is easy to imagine what the town was like in its heyday as the first film capital of the West.

Dan Faris provided some information that was used to prepare these notes.

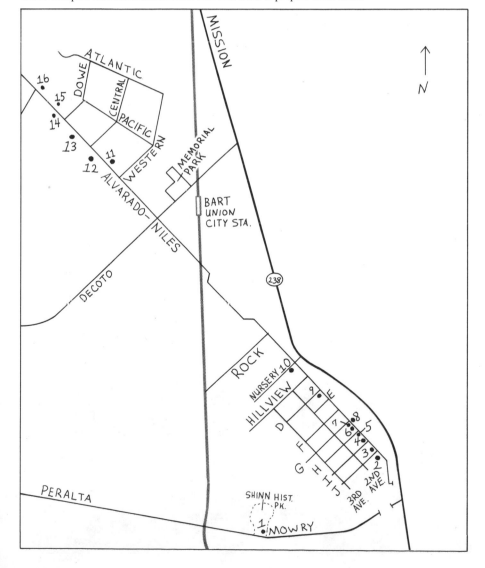

*FREM A-11*

1    Shinn House, Shinn Historic Park. 1269 Peralta Blvd. This early-Gold-Rush-Era estate was started by a prominent nurseryman named James Shinn, who arrived in Niles in 1856. The park grounds contain an earlier pioneer home, the Sim Cottage of 1850, in addition to Shinn's own Victorian farmhouse. The Shinn House is open to the public for special tours (arranged through Fremont Recreation and Leisure Services). 1876.

2    "Joe's Corner." J St. and Niles Blvd., southwest corner. This Spanish Colonial Revival commercial building has a Mexican-style open sidewalk-bar behind a Mission-style arcade. The bar is lined with fine Mediterranean glazed tile. The humorous weather vane (a cowboy roping a steer) atop the square tower at the corner reflects Niles' former prominence as the location for countless silent westerns. 1920.

3    I.O.O.F. Building. J St. and Niles Blvd., northwest corner. This is a dignified, brick, neo-Classic building that has cement crests on the second floor and a Mediterranean tile roof. c. 1900–1910.

4    Ellsworth Building. 37597 Niles Blvd. at I St. A rare example of a Moorish Revival office building, this was the first professional building in town. Named for one of Niles' founders, it housed the offices of the local judge, lawyers, and dentists. The unusual facade of this structure is made of wavy brickwork covered by plaster to make it look like adobe. The second-story windows end in Moorish pointed arches, and on the I Street side is a fine glazed-tile, pointed-arch inset above the door, with Islamic geometric patterns. 1926.

5    Niles Hotel. 37507 Niles Blvd. at H. St. This wood-frame neo-Classic hotel has a false-front cornice that is decorated by an egg-and-dart frieze, as well as massive Baroque-style plaster medallion ornaments under the bays. Above the door is a huge crest with a swag and two horns of plenty, and cherub heads top the Roman-style capitals of the flanking columns. c. 1900.

6    Late-Victorian house. 37445 Niles Blvd. The boxy, Stick-style bay is topped by a mansard roof. c. 1890.

7    Queen Anne cottage. 37425 Niles Blvd. This dimuntive house has a picket fence, and wave-pattern shingles adorn the gable. Next to it is a tiny, false-front, late-Victorian commercial building that now houses a barbershop. c. 1885–1895.

8    Victorian residence. 37364 Niles Blvd. With its red-stained wood sideboarding and small outbuilding in back, this false-front structure — one of the oldest in Niles — is reminscent of Scandinavian country houses. c. 1875–1885.

*FREM A-5*

*FREM A-15*

9      Cast-iron fence. 36967 Niles Blvd. This superb fence, with its flying-horse medallions and pineapple-like finials, came from a mansion near Oakland's Lake Merritt. That mansion was torn down to make way for a freeway. c. 1870s.

10      Vallejo Adobe. On the grounds of the California Nursery at Niles Blvd. and Nursery Ave. The oldest residence in the East Bay was built to secure the land grant of Jose de Jesus Vallejo, General Vallejo's brother and the first secular administrator of Mission San Jose. The simple grace and beauty of its whitewashed adobe walls, latticed windows, and clay-tile roof bespeak an era of rustic tranquility. Note the thick, clasping buttresses along the sides; these enabled this venerable structure to survive several earthquakes. c. 1843.

## Detour — Worth a Side Trip

To get an idea of what life was like in Niles Canyon in the late nineteenth century, continue north along Niles Boulevard to where it becomes Alvarado–Niles Road above Decoto Road. There you can view several fine examples of Victorian Era farmhouses.

11      Transitional Queen Anne/Colonial Revival late-Victorian cottage. 33367 Alvarado-Niles Rd. Now this cottage houses the Union City Chamber of Commerce. The curved, columned porch is a rare touch of elegance for such a modest residence. c. 1895–1900.

12      Craftsman bungalow. 33330 Alvarado–Niles Rd. This simple, clapboarded building was painted recently. One of the best-preserved water towers in the area is in the back, complete with storage tank on top. c. 1905–1915.

13      Queen Anne raised-basement cottage. 33121 Alvarado–Niles Rd. A large, slope-roofed barn sits in the back, and a water tower stands on the side lot. c. 1890.

14      Queen Anne cottage. 32941 Alvarado–Niles Rd. This small, tastefully trimmed cottage is in its original setting — which, including the barn in back and the two flanking palms in front, remains intact. c. 1890–1895.

15      Cluster of late-Victorian farm buildings. Included are a board-and-batten wood-frame house; a two-story storage tower with latticed windows and a hoist in back; and a small board-and-batten barn. c. 1885–1895.

16      Queen Anne raised-basement farmhouse. 32766 Alvarado–Niles Rd. Delicate spindlework may be seen across the porch. The plain, wood-frame residence in the back of the lot may have been the original farmhand's quarter. c. 1890.

*FREM A-14*

# Fremont Tour B

## Mission San Jose

### Tour Notes

The Spanish Mission de San Jose, what remains of it, is the oldest existing building in the entire East Bay. The settlement at the mission was the first European community to be established in the area. The mission was founded under Father Fermin Francisco de Lausén on June 11, 1797, and over the next thirty years a constant building program saw the construction of a compound of buildings which included several dormitories, soldiers' barracks, school rooms, workshops, storehouses, and a church. Only the main portion of the friars' residence along Mission Boulevard survives today.

By the 1820s, Mission San Jose had become one of the most prosperous and productive of all the California missions. Its huge herd of livestock included 18,000 head of cattle and 20,000 head of sheep. In the early 1830s, the population of Indian residents (or neophytes) at the mission reached a height of nearly 1,500; but after the 1834 secularization, and when the U.S. annexed California after the Mexican War, it declined even further. Finally, the remaining holdings were

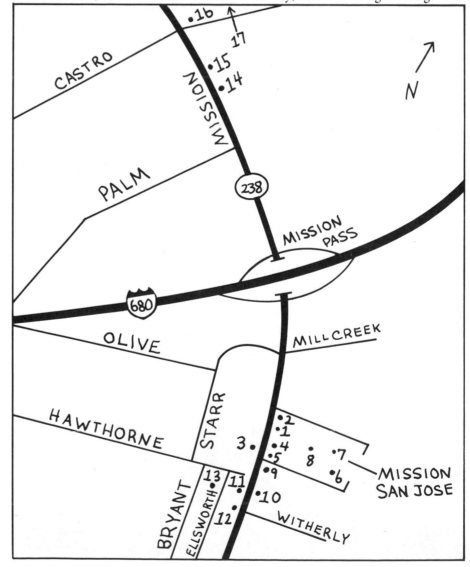

consolidated into St. Joseph's Parish, which was created in 1853. In 1868 there was a severe earthquake; most of the standing structures from the old mission were reduced to rubble, and eventually cleared away.

Meanwhile, in the years following the Gold Rush, an American community was slowly growing up around the mission site. By the late 1800s, a few dozen wooden Victorian residential and commercial buildings were erected along Mission Boulevard and the side streets to the west. After 1900 there was some residential development in the district, but basically the architectural character of the community has changed little since the early years of this century.

Mission San Jose was a separate, unincorporated community until it was incorporated into the city of Fremont in 1956. Today, the Mission San Jose District includes the remains of the old mission and its graveyard, the buildings and grounds of the Sisters of St. Dominic Convent behind it, and a number of interesting Victorian structures in various styles along Mission Boulevard. Walking through this richly historic district offers a vivid sense of what life was like in a rural California community during the nineteenth century.

---

These notes were written with information provided by Father Abeloe of the Mission San Jose Parish.

1    Old St. Joseph's Parish Church. Mission Blvd. at Washington. Designed by a French priest, Father Julien Féderey, this imposing, wooden Norman/ Gothic Revival church was built to replace the adobe mission church destroyed in the 1868 earthquake. The church has finely carved tracery on the door, a delicate stained-glass rose window, a soaring, tapered spire, and a brick foundation. Sadly empty at this time, present plans call for moving the building to another location so that the old mission complex can be completely reconstructed. 1868–1869; spire finished c. 1890.

2    Old Mission San Jose Graveyard. On the grounds around Old St. Joseph's Church. Using a variety of popular nineteenth-century designs, this is a fascinating collection of wooden gravemarkers and marble tombstones, including urns, Gothic gables, and crosses. Many of the graves are enclosed by Victorian cast-iron fencing, and some of the tombstones date from before the Civil War. Established about 150 years ago, this was originally the mission graveyard. Many Indian residents were buried here.

*FREM B-1 and 2*

*FREM B-5*

3    False-front Victorian commercial building. 43279 Mission Blvd. There is a Carpenter Gothic, icicle-pattern bargeboard along the wooden awning. c. 1875–1885.

4    Stick-style two-story house. 43274 Mission Blvd. Once the rectory of St. Joseph's Parish Church, this excellent building will soon be moved to Anza Street, two blocks away. 1890.

5    Friar's Residence, Mission San Jose. Mission Blvd. at Washington. This post-and-beam, adobe-walled building — the oldest standing structure in the East Bay — was constructed as a residence hall for the Franciscan friars of the mission (about one third of the original building at the northern end was destroyed in the 1868 earthquake). The original, handmade, adobe-brick walls are most visible through the whitewash on the facade at the southern end. The covered walkway along the northern wing of the building displays the traditional Spanish Colonial method of projecting roof beams, or vigas, supported by heavy wooden posts. Its lawn is landscaped, and one of the original cast-bronze bells in front comes from Mexico. In all, the atmosphere is one of simple, time-worn beauty. The building is open to the public as a museum, now, on weekdays and Saturdays. c. 1810.

6    Sisters of St. Dominic Convent. South wing, behind Mission San Jose. This impressively scaled, three-story, mansard-roofed, French Second Empire building originally housed the St. Thomas Seminary. Although it was stuccoed over in later years, the original wood and stone trim around the arched windows remains; so do the clasping buttresses that line the facade. When the convent was created in about 1901, the building became a nuns' residence. c. 1880.

7    Dominican Convent. North wing, behind Mission San Jose. This is the newer of the two nuns' residences on the convent grounds. Using a brick version of the Spanish Colonial style, the structure has a superb, glassed-tile, Baroque pavilion above the main door, complete with winged cherubs' heads and spiraled columns. c. 1930s.

8    Mater Dei Shrine. Dominican Convent grounds. This is a small, stone, neo-Gothic shrine, with miniature mock turrets, cherub's heads, and twisted finials on all the gables. Inside is a very ornate, Baroque, gilded chapel. Notice the lovely flower beds and tree-lined drives along this part of the convent grounds. 1922.

*FREM B-9*

9    Large neo-Classic "Pioneer box." 44342 Mission Blvd. Shelf molding stands out above the windows and a bracketed cornice projects from the second floor. In the early years of the community, this building served as a hotel. c. 1870s.

10    Small neo-Classic "Pioneer box." 44352 Mission Blvd. Note the square-latticed windows and the pedimented roofline. c. 1870s.

11    Neo-Romanesque commercial building. 44363 Mission Blvd. This brick building has three massive, rimmed arches and a Dutch-Baroque-style, false-front gable. Note the beam anchors, visible on the second floor. c. 1895–1905.

12    Victorian wood-front commercial building. 44377 Mission Blvd. This unwieldy building has a good six feet of false front, and a touch of neo-Classic trim on the facade. c. 1880s.

13    Ellsworth House. 44347 Ellsworth Rd. This boxy, hipped-roofed, two-story, Stick-style house has a Gothic, high-peaked gable decorated with a pendant-and-crossbar design. It is now a natural foods store. c. 1870–1880.

*FREM B-10*

## Detour — Worth a Side Trip

14    Late-Victorian farmhouse. 41252 Mission Blvd. The hipped roof is topped by a pair of ornate finials. Two old palm trees flank the front yard, and directly behind the house stands an impressive water tower, complete with working windmill and pumping apparatus. c. 1890.

15    Almost-Prairie-style bungalow. 41200 Mission Blvd. Covered in textured stucco, this bungalow has sweeping horizontal lines. Fine, beveled, leaded-glass windows are set into the facade, and a large windmill-powered water tower stands in the back of the lot. c. 1915–1920.

16    Small Queen Anne raised-basement cottage. 41100 Mission Blvd. at Castro Lane. The original farm buildings are behind it. c. 1890s.

17    Stick–Eastlake farmhouse. 39270 Mission Blvd., just north of Stevenson Blvd. This refined house has varied geometric patterns in the upper story, shingles and a pendant in the front gable, and a diminutive icicle bargeboard on the side gable. In the back of the lot is a mellow, weathered redwood barn. c. 1880–1890.

*FREM B-11*

# Hayward

Population: 100,000. First settled: 1851, at what is now A and Main Streets. Incorporated: 1876. Area: 37.67 square miles. Architectural characteristics: There are several good Art Deco and Moderne civic buildings in the central business district, as well as several turn-of-the-century neo-Classic brick commercial structures and a number of Spanish-Colonial-style buildings. A few Victorian residences are left in the downtown area, and some fine Victorian mansions are scattered along the city's northern and western fringes.

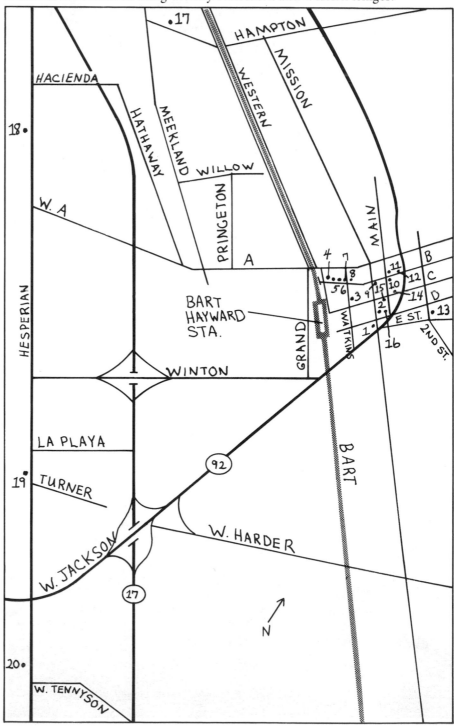

## Tour Notes

The area that was to develop into the City of Hayward first entered recorded history as a grazing land for Mission San Jose. In 1834, the Mexican Congress opened the area up to settlement, and in 1838 Don Guillermo Castro built a hacienda at what is now the site of the old City Hall, on Mission Boulevard between C and D Streets. Don Castro eventually became the largest private stock-raiser in the East Bay, shipping 4,000 head of cattle a year to San Francisco.

William Hayward, for whom the town was named, arrived in 1851 and settled at what is now A and Main streets. In his tent he set up a store, which doubled as a stagecoach stop. Eventually, this modest enterprise grew into a resort hotel and restaurant, attracting San Francisco tourists who sought a bit of rustic charm. In 1852, Don Castro sold off town lots, and the town was platted in a characteristic nineteenth-century grid pattern. In 1865, when Alfred A. Cohen and F. D. Atherton bought up the rest of Castro's land and brought in settlers from the East, the Southern Pacific Railroad arrived. After that the population of the new community grew steadily, and Hayward was incorporated as a city in 1876. In the years around the turn of the century, Portuguese immigrants were brought in as itinerant workers to help build the town; by around 1900 they made up one-fifth of the city's population. Development continued at a fairly even pace in the early years of this century. Most of the current commercial structures in the central business district were built between 1910 and 1940.

After World War II, Hayward, like most other Southeast Bay communities, experienced a real estate and population boom, leading to large-scale tract home development in its outlying areas. However, enough of the older, late-nineteenth- and early-twentieth-century buildings remain in the central business district to give some idea of what the town was like in its earlier days. But most interesting of all is the handful of really fine Victorian homes and estates that still stand in scattered locations along the fringes of the modern city.

1    Portuguese Hotel. 22801 Mission Blvd. at D St. This hipped-roof, neo-Classic Victorian hotel once housed itinerant Portuguese laborers who helped build the community in its early years. There is a nice bracketed frieze along the cornice. Now the building is a thrift shop. c. 1880.

*HAY-2*

*HAY-13*

2     Old City Hall. 22738 Mission Blvd. Truly one-of-a-kind building, this concrete structure combines Art Deco vertical-slab lines with unique ornamentation: foliated capital pilasters; a frieze showing Roman, clad figures with farm implements; and cattle heads, flanked by snakes wrapped around urns on the upper corners. The ubiquitous cattle heads also adorn the keystones above the arched windows in the recessed wings. c. 1935–1940.

3     Hayward Post Office. 822 C St. at Watkins. This small one-story building is Louis A. Simon's very stripped-down version of the W.P.A. Moderne style. 1936.

4     Raised-basement Queen Anne cottage. 714 B St. Note the pleasant decoration and the hipped roof. c. 1890–1895.

5     Large Queen Anne house. 722 B St. Notice the lacy spindlework on the porch, heavy stickwork around the windows, and cast-iron cresting at the top. c. 1885–1895.

6     Stick–Eastlake house. 750 B. St. This fairly plain house was remodeled recently — note the brick facing on the ground floor. c. 1890s.

7     Colonial Revival house. 762 B St. This gambrel-roofed house has fish-scale shingles and in indented, balustraded balcony on the ground floor. c. 1900.

8     Late-Victorian wooden commercial building. Watkins and B St., northeast corner. Note the large, pedimented gable on the front. c. 1890–1900.

9     Classical Revival building. 903 B St. at Mission Blvd. This brick-and-stone building originally housed a bank. The upper floor retains its finely detailed colonnade with Ionic, voluted capitals. Around the 1940s the ground floor was remodeled in Moderne fashion, with glazed tile and a "streamlined" marquee. Now it houses a loan office. c. 1912.

10     Green Shutter Hotel. B St. at Main, southeast corner. A sizeable brick hotel with a stuccoed-over Georgian Revival facade, its main entrance (on B Street) has an impressive, wooden, radiating famlight and flanking, embedded columns. The green-shuttered, latticed windows give the upper floor an esthetic cohesiveness. In the 1940s, the entrance at 22626 was remodeled in an interesting Streamlined Moderne design. c. 1915–1925.

11     Late-Beaux-Arts bank building. 1004 B St. at Main. Touches of early Art Deco decorate the gladiola-leaf finials above the cornice. Now it is the Sumitomo Bank. c. 1925.

*HAY-14*

12      Masonic Temple. 1074 B St. This exceptionally refined, neo-Classic design in brick has stone trim in the form of pilasters, swags above the second-floor windows, and a zigzag-patterned, brickwork frieze below the cornice. The ground floor was remodeled recently. 1924.

13      All Saints Catholic Chuch. 2nd and E Sts., northeast corner. This is a fabulous, Spanish-Baroque-style cathedral with immense bell towers and lavishly molded details above the entrance. The interior has massive marble columns and a Renaissance-style valuted, arched ceiling. 1909–1910.

14      Pratt Mortuary. 1044 C St. Here is a good example of the Mission Revival style (minus the bell tower) in a commercial structure. Now it is owned by Guerrero and Steiner. c. 1925–1935.

15      Hayward Area Historical Society. C and Main Sts., southwest corner, Originally built to house a U.S. post office, this one-story, red-brick building with Romanesque arched windows has several large, marble urns perched along the edge of its clay-tile roof. A nice, Spanish Baroque, tiled drinking fountain graces the wall of the arcaded entrance on Main Street. 1927.

*HAY-17*

16      Veteran's Memorial Building. 22737 Main St. This late-W.P.A.-Zigzag-Moderne structure has Art Deco geometric motifs embossed on the upper walls of the wings and on the frieze along the top of the central pavilion. Medallions with faces of men and women in varius branches of the armed services adorn the facade above the second-floor windows. A howitzer from the days of World War I sits on the left side of the front lawn, just begging for children to clamber over it. c. 1935–1940.

**Detour — Worth a Side Trip**

17      Meek Mansion and Estate. Boston at Hampton Rd. (Take Mission Blvd. north to Hampton; then go left to Boston.) This breathtakingly beautiful Italianate-villa-style mansion is built on an impressive scale. The central, mansard-roofed, four-story tower dominates the design. on the flanking project-ing pavilions, the Italianate carved and sawn-wood detailing is made to look like stone. In all, the building has a feeling of classical Renaissance symmetry. Meek was an early pioneer in the citrus-fruit industry. The land around the house was the Meek Estate, and it includes a fine circa-1900, Mission Revival, star-shaped fountain in front of the main entrance. The grounds, landscaped with lovely gardens are now a park, open to the public. Mansion tours are given on request: call (415) 881-6700. This is a national and state historic landmark. 1869.

18      McConaughy Home and Estate. 18701 Hesperian Blvd. in San Lorenzo. (Take Hampton west to Paseo Grande; then go west on it over the Nimitz Freeway to Hesperian Blvd; then go south past Bockman.) This large, hipped-roof, Stick–Eastlake farmhouse has a wide, curved veranda as well as iron cresting on the second floor and the rooftop. Once part of a large farm estate, this is now open to the public as a furnished-house museum, under the Hayward Area Recreation and Parks District. Hours are 1 to 4 P.M., Thursday through Sunday. 1886.

*HAY-18*

19      Old Mohr Home. Hesperian Blvd., Just north of the Chabot College Campus. (Take Hesperian Blvd. south past Winton Ave.) This late-Victorian farmhouse has a similar stylistic flavor to the McConaughy Home. 1880.

20      Oliver Homestead. Hesperian Blvd. near Tennyson Rd. (Go south on Hesperian to Sleepy Hollow. The estate is on the right.) This is an Italianate-style mansion set into a spacious, landscaped lot. Mr. Oliver owned a local salt-works business. c. 1875–1885.

# Kensington–Thousand Oaks

Population (Kensington only): 6,500. First settled: By squatters in the post-Gold-Rush Era, c. 1860s. Incorporated: An unincorporated district of Contra Costa County. Area: 1.1 square miles. Architectural characteristics: Almost entirely residential, with a variety of small Period Revival homes and many Mediterranean-style houses and bungalows. Several larger architect-designed homes stand along the winding roads to the west of Arlington Avenue. The

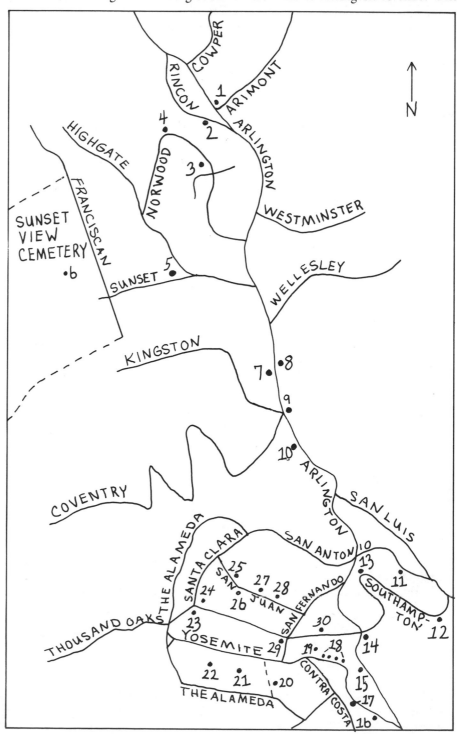

# Kensington-Thousand Oaks Tour

Thousand Oaks area (now part of Berkeley) contains a large number of substantial, early twentieth-century homes designed by renowned Bay Area architects.

## Tour Notes

The unincorporated community of Kensington was part of the Francisco Castro land grant created in 1823, which Castro later subdivided among various members of his family and their in-laws. The area that is now Kensington originally was called Rancho San Pablo; by the time Anson Blake bought part of it in 1892, it was almost completely overrun by squatters. Blake waited until 1922 to finally move to Kensington, and then he built a magnificently landscaped estate with a large, Italian-Renaissance-style villa that is still the finest home in Kensington today.

Full-scale development of Kensington did not begin until after 1906. The impetus was provided by the thousands of homeless families who flocked to settle in the East Bay after the San Francisco earthquake. In 1911 the first subdivisions, Kensington Park and Berkeley Park, were begun, and about that time streetcar tracks were laid along Arlington Avenue. But population grew very slowly at first; by 1920, the grand total was only 226. The Berkeley fire of 1923 gave another, more substantial, spurt to settlement in Kensington, and during the next decade or so many of the larger architect-designed homes were built, mostly in variations of Mediterranean and Spanish Colonial styles. Residential construction has continued to the present day, but most of the architecturally interesting buildings on the streets around Arlington Avenue were completed by the 1930s.

Thousand Oaks also began as an unincorporated community that previously had been a portion of a Spanish land grant. In 1905, the area was first subdivided as part of a planned development by Mark Daniels, the famous landscape architect. Daniels integrated the natural, rocky, Mediterranean-type landscape into the settings for the well-designed homes commissioned by the many prominent residents who settled there in the 1910s and '20s. Thousand Oaks was incorporated into the City of Berkeley in 1924. Today, the neighborhood still retains its eclectic architectural character, and within its rustic, rolling foothills you can find many attractive homes designed by such famous First Bay Tradition architects as Julia Morgan, Bernard Maybeck, and John Hudson Thomas.

Trish Hawthorne gathered the information for some of the entries in the Thousand Oaks section.

KEN-2

1     Miller House. 53 Arlington Ave. at Arimont. This attractively landscaped Spanish Colonial house, set high on a terraced lot, has Renaissance arched windows and porch. 1935.

2     Anson Blake House. 70 Rincon Rd. (just off Arlington Ave.). This opulent, Italian-Renaissance-style villa was built for Walter Bliss, one of the "founding fathers" of Kensington. The two-story, stuccoed facade, with its Renaissance loggia on the north wing and restrained, neo-Classic detailing on the second floor, is impressive indeed. However, the ten-and-three-quarter acres of magnificently landscaped grounds are really the main attraction. The long, tree-lined reflecting pool leading up the main entrance recalls images of Baroque, European palaces. In 1957, Mrs. Blake gave the lavish gardens to the university, for the Landscape Architecture Department to use as a horticultural station. Today, over 2,500 individual species and varieties of plants grow in these spectacular gardens. After Mrs. Blake's death in 1962, the university received the house, which it used as a graduate women's residence for two years. Restored and remodeled in 1969, the home became the university president's house. 1922–1924.

*KEN-4*

3        Spanish Colonial Revival house. 54 Norwood Ave. at Arlington Ct. Note the Monterey-style balustraded balcony, superbly set in a huge lot overlooking the Golden Gate Bridge. 1925–1935.

4        John Hudson Thomas House. 31 Norwood Ave. at Norwood Pl. John Hudson Thomas designed his own house as a multigabled, neo-Tudor-style structure, with more Period Revival flavor than most of his earlier work. The fairly clean, stuccoed surface, topped by shingling on the roof and punctuated by a wide overhang above the main entrance, indicates Thomas' original hand in designing his own residence. The well-landscaped lot with stone terracing offsets the house nicely. c. 1930.

5        Novitzky House. 15 Sunset Dr. The builder designed this part Craftsman, part log-cabin house for himself. The gambrel roof lends a note of historic sophistication to this otherwise rustic edifice. 1930.

6        Sunset View Mausoleum. On the grounds of Sunset View Cemetery, Sunset at Franciscan. Enter the cemetary grounds through the footpath at the end of Sunset to view the fine, Renaissance-style mausoleum made with marble brought from Europe. 1927.

7        Roth Realty. 264 Arlington Ave. The oldest building on the Kensington end of Arlington Avenue, this solid, Dutch Colonial Revival house has rusticated-stone walls, a coach porch on the south end, and a gambrel roof. Originally called Fellowship House, it was used by the Arlington Community Church for many years. c. 1910.

8        Colonial Revival house. 261 Arlington Ave. The house has side dormers and a gambrel roof. The attractive yard is enclosed by a white picket fence. c. 1925–1935.

9        Pharmacy Building. 299 Arlington Ave. at Amherst. William R. Yelland designed this Spanish Colonial Revival commercial building, which has a five-sided corner wing. 1928.

10       "Southwest Revival" house. 322 Arlington Ave. (at the Berkeley city line). This unusual house has a Mission Revival porch on a Taos, New Mexican Pueblo-style front with fake projecting beam ends. c. 1925–1935.

11       Spring Mansion. 160 San Antonio Ave. John Hudson Thomas built this palatial, sublime, neo-Classic residence for one of the first and most prominent residents of Thousand Oaks. The various elements — white, stuccoed walls;

*KEN-7*

*KEN-11*

exaggerated Beaux Arts design; geometric detailing on the corner volutes and terraced garden stairs; and Prairie School influence in the horizontality of the facade — all combine to mark this house as a highly personal statement by the architect. For many years, the estate housed Williams College (a private school). 1912.

12    Jerolemon House. 168 Southhampton Rd. Bernard Maybeck combined this house and studio in two wings, joined at the entrance. Constructed immediately after the Berkeley fire of 1923, the building reflects Maybeck's rekindled concern for using fireproof materials, especially in the metal sheathing of the wide, split eaves. 1923.

13    Natchreib House. 111 Southhampton Rd. Warren Perry, U.C.'s architect of that time, designed this magnificent Spanish-Colonial-style house. Its impressive squared tower and sheltered, Spanish-style patio recall images of the Alhambra Palace in Granada, Spain. 1928.

14    Tudor Revival house. 611 Arlington Ave. This is not just another Tudor Revival house. The superb craftsmanship, original arrangement of the stone, and timber work on the facade are most pleasing. c. 1915–1925.

15    Craftsman-style house. 726 Arlington Ave. There is a touch of the Swiss Chalet style in this refined house, which its owner attributes to Bernard Maybeck. c. 1910–1920.

16    Tudor and Jacobean Revival house. 1966 Yosemite Rd. Many local residents believe that this sophisticated blend of styles, rendered in stone and brick, was designed by Timothy Pfleuger, the architect of the Oakland Paramount Theater. 1926.

*KEN-14*

17    McGregor House. 1962 Yosemite Rd. Julia Morgan designed this pleasant, high-gabled, stucco-surfaced house, which uses its modest lot to maximum effect. 1920.

18    Four Tudor-Revival-like houses. 1941–1947 Yosemite Rd. In the later stages of his career, John Hudson Thomas designed these beautifully landscaped houses as speculative housing. 1928.

KEN-17

19    Sill House. 1936 Thousand Oaks Blvd. This large, Mediterranean Revival house is set on a high, raised lot, and shows touches of architect John Hudson Thomas' characteristic geometric ornament. The dense foliage around the entry stairs almost totally obscures the facade from the street. 1913.

20    Leavens House. 1900 Yosemite Rd. This is a good example of the First Bay Tradition work, done by Walter Stileberg, the man who was Julia Morgan's chief draftsman for a number of years. 1923.

21    Murdock House. 1874 Yosemite Rd. This is a fairly characteristic early design by John Hudson Thomas. 1911.

22    Mark Daniels House. 1864 Yosemite Rd. Jeffery Bangs designed this for Daniels, the man who first planned the Thousand Oaks subdivision. c. 1914.

23    Large Craftsman bungalow. The Alameda at Thousand Oaks Blvd., southeast corner. c. 1910.

24    George Friend House. 597 Santa Clara Ave. This is done in the Tudor Revival style. c. 1914.

25    Jones House. 1827 San Juan Ave. Bernard maybeck's solid craftsmanship is evident in the overhanging, beamed eaves and wood-shake surface. 1916.

26    Harold Leupp house. 1838 San Juan Ave. This has a dignified Colonial Revival design. 1913.

27    Cooper House. 1831 San Juan Ave. William C. Hays designed this fine, First Bay Tradition house with neo-Classic detailing. The "elbow"-angled floor plan embraces its tree-shaded lot beautifully. c. 1915.

28    Italian Renaissance Revival house. 1853 San Juan Ave. c. 1920.

29    Tudor Revival house. 686 San Fernando Ave. Edwin L. Snyder designed it. 1920.

30    Ralph Elste House. 1937 Thousand Oaks Blvd. Julia Morgan was responsible for this basically Mediterranean Revival house. Beautifully sited, its unusual floor plan was dictated by the client's mysterious insistance that no room was to contain four 90-degree angles. 1915.

**Detour — Worth a Side Trip**
31    Tilden Park Carousel. (Go south on Arlington Ave. to Marin; turn right onto Spruce; when you pass Summit Reservoir, go down Canon to Valley; turn right and continue until you see the carousel sign on the left side.) Built in 1911 by the nationally renowned Hershell Spielman Company of New York, this gem of folk art from the golden age of carousels found its way to Tilden Park in 1948. The forty wooden animals on the original outer rows of the machine comprise no less than fourteen varieties of hand-carved, gaily painted creatures, both real and mythical. There are two band organs, including a circa-1910 model with gilded scrollwork and a wooden figure of an Edwardian band leader. The shed housing the machine has an almost-geodesic-dome design, which was copied from the shed in Griffith Park, Los Angeles that previously (1937) housed this same carousel.

       This joyous creation was threatened with demolition and removal in 1976. Happily, a grass-roots East-Bay-wide movement saved it by persuading the Tilden Park Board to purchase and agree to restore the machine, proving that historic preservation can succeed to everyone's benefit. Now a national registered historic place, the carousel is open to the public from 10 A.M. to 5 P.M. on Saturday and Sunday, and daily during summer vacation. For 35 cents a ride, there's no greater thrill for children of any age.

# Oakland

Population: 335,000. First settled: 1849, near the west shore of Lake Merritt. Incorporated: 1852. Area: 79.14 square miles. Architectural characteristics: Several good examples of Gothic Revival buildings are scattered throughout the central area of the city. Some of these are the oldest buildings in the East Bay. All the other Victorian styles are well represented in the flatland neighborhoods, especially just east of Lake Merritt and to the west of Grove Street. Many fine Colonial Revival and Brown Shingle homes dot the streets of most neighborhoods from North Oakland to Fruitvale. The downtown area contains one of the best collections of Art Deco and Streamlined Moderne buildings in the western United States.

## Areas Covered by Walking Tours
    A: Downtown
    B: Preservation Park—Victorian Row
    C: Oak Center Area
    D: West Oakland
    E: Lake Merritt
    F: Brooklyn Area
    G: San Antonio Park Area
    H: Fruitvale

Oakland, the giant of the East Bay, is probably one of the most maligned of all major U.S. cities. But an objective look at the place will reveal a city that contains within its boundaries an unusual variety of cultural, historic, and architectural resources, despite its share of urban problems. From the glistening waters of Lake Merritt, enshrouded by mist and encircled by joggers in the early morning hours, to the magnificent marquee of the Paramount Theater, its neon lights reflecting their colors at night in the gleaming tile of its magnificent facade, Oakland has much to be proud of.

Oakland began with three tranquil decades of Mexican rule, as part of the Luis Peralta Land Grant. But in the Gold Rush year of 1849, Oakland's development into a city started off with a bang: before the year was out, the town had grown from a collection of tents to a community of several substantial wood-frame buildings, including a city hall. Oakland grew at a fairly rapid rate during the 1850s, as hundres of sturdy houses were built for the influx of immigrants. A number of these people became wealthy and erected impressive Victorian mansions for themselves. One such was Dr. Samuel Merritt, who helped create the lake that was to bear his name. In 1852, Oakland was incorporated as a city; two years later, the passage of ordinances prohibiting bull fights heralded the advance of Anglo Saxon civilization.

The 1860s and '70s were a boom period for Oakland. The population doubled between 1862 and 1866, and when the transcontinental railroad terminus was located in the city in 1869, a spurt of commercial construction developed along Broadway between 10th and 7th Streets, in the area now known as Victorian Row. By 1874, the population had grown to nearly 20,000. In that decade, most of the great grove of oaks from which the city took its name were felled to make way for residential and business development.

Toward the end of the nineteenth century, Oakland became known as a city of graciously designed houses with large, lush gardens. Some of the best examples line the west shore of Lake Merritt, of which only the Camron-Stanford House remains. At the turn of the century, Oakland was the working territory of such illustrious people as Jack London, Bret Harte, Frank Norris, Isadora Duncan,

*OAK A-28*

Gertrude Stein, and Julia Morgan. By then, the city included the outlying flatlands east and west of downtown.

The earthquake of 1906 left more than 100,000 San Franciscans homeless, and Oakland became the permanent residence for many of them as new homes and apartment houses were constructed to provide living quarters for thousands of these new refugees. Nearly a third of Oakland's present housing stock was erected between 1910 and 1920, and it was during this period that the huge Oakland Hotel and many of the elegant Mediterranean-style and neo-Classic apartment houses near the lake were built. The central business district also experienced a major boom in those years, when such high-rise office structures as the Central Bank Building and the Federal Building were constructed along Broadway.

The 1920s and '30s saw the last major period of architectural development in the flatlands (until the "urban renewal" of recent years). Such great Art Deco buildings as the Fox and Paramount Theaters and I. Magnin's and Bruenner's Department Stores went up at that time, and gave the downtown area a distinctively Deco flavor.

One of the most encouraging signs of vitality and renewed faith in a community's future is the ability to appreciate and make imaginative use of its architectural heritage. By this standard, Oakland has done quite well. The saving of the Paramount and the Fox, the Urban Homesteading Program in West Oakland, the Preservation Park Project near Grove Street, and the Victorian Row restoration at the foot of Broadway are all positive signs of the pride Oakland takes in its considerable architectural legacy. If you are not familiar with the extent and quality of that legacy, the eight walks provided here will help you to discover and enjoy it for yourself.

*OAK D-22*

## Tour Notes

Aside from making an occasional visit to one of its larger department stores or an evening's performance at the Paramount Theater, many Bay Area residents think of Oakland's downtown as an area with little worth seeing. But Oakland contains in its central business district one of the finest collections of Art Deco buildings in the western United States. Certainly, it offers a better concentration of this fantastic genre than any single section of its rival city across the Bay. In addition to the much-acclaimed Paramount Theater, this area has many other architectural treasures from the 1920s and '30s, such as the Fox Theater, the Oakland Floral Depot, the Howden Building, and I. Magnin's and Breuner's Department Store buildings.

Only a handful of structures from the Victorian Era survive in downtown Oakland to show us what this city's nineteenth-century urban fabric was like. But just before and after World War I, Oakland had a building boom in the area along Broadway, between 12th and 18th streets, and this led to the construction of

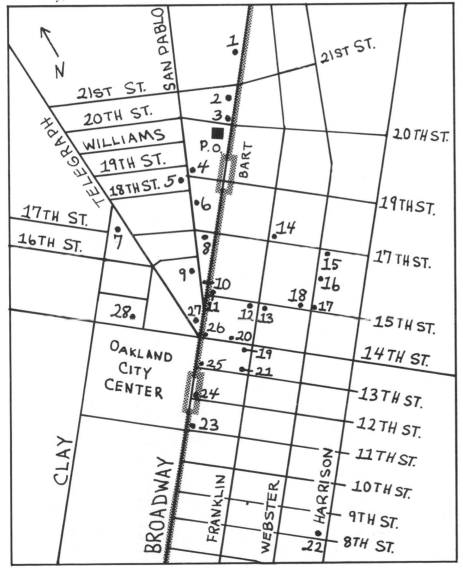

many eclectic skyscrapers that remain today, the most prominent of which is the Oakland City Hall. Triangular lots were created by the convergence of side streets onto Broadway and San Pablo Avenue, and during this period a number of interesting "flat iron"-shaped commercial buildings were erected, the most outstanding example of which is the marvelously ornate Cathedral Building at 15th and Broadway. Anyone who still thinks that "There is no there, there" in downtown Oakland will be pleasantly surprised by the following walking tour.

1     John Breuner Company Building. 22nd and Broadway. Albert F. Roller designed this massive, Art-Deco-style cube, sheathed in sea-green terra cotta that undulates in a strong, slabwork pattern across its block-long facade. Just above the entrance is a heroically scaled bas-relief scene depicting two bare-chested laborers hard at work putting the finishing touches on a carved, wooden chair; this is typical of the allegorical panels used on many Art Deco buildings. The structure used to house a department store, but its new owners recently restored it to use as a multitenant office building. 1931.

2     Paramount Theater. 2025 Broadway. Designed by Miller and Pfleuger, this is Oakland's premier Art Deco building and the showcase for the Oakland Symphony. On the exterior is a tile-work mosaic design with two giant, Byzantine-style figures controlling several smaller characters who represent various fields of entertainment. Inside the lobby, architect Pfleuger's stunning fantasy of Freudian sexual symbolism holds forth, including a "fountain of light" rising above the entrance doors. The auditorium, a show in itself, has huge, bas-relief murals in stamped metal depicting nude figures posing in an earthly paradise. Guided tours are given for $1 per person on the first Monday of the month at 2 P.M. and on the second and fourth Tuesdays at 11 A.M., except holidays, or by special arrangement through the box office. 1931.

3     I. Magnin's Department Store. 20th and Broadway, northwest corner. The glorious, deep-green, glazed terra-cotta surface of this building with its sweeping vertical slabs presents what is probably the most classic essay in the "Streamlined Moderne" phase of the Art Deco movement. 1931.

4     Oakland Floral Depot. 19th and Telegraph, northeast corner. A gleaming-blue tile facade rises into a battlement of Babylonian stepped pyramids, topped by silver fountain-spray finials. c. 1930.

*OAK A-5*

5     Fox Oakland Theater and Office Building. Telegraph Ave. at 19th. Weeks and Day designed this imposing, early-Art-Deco movie "palace" — a fantastic admixture of Hindu and Islamic motifs, with a dash of Babylonian thrown in. Stainless-steel columns and exaggerated scrollwork embellish the entrance around the ticket booth, and the interior, with two huge, Buddha-like figures on ornate pedestals, has a Javanese/East Indian flavor. The Fox Oakland was the first sound movie theater west of Chicago and by far the largest and most lavish in the East Bay until the Paramount was built. Recently, after several years of forlorn vacancy, a family from Piedmont purchased it at public auction, and plans are underway to restore it as a combined office building and performing arts center. 1926–1928.

6     Singer Sewing Shop. 1721 Telegraph Ave. A superb frieze of green terra-cotta tilework in zigzag geometric design greets the passerby who looks up above the window level of this small retail store. c. 1930.

7     Smith Brothers' Apothecary Shop. 17th at San Pablo. This exquisite gem of a neo-Classic commercial building in brick and stone has a "flat iron" shape.

*OAK A-14*

According to the current owner's research, this originally was built as a drugstore by the Smith brothers, of cough-drop fame. c. 1892.

8      Cathedral Building (formerly the Federal Building). Telegraph at Broadway. Benjamin G. McDougall designed this "flat iron" skyscraper, which has French-Gothic-Chateau-style ornament. The small lobby has wonderful marble, Gothic tracery patterns above the burnished-bronze elevator doors. 1913.

9      Latham Memorial Fountain. Telegraph Ave. at Broadway. This bronze Beaux-Arts-style monument to one of Oakland's early pioneer families forms an interesting contrast to the fast-food outlet behind it. 1913.

10      Liberty House Department Store. Broadway at 16th. From the outside, this is a fairly utilitarian commercial building; but from the top floor, you can see a splendid glass-and-steel dome set into the ceiling, with a fine neo-Classic tile frieze around it in Beaux Arts fashion. 1910–1913.

11      West Coast Furniture (formerly Roos/Atkins). 1520 Broadway at 15th. A subdued, flesh-colored terra-cotta facing with Gothic decorative patterns enhances the design of this structure. 1932.

12      Pearson Realty Office. 401 15th St. at Franklin. This Italian Renaissance Revival office building has a terra-cotta facade, embellished by fascinating sculptured figures. c. 1915–1925.

13      U.S. Post Office. 15th at Franklin, southeast corner. This colorful Spanish Colonial Revival building has a mock domed tower at the corner. c. 1920.

14      First Christian Science Church. 17th and Franklin, northwest corner. Architect Henry Schultze created one of the best examples of a rusticated-stone Romanesque Revival church in the East Bay. In the apse and nave are several spectacular stained-glass windows that a renowned company in Chicago made expressly for this congregation. 1899–1900; dedicated 1902.

15      Howden Building. Webster and 17th, southeast corner. A striking combination of highly polished orange and black tiles covers the facade of this unusual building, with its mixture of Spanish Baroque and highly original Art Deco motifs, was intended as a three-dimensional advertisement for the Howden Tile Company, its owner ironically went broke trying to complete his next major job — the Leamington Hotel, two blocks up the street. c. 1926.

*OAK A-21*

16      Cook's Union Hall. 1608 Webster St. This sophisticated Georgian Revival design could have been plucked right off the streets of Philadelphia. c. 1920–1930.

17      White Building. 15th and Franklin, southeast corner. This Gothic Revival office building shows the Chicago School influence in its use of alternating bays and piers. c. 1910–1920.

18      Y.W.C.A. 1515 Webster at 15th. One of a series of commissions that Julia Morgan did for the Y.W.C.A., this is an Italian-Renaissance-Revival design whose arched windows have attractive, bas-relief tile friezes depicting Mediterranean fruits. Inside, below the skylighted ceiling, is an arched and colonnaded atrium, around which runs a frieze carved with inspirational mottoes. 1915.

19      Financial Center Building. 14th and Franklin, southwest corner. The soaring, concrete slabs of this Art Deco skyscraper project an image of financial solidity. The recessed entryway, spanned by an ornate arch with ram's-head corbels, has a fine Zigzag-style hanging light fixture. 1929.

20      Art Deco commercial building. 440 14th St. This green-and-yellow tiled building was once a high-quality haberdashery, as indicated by the Zigzag-style glass panels above the west entrance advertising "top hats," "neckties," and "Borsalino hats." c. 1930.

21      Oakland Tribune Building. 13th and Franklin, southwest corner. Edward T. Foulkes designed this mellow yellow-brick skyscraper. Its copper-sheathed, French-Chateau-style roof has been a symbol of Oakland for many eyars. 1923.

22      Neo-Gothic terra-cotta structure. 8th and Harrison, northwest corner. Formerly a moving van company office building, this outlandish structure is encrusted with Gothic tracery, finials, grapevine patterns, and humorous gargoyles. Currently, it is being refurbished, with city aid, as a Chinatown community and business center. c. 1925.

23      Security Bank Building. 11th and Broadway, northeast corner. This Beaux Arts, Renaissance Revival, high-rise building is similar to many turn-of-the-century designs by the famous New York firm of McKim, Mead, and White. c. 1900–1905.

24      Bank of America Building. 12th and Broadway, northeast corner. Reed and Corlett designed this interesting, late-neo-Classic skyscraper, which has wide cornices and a frieze of bas-relief oak trees symbolizing the city of Oakland. 1923.

25      Neo-Classic skyscraper. 13th and Broadway, northeast corner. Here is one of the city's oldest high-rise buildings — an eleven-story, yellow-stone skyscraper, with Renaissance-style arches and pilasters on the upper floor. c. 1900–1925.

26      Central Building. 14th at Broadway, northeast corner. This brick-sheathed, neo-Romanesque skyscraper is immense. c. 1915.

27      First National Bank Building. San Pablo at 14th. Yet another "flat-iron" commercial building, this one is dressed in pristine-white stone and sports a richly ornamented clock at the corner. 1905.

28      Oakland City Hall, 12th and Clay, southeast corner, Palmer, Jones, and Hornbostle designed this superb Beaux Arts skyscraper. Note the Baroque-style clock tower, and look carefully at the columned entrance, eagles on the first-level parapet, and horns-of-plenty lamp pedestals — they'll give you some idea of Oakland's grandiose self-image in the early years of this century. 1911–1914.

**Detour — Worth a Side Trip**

You can find three of the East Bay's best Gothic Revival buildings just north of downtown Oakland.

29    St. Francis de Sales Catholic Cathedral. Grove at 21st St. This French-Gothic-style church, the site of the archdiocese of Oakland, has imposing masonry, a lofty, soaring spire, and large rose windows. 1891.

30    St. Augustine's Episcopal Church. 29th and Telegraph. Reverend Bakewell designed this gorgeous, red-stained wooden Carpenter Gothic church. A pleasantly tapered spire nestles between tall trees. Inside, the impressively beamed nave has several exquisite Victorian stained-glass windows. 1893.

31    Mosswood Cottage. Mosswood Park at Broadway and MacArthur, southwest corner. Without a doubt, this is the finest Gothic Revival house in the East Bay, and the oldest recorded house in Oakland. Designed by R. S. H. Williams, its multiple, high-peaked gables, lined with a variety of scalloped and snaking bargeboards and topped with steeple-like finials, create a strongly Romantic image. 1864.

And further up Broadway, near 42nd Street, is Oakland's oldest standing high school building:

32    Oakland Technical High School. 4351 Broadway. John T. Donovan did this almost-mannerist rendering of a neo-Classic, Beaux Arts design, with magnificent landscaping and a massive, colonnaded entryway. The only pre-1933 high school in Oakland to survive the ravages of the earthquake safety program, this building's facade is being saved intact, while the interior is being remodeled. 1914.

*OAK A-18*

# Oakland Tour B

## Preservation Park— Victorian Row

### Tour Notes

The Preservation Park Project in West Oakland involves a corridor of land that runs between Grove and Castro, from 11th to 14th streets. Preparation for the completion of the Grove–Shafter Freeway has caused dozens of houses to be moved from the freeway's path. Many of these houses have been relocated here, and plans for restoring them to their original historic character and using them for much-needed housing are underway. Many nineteenth-century structures still stand in their original state in this area and its neighboring streets. Anchoring the neighborhood are two of Oakland's most outstanding Victorian buildings: the 1868 Pardee Mansion and the Romanesque-style First Unitarian Church.

Officially, the term "Victorian Row" only covers one block of 9th Street west of Broadway. But in this guide, it refers to the superb rows of Victorian commercial blocks that line Broadway and Washington between 10th and 7th streets. Plans to use a combination of private and government funds to restore much of this business district have been approved; the buildings will be occupied by

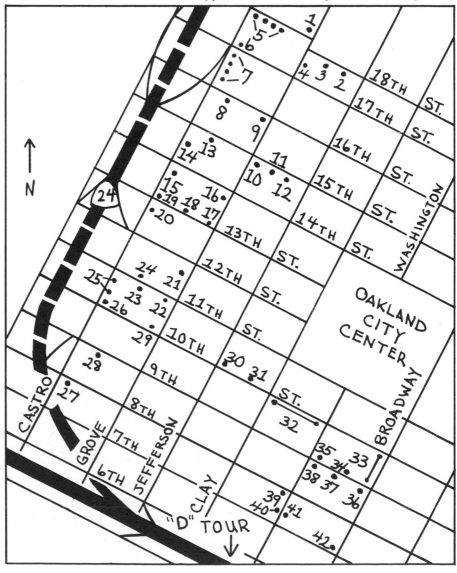

various small businesses, professional people, and community organizations. One such structure, the 876 Dunn's Block Building, has already been restored by a private investor, and the City of Oakland has chosen the multigargoyled Nicholl Block as the next one slated for renovation.

It is encouraging indeed to see the City of Oakland investing in its rich nineteenth-century architectural heritage, through such projects. Few other California cities have a greater treasure trove of Victorian buildings than the Preservation Park and Victorian Row districts offer. Taken together, these two areas provide a vivid record of nineteenth-century urban life. Learn and enjoy.

*OAK B-15*

1    Bracketed Italianate house. 1807 Grove St. at 18th. c. 1875.

2    Bracketed Italianate cottage. 623 18th St. This small, raised-basement cottage has a square bay topped by a small mansard roof. c. 1875–1885.

3    Late-Victorian triplex. 629 W. 18th St. Note the Queen Anne decorative trim. This was one of the oldest apartment houses in the city. c. 1895.

4    Queen Anne duplex. 1734 Grove St. at 18th. The original stained-glass transoms still show the old addresses. c. 1890s.

5    Row of modest Bracketed Italianate houses. 678, 684, 690, and 696 18th St. The houses are in varying states of renovation. c. 1880.

6    Colonial-Revival-style quadriplex. 678–672 17th St. at Castro. This nice building has three porticos. c. 1900–1910.

7    Row of raised-basement, Stick–Eastlake cottages. 1626, 1622, 1618, and 1614 Castro St. The squared bays have a variety of window designs. c. 1880–1890.

8    Late-Victorian house. 665 W. 16th St. This large house has clapboarding and a balustraded double portico. c. 1895.

9    Pilgrim Rest Missionary Baptist Church. Grove St. at 16th, southwest corner. This stuccoed-over Gothic Revival church has a stained-glass rose window in the east end and ornately trimmed Gothic arch windows on the north face. Note the wooden Gothic Revival entry gate at the south end. c. 1885–1895.

*OAK B-16*

*OAK B-19*

10    Bracketed Italianate house. 1432 Grove St. at 15th. This dignified house has refined detailing on the facade and angled bays. c. 1875–1885.

11    Boxy Italianate house. 627 15th St. Notice the stick trim around the windows and fancy bracketed hood above the doorway. c. 1800s.

12    Bracketed Italianate house. 619 15th St. This very vertical house has a pedimented gable. c. 1870–1880.

13    Late-Victorian duplex. 663 15th St. This unusual building has recessed porticos on either end and double, bracketed cornices across the facade. c. 1890–1895.

14    Queen Anne/Stick–Eastlake house. 1416 Castro St. There is superb detailing on the porch and main gable of this solid house. c. 1880s.

15    First Unitarian Church. 14th and Castro, southeast corner. This is the earliest, and certainly the most outstanding, example of a Romanesque Revival church in the state of California. The massive corner bell tower, Romanesque arches, and imposing brick-and-stone walls create a feeling of medieval solidity. Inside the spectacular nave are the longest redwood beams in the East Bay and several exquisite, stained-glass windows that are among the finest in the state (notice especially the "Sower" window in the south end). This church, designed by Walter J. Matthews, has hosted a number of historic persons and events within its walls. Isadora Duncan is said to have performed her first public dance here; the UNESCO organization of the United Nations was founded here in 1945; Swami Vivekananda, the spiritual "father" of the Vedanta Society, spent time here (thus making it holy ground to all his followers); Jack London, Bret Harte, and Frank Norris discussed literary matters in the conference room in the east wing at the turn of the century; and Herbert Hoover and William Howard Taft lectured in the same room. Now it is a city, state, and national historic landmark. 1886–1890.

16    Green Street Library. Grove St. and 14th, southwest corner. Here's a splendid Beaux-Arts-style building, with a symbolic bas-relief open-book decoration in the medallion above the entrance. The interior has a sumptuous, wooden staircase on the ground level, and columns around the fancily decorated walls on the second floor. 1900–1902.

17     Pierre Remillard House. 654 13th St. This large Queen Anne house has a wide, rounded corner tower and "branchwork" detailing on the rear corner porch. 1880.

18     Oakland Ensemble Theater. 660 13th St. A. Page Brown blended half-timbered Tudor Revival elements with a Colonial Revival side portico and gambrel gables. 1890.

19     Bracketed Italianate house. 682 13th St. at Castro. Narrow windows and delicately stenciled scrollwork on the porch and angled bay adorn this refined house. c. 1875–1885.

20     Bracketed Italianate house. 13th at Castro, southeast corner. This was moved from across the street for renovation, as part of the Preservation Park Project. c. 1870s.

21     Raised-basement Queen Anne cottage. 1119 Grove St. This house is absolutely crammed with ornamental detail. c. 1890.

22     Bracketed Italianate house. 653 11th St. at Grove. A charming house, this has a pedimented gable and a balustraded portico. c. 1885.

23     Transitional Victorian house. 663 11th St. Narrow clapboards, columned porticos on the front and side, and a wide-angled corner turret topped by a weather vane can be seen on this immense home. 1885.

24     Pardee Mansion. 672 11th St. at Castro. An enchanting island of Victorian antiquity, this beautiful house with its picturesque grounds is Oakland's best remaining example of a Bracketed Italianate villa in its original setting. The round, arched windows, bracketed pediments, Classical balustraded portico, and central cupola are all hallmarks of this most graceful of Victorian styles. The wood siding is scored, and quoins have been placed on the corners to give the proper Renaissance appearance of stone construction. Be sure to walk around the back of the lot — and look over the picket fence and lovely garden at the original water tower and the carriage house complete with bracketed cornice and a "running horse" weather vane. This mansion, owned by the prominent George Pardee (who became mayor of Oakland in 1893 and later served as governor of California between 1902 and 1907) is now a city and state historic landmark. 1868.

*OAK B-24*

25     Two Stick–Eastlake-style houses. 1010 and 1014 Castro St. The machine-cut ornaments and garages were added later. c. 1880–1890.

26     Stick–Eastlake house. 696 10th St. at Castro. This large, attractively maintained house has heavy, sweeping brackets, several stained-glass windows, and an intact cast-iron fence. c. 1890.

27     "Pioneer saltbox"-style house. 8th St. at Castro, southeast corner. Undoubtedly among the first homes in the area, this rare-style house has a slender, pillared portico and a lean-to in back. c. 1860s. Demolished.

28     Carpenter Gothic Revival cottage. 669 9th St. This is one of the few Gothic Revival residences left in West Oakland, and one of the oldest houses in the neighborhood. The garage underneath was added later. c. 1865.

29     Lutheran Church. 10th St. at Grove, northwest corner. This Gothic Revival Structure has an open, arched tower, paired-arch windows, and sweeping buttresses along the nave. 1900.

30     Carles Apartments. 1006 Jefferson at 10th. This is a brick neo-Classic building with a nice arched and columned entryway and a stained-glass transom depicting a Viking ship. c. 1910.

31     Stucco commercial building. 576 10th St. Originally used by Fong Wan, herbalist, this building has "Chinatown"-style balconies and pagoda roofs. c. 1915–1925.

32     Swan's Market. 10th St. between Washington and Clay. Across from the "housewife's market," this unusual retail building has colorful fruit medallions and garland-decked urn decorations on its glazed-tile facade. Originally, it was called the Free Market. 1917.

33     Delger Block. Broadway between 10th and 9th sts. This is an angled-bay, Italianate-style commercial block. The cast-metal owls on the roofline were added later to scare away pigeons. At 696 Broadway, in the middle of the block, is the Upstairs Art Gallery; most of its original Victorian interior is intact, and it is open to the public. 1868–1882.

34     Portland Hotel. 476 9th St. Yet another Italianate-style commercial building, this one designed by William Stokes to have wide, squared bays, topped by triangular pediments. Look up above the entrance at the cast-iron lions' heads with brass rings through their teeth — obviously, visiting Texans used them to tie up their horses. This was originally the Henry House, built by Ashum C. Henry, a prominent local banker. 1877.

35     Nicholl Block. Washington and 9th St., northeast corner. The brick, Italianate-style facade of this most unusual of all commercial buildings in this area has ornate, angled bays and a central pavilion that rises to a false-front pediment. But the building's truly unique feature is the amusing hose of carved devil's-head gargoyles, some leering, some sticking out their tongues, that decorate the tops of the third-floor windows. Currently, it's being restored by the city-administered Victorian Row Project, which includes plans to restore the rest of this block of 9th Street, as well. 1875–1876.

36     Wilcox Block. 9th and Broadway, southwest corner. This neo-Classic business building is reputed to be Oakland's first brick structure. c. 1860–1868.

37     Italianate-style commercial building. 461–471 9th St. Another brick building — used as the Oakland Post Office from 1875 to 1877, its stucco surfacing and metalwork were added in the twentieth century. c. 1875.

38     Two neo-Classic brick buildings. Washington and 9th St., southeast corner. William Stokes, the architect of the Portland Hotel (across the street), designed these brick buildings. 1865–1879.

39     Italianate-style commercial building. 8th St. at Washington, southwest corner. This one is done in wood with a five-sided corner bay. c. 1875–1880.

40     Dunn's Block. 721 Washington St. The rich facade of this superb, Italianate-style, angled-bay commercial building has been restored excellently by its private owner. Notice the benign, smiling gargoyles that decorate the voluted and stenciled brackets along the cornice (compare with the Nicholl block). Around the entrance is a fine cast-iron decorative piece made in San Francisco. These days, cast-iron entrance pieces are relatively rare in the Bay Area. The Victorian Row District has several; most are encrusted with several layers of paint. 1875.

41     Peniel Mission. 722 Washington St. This well-maintained, neo-Classic commercial block has alternating squared and angled bays, which are decorated with stickwork and miniature triangular and curved pediments. c. 1875.

42     Dahlke's Bar and Restaurant. 7th St. and Broadway, northwest corner. This Italianate-style building was remodeled in 1904, when Dahlke's Bar moved

in. The magnificent, carved-cherrywood, mirrored mantel behind the bar was made by a German in 1868 and brought from another bar across the street. Notice the attractive stained-glass windows at the doorway. c. 1875.

## Detour — Worth a Side Trip

43      Bret Harte Boardwalk. 567-577 5th St. (Go down Broadway under the freeway to 5th, and turn right to Clay St.) This row of nicely restored, pedimented, Italianate houses contains restaurants and shops. Bret Harte lived near here for a number of years. 1870.

44      Jack London Square. Along the Embarcadero to the waterfront, between Washington and Webster sts. (Go down Broadway past Embarcadero.) An area of mixed commercial, restaurant, and industrial buildings, this once was the heart of Oakland's waterfront, and as a young man at the turn of the century, Jack London spent much of his time here. A number of interesting nineteenth-century brick warehouses sit just off the square between 3rd Street and Embarcadero. In the square itself sits the circa-1880 Last Chance Saloon, one of London's favorite haunts. In front of it is a genuine, circa-1890s log cabin that was brought from the Klondike; London lived in it while he prospected during the Gold Rush. Up Washington Street, at the northwest corner of 3rd, is the 1915 Western Pacific Railroad Station, a concrete Beaux-Artes-style gem with an inviting arcade. This entire area has been largely restored in recent years, and the resulting stores, bars, and restaurants are doing a thriving business.

*OAK B-34*

# Oakland Tour C

## Oak Center

### Tour Notes

If you have driven to downtown Oakland on the Grove–Shafter Freeway, you probably have noticed several blocks of recently restored Victorian homes on your right, between about 20th and 10th Streets. This heavily blighted yet historic neighborhood is being rehabilitated under a federally funded project known as "Urban Homesteading," which cities across the nation are using to restore many of the inner-city communities that have fallen victim to urban decay. The concept behind this program is a simple one: low-income families are allowed to purchase delapidated homes in older neighborhoods, and are given low-interest, federally subsidized loans to fix them up. Since these families are required to live in these houses for a number of years afterwards, family-oriented community stability is brought back into areas that had been all but abandoned as decent places to live. At the same time, the historic character of these older areas is preserved for everyone to enjoy. Urban Homesteading has met with a remarkable degree of success in many big eastern cities, such as Baltimore; and Oakland's own achievements, under the city-administered Oakland Redevelopment Agency's projects on such sections as Chestnut Street between 14th and 16th, were featured in a July 1977 photo essay in the *American Heritage Magazine*.

Scattered throughout these streets of "near"-West Oakland, between the Grove–Shafter and the Nimitz freeways, are some superb gems of Victorian architecture, such as the magnificently restored, Italianate-style Canning Mansion at 46th and Myrtle streets, which still has its original Italianate-style carriage house in back. In this same area is a venerable homestead that is certainly one of the oldest remaining buildings in Oakland — the De Fremery Mansion, which is set in a spacious lot between 16th and 17th streets, along Adeline. A walk through this historic district, whith its endless variety of nineteenth-century domestic architecture, will reward anyone who's interested in getting a taste of what a well-designed Victorian urban community looked like.

*OAK C-4*

1    Two large Colonial Revival duplexes. West St. at W. 18th, southeast corner. Originally, these formed one mammoth quadriplex. Then they were separated and moved here from the other side of the Grove–Shafter Freeway. Note the sophisticated, carved, Corinthian pilasters on the corners, doors, and windows. c. 1900–1910.

2    Queen Anne cottage. 1824 West St. at 19th. This cute house has a small corner turret, and a cut-out icicle pattern above the door. c. 1890–1895.

3    Two-story Eastlake/Queen Anne house. 769 W. 19th St. This outstanding house, with its rich texturing of sawn-wood ornament, was restored recently. c. 1885–1895.

4    Row of Queen Anne houses. 700 block of W. 19th St., even side. Numbers 792 and 798 are raised-basement cottages; 782–770 are two-story houses that were restored recently. c. 1885–1895.

5    Colonial Revival house. West St. at W. 19th, northeast corner. Pilasters line the rounded corner of this excellent home. c. 1900.

6    Row of very unusual Colonial-Revival/Mediterranean-style duplexes. 825, 829, 841 W. 19th St. These are three houses of the original row. The Baroque cartouches on the corners and above the entries are unique. c. 1905–1915.

7    John Missionary Baptist Church. 1909 Market at 19th. This impressive, Spanish Colonial church has twin bell towers and lavish Baroque decoration, especially on the portico. Originally a Catholic church, it was moved from near Freeway 580 several years ago, at which time it received its current, dazzling color scheme. c. 1905–1915.

*OAK C-3*

8    Transitional house. 1936 Market at 20th. This home has a Queen Anne corner turret, a Colonial Revival curved porch, a balustraded "bulging bay," and fine, leaded windows. c. 1900–1905.

9    Raised-basement Italianate cottage. Note the hood molding above the door. c. 1870–1880.

10    Large Italianate house. W. 20th St., just south of Curtis, odd side. An unusual design with odd bracketing on the wide, flat, projecting cornice; split pilasters at the corners; and a pediment above the squared bay on the side. c. 1870–1880.

OAK C-5

11    Six Queen Anne cottages. 2000 block of West St., even side. These very nice cottages still have most of their original ornament. Number 2008 has Gothic arches on its porch; 2010 and 2014 have excellent, hand-carved scrollwork friezes (2014 recently underwent a fine restoration); and 2024 and 2030 have "mini-villa"-style squared corner turrets with pyramidal spires topped by metal finials. c. 1885–1895.

12    "Pioneer box." 832 W. 21st St. This utterly charming diminutive home has wide sideboarding, narrow shelf-molding, and a tiny porch. c. 1870s.

13    Two rare "Midwest-style," raised-basement, Italianate cottages. 868 and 871 W. 21st St. Two of the oldest homes in West Oakland, these have wide, balustraded porches and porthole windows in their pedimented rooflines. c. 1865–1875.

14    Queen Anne cottage. 878 W. 21st St. This very fancy cottage has an unusual, beaded swag-pattern in its spindles above the porch. A tall redwood barn stands in the next lot over. c. 1890.

15    Three raised-basement "Pioneer boxes." 815, 825, 835 W. Grand St. Each house has varying degrees of bracketing and shelf molding. c. 1870s.

16    Italianate house. 970 W. 21st St. This truly unique home has Gothic-like crenelation above the attic windows, as well as an odd, rectangular tower that has its own door, which leads onto a small balcony above the second floor. c. 1870s.

17    Two fine Queen Anne cottages. 2130 and 2126 Linden St. Notice the wealth of carved and machine-cut ornament, and an interesting arched-porch treatment. Number 2126 has a regal-looking carved head above the attic window. c. 1885–1895.

18    Hipped-roof "Pioneer Box." 2015 Filbert St. c. 1870–1880.

19    Queen Anne house. 1930 Filbert St. This huge house has heavy "stick and ball" spindling above the porch. c. 1890–1895.

20    Raised-basement Italianate cottage. 1909 Filbert St. Bracketed pediments are set into the hipped roof of this double-bayed home. c. 1870s.

21    Large Queen Anne house. 1902 Filbert St. This home has intricate ornamenting in the gables, especially on the bargeboards. c. 1885–1895.

22    Two-story Bracketed Italianate house. 982 W. 18th St. The curved, Colonial Revival portico was added later. c. 1875–1885.

23    Gothic Revival cottage. 964 W. 18th St. One of the few Gothic cottages remaining in Oakland and one of the oldest homes in this area, this home has a steeply pitched central gable, miniature brackets, and tall, narrow, angled bays. The original gilt-lettered address can be seen on the transom behind the small, pilastered porch, and wave-pattern bargeboards line the side gables. c. 1860s.

24    Queen Anne house. 918 E. 18th St. This is one of West Oakland's best, and the setting is superb. The bas-relief ornament along the chinmey is especially nice. c. 1890–1895.

25    Stick-style house. 1725 Myrtle at 18th. This is an odd, horizontal, solid-looking home. The heavy, curved bracketing along the wide eaves has an uncommon shape. c. 1880s.

26    Late-Victorian house. 1631 Myrtle St. A *Scientific American Builder's Edition*-appearance distinguishes this large home, in its combination of stained-glass windows, half-timber trim, and stipled stucco surfacing in the gable. c. 1895.

OAK C-13

27      Queen Anne house. 1628 Myrtle St. A filigree of "cake-icing" ornament decorates the entire upper portion. c. 1885–1895.

28      Canning House. 954 W. 16th St. at Myrtle. Here stands a Bracketed Italianate mansion of rare quality. The delicately incised details on the porch columns and the intricate, geometric decorations along the porch's bay and cornice gave an extremely beautiful effect. Recently, the house was excellently restored, and now it has an appropriate, period color-scheme. The original pedimented, "Italianate-style" carriage house can be seen from Mytrle Street. c. 1875–1880.

*OAK C-23*

29      Bracketed Italianate house. 972 W. 16th St. There is a curved bay on the right side. c. 1875–1885.

30      Solid Stick-style house. 974 W. 16th St. at Filbert. The high-peaked gable above the porch has a Gothic flavor. c. 1875–1885.

31      Large Bracketed Italianate house. W. 16th St. at Filbert, northeast corner. This house has a wide, squared-columned porch, and the horizontal banding in the wood siding is made to look like Renaissance-style stone facing. c. 1870–1880.

32      Queen Anne house. 1630 Filbert St. This attractive home has half-timber trim on the second floor, a right side-overhang, a tall, corbeled chimney, and a very ornate, gabled porch. c. 1880–1890.

33      Another *Scientific American* version of a late-Victorian house. 1710 Filbert St. An odd-shaped column at the entry, wide, sweeping brackets on the canted first floor bay, and half-timber trim on the second floor embellish this design. c. 1895.

34      Queen Anne house. 1843 Chestnut St. This fine, "midwestern"-looking house has a curved porch on the right side and pipestem columns on the corner tower. c. 1885–1895.

35      Bracketed Italianate house. 1804 Adeline at 18th St. This pediment-gabled house has quoins at the corners. c. 1870s.

36      De Fremery House. Adeline between 17th and 18th Sts. If the older of two possible dates is correct, then this is Oakland's oldest remaining house. The style is a mixture of late Gothic (with its high-peaked central gable) and "Midwest Italianate" (with its Tuscan-columned porch around three sides, and its upper arched and lower square-latticed windows). James De Fremery was a Dutch immigrant who came to California in 1849 and later founded the first legal bank in the state. He gave the home and grounds to the city in 1907, and it is now open to the public as a recreation center and park. 1860 or 1867.

*OAK C-28*

37      Eastlake/Queen Anne house. 1527 Union St. at 16th. Note the cheerful array of vibrant ornamentation. c. 1885–1895.

38      Bracketed Italianate house. 1430 Union St. The porch has a Gothic arch. c. 1880.

39      Two Queen Anne cottages. 1228 and 1222 Union St. These clapboarded, turreted homes have Colonial Revival porches. c. 1895–1900.

40      Brown Shingle house. 1183 W. 12th St. There are twin, Elizabethan-looking, high-peaked gables; a neo-Classic portico at the entrance; and a tall, sentinel-like palm tree. c. 1900–1910.

41      Queen Anne cottage. 1125 W. 12th St. Like many in Alameda, this Oakland cottage has an exceptionally rich array of ornament. c. 1885–1895.

*OAK C-36*

42      Raised-basement Italianate cottage. 1085 W. 12th St. at Chestnut. This double-bayed cottage is loaded with decoration. c. 1875–1880.

43      Late-Victorian house. 1003 W. 12th St. at Filbert. Here is a highly unusual, wide-fronted house, with its Italianate windows and bays, fish-scale shingles on the left-corner gable, and a Queen-Anne-like hexagonal spire on the right. c. 1885–1890.

44      Bracketed Italianate house. 1101 Filbert St. Heavy trim around the windows and double oak doors characterize this boxy house. c. 1880.

45      Raised-basement Italianate cottage. 1034 W. 10th St. A good example of its kind, this pedimented cottage has delicate incising above the windows. c. 1875–1880.

46      Stick-style house. 1084 W. 10th St. The bracketing on this home is ornate. c. 1880–1890.

47      Neo-classic Victorian house. 1028 Adeline St. This boxy home has a square-columned, midwestern, "Greek Revivalish" porch. c. 1870–1875.

48      Raised-basement Italianate cottage. 1027 Adeline St. Now open to the public as the Oakland Better Housing, Inc., headquarters, this building has pediments above the roof and door, and some old, flanking palms. c. 1875–1880.

49      Stick–Eastlake house. 1036 Adeline St. This uncommonly ornate home has finely carved, oak double doors. c. 1875–1885.

50      Transitional Queen Anne/Colonial Revival house. 1131 Adeline St. at W. 12th. Notice the gambreled side-gable, and a spindled mini-balcony on a dormer set into the sloping overhang above the porch. 1895–1905.

*OAK C-41*

51      Two Queen Anne houses. 1223 and 1221 Adeline St. Neither of these well-designed homes has a tower. Number 1221 now houses the Oak Cultural Center, and is open to the public. c. 1890.

52      Italianate house. 1433 Adeline St. This is an extremely vertical home, with narrow windows in an angled bay, as well as delicate, incised vine-patterns on the pilastered corners and above the second-floor windows. Note the fancily trimmed porthole window on the right side. c. 1870s.

Finished at last! Take a well-earned rest.

## Tour Notes

# West
# Oakland

The West Oakland area between the Oakland Army Base and Highway 17 originally was named Point Oakland. Its rural-like setting lured many retired civil servants from across the Bay to build homes. When the Central Pacific and Northern Railway lines came into the area in the 1870s, this district was called Prescott. Full-scale residential development then ensued, as hundreds of railroad employees moved into the area. Within a decade or so, by about 1885, Prescott was settled thoroughly, and nearly a third of its residents worked for the Central Pacific Railway. Since the turn of the century, little significant architectural change has occurred in the area.

At first glance, this part of West Oakland shows some remarkably intact blocks of Victorian homes that are in various states of delapidation. But a closer look reveals a number of houses that have been kept up well; in fact, nearly all the housing stock here is structurally sound enough to be fully restored. It's hoped that the City of Oakland and other private and public agencies can soon find the resources to undertake a large-scale revitalization of this district, similar to the one now going on in the Oak Center Project area. It's not only the low-income, minority, neighborhood residents who could benefit immensely from such a project, but also the greater community of citizens interested in historic preservation. In the meantime, the student of nineteenth-century architectural history will find this district exceptioally rich in examples of nearly every type of Victorian residential structure, ranging in style from several early Pioneer boxes (some with an almost Greek Revival flavor) to the full-towered Queen Anne house.

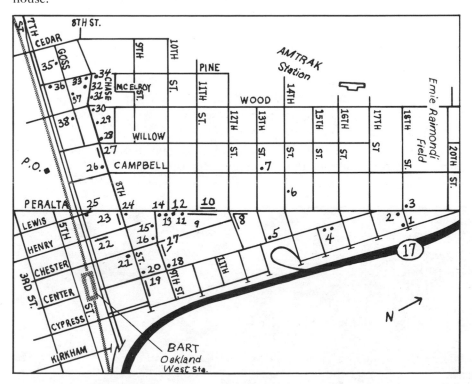

1    Queen Anne cottage. 1409 W. 17th St. at Cypress. The wealth of ornament includes a neo-Classic garland frieze. c. 1890–1895.

2      Italianate raised-basement cottage. 1421 W. 17th St. Note the unusual "Moorish" cupped bay. c. 1880.

3      Late-Victorian duplex. 1701 W. 17th St. at Peralta. This boxy structure has a latticed-fenced bancony across the second floor, ending in miniature urns at either end. c. 1880–1890.

4      Two "flat-front," false-front, raised-basement Italianate cottages. 1524 and 1510 Center St. The period trim is good. c. 1870s.

5      Bracketed Italianate duplex. 1301 Center St. at W. 13th. This fine building has a proper Classic portico. c. 1870–1880.

6      Bracketed Italianate house. 1628 W. 14th St. This brightly painted, false-front is similar to San Francisco rowhouses. c. 1875.

7      Bracketed Italian house. 1305 Campbell St. A spacious lot surrounds this large house, which was shingled around the turn of the century. c. 1875–1885.

8      Raised-basement Stick–Eastlake cottages. Peralta at W. 12th, southeast corner. This extremely rare, half square-block of cottages runs from 1214 Peralta to 1466 W. 12th Street, around the corner. The Peralta structures are almost intact, with robust, incised vine patterns in their gables. These cottages were almost certainly built for employees of the Central Railway Company or the later Western Railway Company. c. 1880–1890.

9      Bracketed Italianate houses. 1144–1020 Peralta. Most houses in this incredible, two-block-long stand still have their original ornament (1028 is an Eastlake/Queen Anne house). This unique row gives some idea of the original architectural character of other nineteenth-century neighborhoods in Oakland. c. 1875–1880.

10      Four raised-basement Queen Anne cottages. 1117–1101 Peralta. This row of cottages, with multitextured decorative surfacing in their gables, is quite well preserved. c. 1885–1895.

11      Italianate mansion. 1004 Peralta. Set back on a large lot, this interesting house has incising on its portico, a porthole n the right side, and a Stick-style porch along its right-hand wing. Note the arched windows in the doors. c. 1875–1885.

12      St. Patrick's Convent. 920 Peralta. There is sophisticated detailing on the portico and front bays of this impressive Bracketed Italianate residence. A

*OAK D-8*

carpenter who lived across the street originally built this as a home. He willed it to the convent, and when he died in 1883, the building was moved to its present site and skillfully joined to the front portion. Notice the Gothic, arched windows on the left side. c. 1870–1875.

13      Colonial Revival house. 912 Peralta. This high-peaked home has fine Classic details on its upper floors. c. 1895–1905.

14      Turreted Queen Anne house. 902 Peralta at W. 9th. A projecting wooden storefront was added shortly after 1900. c. 1890.

15      Italianate house. 1521 W. 9th St. This large, pedimented home has a tall, square-pillared porch and a large, raised lot. c. 1865–1875.

16      True Light Church of God. 835 Chester St. at W. 9th. This wooden Gothic Revival church has a brick foundation and a soaring spire. c. 1880–1890.

17      Three Bracketed Italianate homes. 1484, 1480, and 1474 Chester. Number 1484 is especially beautiful, and it has an interesting old tree in back. c. 1875–1885.

18      Late-Victorian house. 1454 W. 9th at Center. Italianate arched-windows and portico combine unusually with Stick–Eastlake squared bays and lacy vine-patterns in the gable. c. 1880s.

19      Row of late-Victorian houses. 1400 block of W. 8th St., even side. These houses span the Italianate through Colonial Revival styles. Number 1406 is the best preserved — a large, circa-1895 Queen Anne that recently was restored. c. 1875–1895.

20      Late-Victorian mansion. 1454 W. 8th at Center. This huge, rambling structure could have come straight from an Edward Hopper painting of the 1930s. This curiosity offers a rare combination of Queen Anne gables with Italianate windows and portico. c. 1880s.

21      Late-Victorian commercial block. Chester at W. 8th, southeast corner. Hexagonal turrets project at the front and back of these buildings. Note also the Italianate windows with shelf molding and the Corinthian pilasters around the corner. Now it is a Baptist church. c. 1880s.

22      Block of Victorian homes. 700 block of Henry St., even side. An uncommon stylistic variety exists among these buildings. Number 726 is a neo-Classic, late-Victorian house with a peaked gable, clapboarding, and a Colonial Revival portico (c. 1895). Number 722 is a Stick-style, raised-basement cottage with a Gothic-style, scalloped bargeboard (c. 1875–1885). Number 718 is a wide Queen Anne cottage with stickwork; its original wooden, balustraded stairway is intact (c 1890). And numbers 741 and 710 are fine, peaked-gabled "Pioneer boxes" that have all their original latticed windows in place (c 1865–1875). The cast-iron fencing that runs along most of the block is worth noting, especially in front of number 726 where its leaf pattern has an almost New Orleans quality.

23      Row of four Bracketed Italianate houses. 1555–1561 W. 8th St. One of these excellent houses, number 1561, is loaded with ornament and has an interesting Islamic, poionted, arched balustrade above the portico. c. 1875–1880.

24      Stick–Eastlake commercial building. W. 8th at Peralta, northeast corner. The two projecting, squared bays are decorated with intricate, machine-cut, geometric trim. c. 1880s.

25      Stick–Eastlake commecial block. W. 7th at Peralta, northeast corner. Note the unusual "quilted"-textured paneling on its projecting squared bays, and the Italianate-style curved brackets along its cornice. c. 1875–1885.

*OAK D-12*

*OAK D-17*

26    Engine Company No. 3. 1681 W. 8th St. This neo-Romanesque brick building with wide-spoked, arched windows served as a city fire station until 1953. Now it is a warehouse. 1896.

27    Three Bracketed Italianate rowhouses. 1685, 1687, and 1693 W. 8th St. These resemble similar blocks in San Francisco. c. 1875–1880.

28    Hipped-roof Italianate cottage. 1706 W. 8th at Willow. The original picket fence is in front of its lush lot. Note the lean-to in the back. c. 1870–1880.

29    False-front Victorian store. 1736-42 W. 8th St. There is a veranda, arched windows, and a bracketed cornice on this building. c. 1880–1890.

30    Boxy Italianate house. 1746 W. 8th St. The pleasant period color-scheme of this solid-looking home nicely offsets the molding around the windows. c. 1870–1880.

31    Late-Victorian corner store. 1752 W. 8th St. at Wood. This building has a Queen-Anne-style hexagonal projecting turret, Italianate arched windows, a bracketed cornice, and a pediment on the rear roofline. It recently received a cheerful paint job. c. 1880–1890.

32    Small raised-basement Italianate cottage. 1765 W. 8th St. This one's very cute — note the false front. c. 1870–1880.

33    Two "Pioneer boxes." 1777 and 1781 W. 8th St. These remarkably ancient survivors of West Oakland's earliest days have pedimented roofs and square-latticed windows topped by shelf molding. Number 1777, however, is almost unique in Oakland in its nearly Greek Revival design on the pedimented and pilastered doorway. (Both these houses have been sold to Oakland Better Housing, Inc., and are slated for restoration on their current sites.) c. 1860–1870.

*OAK D-34*

34    Queen Anne/Stick–Eastlake cottage. 1796 W. 8th St. at Pine. This house has much decorative detailing, especially along the trefoil Gothic arch in the small gable over the porch. c. 1880s.

35    Two-story Pioneer house. 1821 W. 7th St. This very old home has a wealth of latticed windows and a "Midwest"-style pillared veranda. c. 1865–1875.

36    Tiny "Pioneer pillbox." 714 Pine St. The windows are latticed, and the wide-lath sideboarding is painted a cheery yellow. c. 1870s.

37    Italianate house. 1762 Goss St. This high-peaked home has ridged bracketing along the gable. c. 1875.

38    Italianate house. 1731 Goss St. at Wood. The false front is thick, and deep, curved brackets support a long, projecting hood above the door. As of this writing, it is in the process of being restored and remodeled. c. 1870s.

# Lake
# Merritt

## Tour Notes

The present boundaries of Lake Merritt were created in 1860, when Dr. Samuel Merritt and others paid for a dam to be built across the estuary between East and West Oakland. During the 1870s and '80s, elegant mansions in a variety of Victorian styles were erected along the lake's western shore, each home surrounded by spacious, painstakingly landscaped gardens. Today, only the Camron-Stanford House remains to remind us of that once-proud procession of grand residences.

In 1906, under the leadership of progressive Mayor Frank E. Mott, New York architect Charles Mulford Robinson poposed that a park be created around the perimeters of Lake Merritt, and many of the current landscape features near the lake were a result of his plan. Most of the large brick and stone neo-Classic apartments along the streets immediately west of the lake were erected in the years between the San Francisco earthquake and 1920. It was then that this area lost its original Victorian residential character and developed instead its current, predominantly Mediterranean Revival architectural flavor.

Some information for this section was obtained from the staff of the Camron-Stanford House Preservation Society and their pamphlet, "A Walking Guide to Lake Merritt."

1    Oakland Hotel. 13th St. between Alice and Harrison. This mammoth yet supremely elegant example of the grand Beaux Artes hotel was designed by Bliss and Fayville. The arcaded ground floor is reminiscent of an Italian Renaissance loggia, and the twin towers flanking the roof of the central pavilion are topped by Baroque-style colonnaded lanterns. Once the host to high-ranking dignitaries, the hotel lost money in the Depression, and in 1947 it was sold to the U.S. government as a veteran's hospital. Vacant since 1963, it is currently being studied for renovation into senior citizens' housing.

2    Alician Apartments. 1450 Alice St. Here is a Mediterranean Revival apartment house with rich, Italian-Renaissance-style details around the massive-columned portico. c. 1915–1925.

3    Tudor Revival house. 1494 Alice. One of the last remaining private homes in the area, this has heavy projecting beams on the porch coach, a curved corner bay, and fine, leaded windows set in a beautiful, carved-oak door. c. 1905–1915.

4    Alison Apartments. 1560 Alice. This brick, Mediterranean-Revival-style building has a Mission-style planter in the courtyard and two interesting stone lions who guard the entrance stairs. c. 1910–1920.

5    Hill Castle Apartments. 1431 Jackson St. Miller and Warnecke designed this ten-story, concrete, Art Deco apartment house. The exterior is distinguished by a coffin-shaped, black marble inlay around the iron grillwork on the door, and ornately molded, neo-Egyptian decorative patterns on the projecting pavilion above. 1933–1934.

6    Darien Apartments. 1505 Jackson St. Also using the Mediterranean Revival style, this building has a nice marble lobby. c. 1915–1925.

7    Myrtle Arms Apartments. 176 15th St. Still another Mediterranean style, this one is done in warm-yellow brick, and has a fine neo-Classic bas-relief design in the panels around the entrance. 1922.

8    Commodore Apartments. 1501 Madison St. Here is another building in the Mediterranean style, with a recessed, skylighted entry flanked by marble columns. c. 1915–1925.

9    Streamlined-Moderne-style duplex. 1504 Madison St. c. 1940.

10    Late-Victorian house. 1448 Madison St. This stuccoed-over home has been stripped of all its ornament, but it still retains its excellent cast-iron fence and entrance gate. c. 1890.

11    Masonic Temple. 1433 Madison at 15th St. O'Brien and Werner designed this Mission Revival building, which comes complete with twin bell-towers sporting dummy wooden bells. 1908.

12    County Courthouse. 13th at Fallon St. W. G. Corlett and James Plachek created this impressively scaled W.P.A. Moderne structure, which rises above the lake like a Babylonian ziggurat in massive concrete setbacks. A delicate metal grillwork pattern adorns the space above the main entrance doors, and twin pairs of eagles, traditional symbols of the government, perch around the flagpole pedestal, atop the roof. 1935.

13    Oakland Auditorium. 10th St., east of Fallon. J. J. Donovan thought up this gargantuan neo-Roman basilica design, whose allegorical details, sculptured in bas-relief along the arcaded facade, symbolize various cultural activities. 1914.

14    Camron-Stanford House. 1418 Lakeside Dr. A lone reminder of the days of Victorian elegance along the lake, this is one of the finest Bracketed Italianate mansions in the Bay Area. The machine-cut Classical details on the wide-angled bays and across the bracketed porch are especially appealing. The house was lived in by five different families before the City of Oakland bought it in 1907 as headquarters for the Oakland Public Museum. After the museum moved into its new location, the house was empty for several years until a volunteer committee of East Bay citizens saved and restored it. Now it is a museum of Victorian life in Oakland, and several of its rooms have authentic period furnishings. Public tour hours are Wednesdays, 11 A.M. to 4 P.M., and Sundays, 1 P.M. to 5 P.M. 1876.

*OAK E-21*

15     Duel Brae Apartments. 1445 Lakeside Dr. Again, the style is Mediterranean Revival, and this time the decor around the second-floor balcony is unusually ornate, as is the fancy tilework below the roofline and between the windows. 1917.

16     Prairie School apartment house. 1497 Lakeside Dr. Designed by Charles W. McCall, the red-stained, exposed rafters of this white-stucco building give it a touch of the Mediterranean. 1916.

17     Colonial Revival house. 1503 Lakeside Dr. The last of this style on the west side of the lake, this white, clapboarded house has a hipped roof and a terraced, columned porch on the side. 1900.

18     Scottish Rite Temple. 1547 Lakeside Dr. This massive, pilastered, concrete, Classical Revival structure designed by Carl Werner stares imperiously across the lake. 1927.

19     Lake Merritt Hotel. Madison at 17th St., northeast corner. Here, Spanish Colonial combines with early Art Deco. 1925.

20     Schilling Gardens. 19th St., just north of Jackson. Here stand the remains of the gardens of the late-Victorian Adolph Schilling Estate. The original iron gates, bearing the initials "A. S." are still visible from the street. 1894.

## Detour — Worth a Side Trip

21     James P. Edoff Memorial Bandstand. North shore of Lake Merritt, near Bellevue Ave. This is a whitewashed, wooden bandstand with delicate, lacy trim. 1918. Just northwest of it is the "Mother Goose"-style Children's Fairyland playpark. 1950.

*OAK E-22*

22     Bellevue–Staten Apartments. 492 State Ave. Designed by H. C. Bauman, this well-designed blend of Spanish Colonial and Art Deco is by far the most elegant apartment house ever   built in Oakland. Its fifteen floors are clothed in rich, warm-red brick; the abstracted Spanish Baroque decorative details are in poured concrete. Along the roof, chess-piece-like finials rise eight feet above the ramparts. The two-floor-high lobby has a richly painted, plaster, coffered ceiling, and panels of squirrels eating acorns (symbolic of Oakland) decorate the bronze elevator doors. The original sales brochure described the Bellevue–Staten as "the last word in ultra-modern Home-Apartment construction." 1929.

# Oakland Tour F

## Brooklyn Area

### Tour Notes

Brooklyn Township was the original name once given to a separate, incorporated town that extended from Lake Merritt to San Leandro, and from the channel off Alameda to the Contra Costa County line. By 1870, when it was incorporated as a town, it had an area of over 24,000 acres and a population of over 1,600. By the time it was incorporated into the City of Oakland, two years later, Brooklyn's population had grown to nearly 3,000. The fine harbor facilities along Brooklyn Basin and the extension of local railroad lines into the area in the 1860s and '70s led to large-scale industrial expansion and residential development in the late nineteenth century.

Today, the area known as Brooklyn still preserves a remarkable degree of its original historic character, and literally thousands of Victorian houses and churches grace its streets. A number of these are truly magnificent in character. This walking tour includes a figurative gold mine of Victorian architecture, and contains some of the best examples of the work of Newsom and Newsom (the famous local firm best known for designing the Carson House in Eureka) left in the East Bay. Since this tour involves an extensive number of both blocks and houses, take it in two parts, resting at the middle. Along the route, you will notice many other structures of historic interest that are not listed here. If your interest in the architecture of this area increases, you may want to contact the Brooklyn Neighborhood Preservation Association, c/o Peter Carlson, 1937 8th Avenue, Oakland, California 94606.

Some members of the Brooklyn Neighborhood Preservation Association helped prepare portions of this tour.

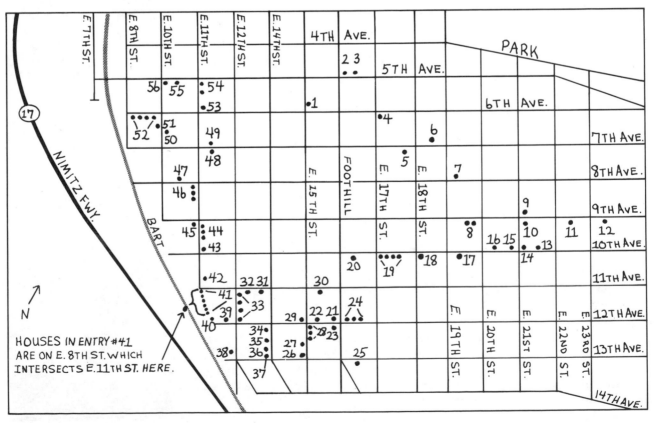

1    Hiram Tubbs House. 544 E. 14th St. at 6th Ave. This visually stunning home is set well back into an ample lot, and was built for a judge of the State Supreme Court. Its original, flanking plam trees remain. The corner turret, fish-scale shingles, and scrollwork vine decoration in the porch gable are typical of Queen Anne, while the latticed windows in the hexagonal left-corner bay and the scrollwork pediment above the attic window show the Colonial Revival influence. c. 1890–1895.

2    Queen Anne house. 448 Foothill at 5th Ave. Curved brackets on the cornice and interesting, machine-cut Queen Anne and Eastlake decor on the gables decorate this large home. c. 1885–1895.

3    Italianate-style house. 1647 5th Ave. This home reveals rare quality, with its ornate "cut-out" wood trim in various patterns around the windows, and its Stick-style, triple-curved bargeboard in the gable. c. 1875–1885.

4    Bracketed Italianate mansion. 604 E. 17th St. at 6th Ave. This richly ornamented structure has a mysterious carved face above the portico at the main entrance. The pleasantly shaded lot is enclosed by one of the best-preserved cast-iron railing left in the city. c. 1875–1880.

*OAK F-12*

5    7th Avenue Baptist Church. 1740 7th Ave. This is a large brick church with neo-Classic detailing and Dutch stepped-gables on the tower and nave. You can read the original Lutheran congregation's name in stained glass, above the main door. c. 1900–1905.

6    Colonial Revival mansion. 1819 7th Ave. This magnificent home has a tremendous, Ionic-columned, Greek Revival portico reminiscent of the White House. The windows have Roman "fasces" motifs in bas-relief, underneath their triangular pediments. There is a superb Palladian window and a blind balustrade above the doorway. This house was built for a wealthy woman, but after it was completed she never lived in it. Instead she headed for the greener hills of Piedmont, which was just opening up to residential development at that time. The building now houses a convalscent home. 1904–1905.

7    Queen Anne cottage. 1937 8th Ave. This charming, well-preserved home is set well above the street on a hilly lot, which is crossed by the original terraced-concrete stairs. c. 1892.

8    Two Queen Anne houses. 1940 and 1950 9th Ave. These probably were done by the same builder. c. 1890–1895.

9    Large Queen Anne house. 2101 9th Ave. at E. 21st St. The palm tree at the corner is the original one, and there are several excellent stained-glass windows set into the building's front and side. 1889.

10    Late-Queen-Anne house. 2106 9th Ave. at E. 21st St. There are Colonial Revival dormer windows in the spire of the hexagonal tower. The row of old palms along the side of the raised lot hint at the grandeur of this neighborhood in Victorian times. c. 1890–1895.

11    Colonial Revival house. 2236 69th Ave. The Palladian windows are very refined. c. 1900–1910.

12    Stick–Eastlake/Queen Anne cottage. 2304 9th Ave. at E. 23rd St. This splendidly robust cottage was designed by the famous firm of Newsom and Newsom. The unusual hexagonal dormer atop the hipped roof, the stenciled bargeboard on the gable of the squared corner bay, and the horseshoe arch and open latticework on the entry porch all demonstrate the originality of the Newsom brothers' work. An appealing color scheme by the son of the current owner enhances the entire design. 1887.

*OAK F-18*

*OAK F-23*

13      Stick–Eastlake house. 2112 10th Ave. This sizeable home, with excellent detailing, has been restored recently. c. 1886.

14      Large Queen Anne house. 2110 10th Ave. at E. 21st St. Note the wide corner tower. This is a fine restoration. c. 1887.

15      Colonial Revival mansion. 2049 10th Ave. at 21st St. A lushly landscaped, raised lot surrounds this superb home. 1905.

16      Late-Queen-Anne house. 2035 10th Ave. The corner porch is curved, and the stained-glass windows are good. 1893–1894.

17      Queen Anne house. 1930 10th Ave. Note the Colonial Revival porch and the solid-oak doors. c. 1890–1895.

18      Queen Anne mansion. 1806 10th Ave. This exquisite building handles its decorative detailing and design elements with great sophistication (after all, it was designed by the Newsom brothers). The noteworthy features include the large, radiant sunbursts in the gables; the wide, arched porch across the front; and the tall, corbeled chimneys. A spacious, raised lot and a delicate pastel color-scheme complete this picture of late-nineteenth-century elegance. 1888.

19      Four Stick–Eastlake, raised-basement, "workingman's cottages." 1730–1704 10th Ave. The gables and porches have excellent stenciled and cut-out ornamentation. 1887.

20      Large Stick/Italianate house. 1636 10th Ave. This house has a San Francisco flavor. c. 1875–1885.

21      Raised-basement Italianate cottage. 1549 12th Ave. at Foothill. This ornate home has curved hood-molding on the windows, a pediment in the roofline, and a shelf motif above the door. c. 1870s.

22      Stick-style cottage. 1537 12th Ave. Note the good complement of stenciled and cut-out geometric details. c. 1880s.

23      St. James Episcopal Church. 1540 12th Ave. at Foothill. This modest yet serene wooden Gothic Revival church has a miniature spire above the lancet-windowed nave. The chapter house next door, the original church building, was moved from E. 14th Street and 17th Avenue when the congregation expanded. Of a simple board-and-batten and high-peaked-gable design, it is very probably the oldest building left in Oakland; it is definitely the only documented structure from before the Civil War. Inside the nave of the main church, the redwood beaming and magnificent stained-glass windows create a marvelous effect. It's now a California state historic landmark. Chapter House, 1860–1861; main building, c. 1870–1880.

24      Three raised-basement, "workingman's," Italianate cottages. 1604, 1608, and 1614 12th Ave. at Foothill. Number 1614 has an extensive false front. c. 1870–1880.

25      False-frong, "shotgun," Italianate cottage. 1625 13th Ave. The small, ornate building is one of the few homes of this type left in Oakland (rooms are arranged from front to back, and there's no hall). c. 1870s.

26      Italianate cottage. 1447 13th Ave. at E. 15th. There are Queen Anne spindles and a brick retaining wall on this unusual home. c. 1880–1890.

27      Gothic Revival cottage. 1235 E. 15th St. Certainly one of the oldest homes in East Oakland, this ancient, clapboarded cottage has squared-latticed windows and a picket fence around the lot. Some of its original pilasters remain on the porch. c. 1865–1875.

28      Three late-Victorian houses. 1200 block of E. 15th St. at 12th Ave., even side. Set up on raised lots, with a well-preserved concrete retaining wll and iron railing in front of them, these homes have a Queen Anne flavor. c. 1890–1895.

29      Brooklyn Presbyterian Church (now Grace Temple). 12th Ave at E. 15th St. Samuel Newsom designed this unusual, immense, Gothic Revival church. Using a squarish "Greek Cross" plan, the church has some of the largest stained-glass windows in Oakland. The tall spire houses the original bells. With its horseshoe-shaped, carved-redwood gallery and its unique, redwood, spoke-like beaming below an octagonal lantern, the interior is simply breathtaking. Currently, the congregation is seeking funds to restore and preserve this superb building. 1887.

30      Raised-basement Italianate cottage. 1524 11th Ave. This delightful cottage is one of the best restorations in the area. The ornamentation is great, and the setting is attractive. c. 1870s.

Pause for a brief rest and some refreshment before going on to the seocnd part of this tour. Now, proceed to:

31      Late-Victorian duplex. 1222 11th Ave. This truly unique building has a Queen Anne flavor to its wide, twin-curved bays at either end, which are covered by fish-scale shingles, and to the spindles across its single-columned, recessed central porch. c. 1895.

32      Two-story, Bracketed Italianate house. 1218 11th Ave. Note the shelf molding above the doors and windows, and the Gothic-detailed, cast-iron fence on the left side. c. 1875–1885.

*OAK F-24*

33      Remarkable Victorian commercial block. 1100 block of E. 12th St., even side. At the southeast corner of 11th Avenue and East 12th Street is a whitewashed, Stick–Eastlake building with intricate patterns on its projecting multisided bays (c. 1880–1890). Numbers 1142 and 1136 East 12th Street are Queen Annes, with projecting, round corner turrets flanking their peaked gables (c. 1890–1895). And at the northeast corner of 12th Avenue and 12th Street is a striking, weathered, Stick–Eastlake structure with a squared corner bay, topped by a pyramidal turret with a metal finial (c. 1880–1890).

34      Bracketed Italianate house. 1227 E. 14th St. This pediment-gabled home has heavy quoining at the corners. c. 1875–1885.

35      False-front Italianate house. 1239 E. 14th St. Note the fine detailing in the frieze and cornice. c. 1875–1885.

36      "San Francisco" Stick-style house. 1241 E. 14th St. Oodles of ornament embellish the facade of this exquisitely restored home. c. 1880–1890.

37      False-front neo-Classic Victorian commercial building. 1241 13th Ave. at E. 14th. There are two cornices on the facade; one is above the pilastered first floor. c. 1875–1885.

38      Victorian commercial building. 1249 E. 12th St. This is one of the most unique Victorian commercial buildings in Oakland. The ground level is spanned by a Gothic arcade; there is a curved bay on the second floor that mixes Queen Anne, Eastlake, and Classical ornaments, and there are mini- "witch's-hat" turrets and twin gables, with oddly curved finials atop the roofline. c. 1885–1895.

39      Classic, hipped-roof "Pioneer box." 1223 12th Ave. The windows are latticed, and the Mission-style stucco arcade was added onto the front around the 1920s. c. 1870s.

40      Italianate house. 1115 12th Ave. at E. 8th St. Note the bracketed portico and the spindle-like brackets along the eaves. c. 1875–1880.

41      Rare block of well-preserved Victorian homes in varying styles. 1100 block of E. 8th St., even side. 1130 is a false-front Italiante with small pediments above the windows (c. 1875–1885). Numbers 1124 and 1120 are neo-Classic Victorian boxes with square-latticed windows (c. 1870s). Numbers 1116 and 1112 are Stick-style cottages (c. 1880s). And 1104 is an unusual, double-bayed, late-Victorian duplex with Queen Anne decor in the gables (c. 1890–1895).

42      Bracketed, false-front, Italianate house. 1042 E. 11th St. This excellent home has a wealth of good ornamentation. c. 1870s.

43      Queen Anne house. 954 E. 11th St. at 10th Ave. Note the Stick–Eastlake trim around the windows and porch. c. 1890–1895.

44      Three very ornate Stick–Eastlake, raised-basement cottages. 932, 922, 916 E. 11th St. Number 932 has Queen Anne details. c. 1885–1895.

45      Neo-Classic Victorian house. 905 E. 11th St. at 9th Ave. This attractive home has a pedimented gable, pipestem columns on the angled bay, and a large oroginal palm plant in front. c. 1880–1890.

46      Three Stick–Eastlake, raised-basement cottages. 817, 809, and 803 E. 11th St. at 8th Ave. All three are good examples of this style, and number 803 has a nice picket fence. c. 1885–1895.

47      "Pioneer box." 1035 8th Ave. Probably the oldest house west of East 14th Street, this clapboarded, two-story home has latticed windows. c. 1865–1870.

*OAK F-36*

*OAK F-52*

48      Stick-style house. 1124 27th Ave. This very vertical home has unique, ridged, Eastlake brackets along the eaves and porch. c. 1880s.

49      Late-Victorian house. 1121 7th Ave. The rounded corner, columned side-portico, and Italianate-style windows and angled bay make for a rather strange combination. c. 1980.

50      Neo-Classic Victorian house. 622 E. 10th St. This fine two-story house has shelf molding everywhere! c. 1870s.

51      Colonial Revival house. 619 E. 10th St. There is unusual scrollwork above the second-floor window of this large, gambrel-roofed home. c. 1900–1910.

52      Row of turn-of-the-century houses. 800 block of 6th Ave., even side. This great block has maintained its original historic character. Number 850 is a large, rambling, Stickish Victorian house (c. 1890–1895). 828 is a cute Colonial Revival cottage (c. 1900–1905). 822 is a Stick–Eastlake/Queen Anne house with spindles above the curved porch, a cast-iron fence along the left side, and a multitude of roving cats in the yard (c. 1890–1895). 812 is a large Queen Anne house with an Eastlake sunburst panel and a fine cast iron fence (c. 1885–1895).

53      Queen Anne mansion. 546 E. 11th St. at 6th Ave. This impressive building has a rounded corner and extensive cast-iron railings around the entire raised lot. c. 1885–1895.

54      Two very large Colonial Revival houses. 534 and 528 E. 11th St. Miniature Ionic colonnades adorn the second floor, and the iron railings and gates are intact. Number 528 has ornate, floral-pattern, stucco panels. c. 1900.

55      Italianate, raised-basement cottage. 1022 5th Ave. The house has redwood double doors; the yard has an old pepper tree. c. 1870–1880.

56      Stick–Eastlake/Queen Anne raised basement cottage. 1014 5th Ave. Behind the cast-iron fence set into the concrete retaining wall is a pleasant yard. c. 1885–1895.

Whew! Now go home and rest your feet and eyes a while before tackling the next tour.

# Oakland Tour G

## San Antonio Park Area

### Tour Notes

In the early Gold-Rush-Era days of this neighborhood, the area in the vicinity of San Antonio Park was inhabited by a number of Mexican families; in fact, it was from them that the park derived its name. But this section of Oakland was not subdivided until the late 1860s; and during the 1870s, '80s, and '90s, many well-to-do and middle-class families settled in the grid-pattern tracts that were being created in the area south of 14th Avenue, between East 20th and East 28th streets. The two perfectly preserved Stick-style houses that sit side by side on the 1800 block of East 24th Street form a striking remnant of those early residential settlements — vivid evidence of the neighborhood's ostentatious character at the end of the Victorian Era. Further east, along 23rd Avenue and East 22nd and East 23rd streets, sit several clusters of attractive late-Victorian and Colonial Revival houses. Some are in excellent condition; others await restoration. Any lover of Victorian residential architecture who has not already thoroughly combed these streets has many pleasant surprises in store.

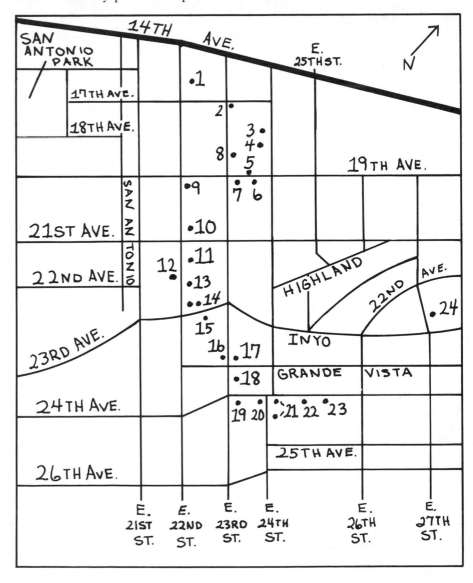

1    Stick–Eastlake house. 1635 E. 22nd St. This solid structure is romantically sited at the top of a hill that commands a sweeping view of the entire Bay Area and is surrounded by lush landscaping. The main gable's stickwork, in half-timber patterns, is very original. This house was part of a large estate that was created in 1868 and had citrus groves on it. The current lot was part of a later subdivision. c. 1885–1895.

2    Large Queen Anne house. 2302 17th Ave. at 23rd St. Fretwork shingling decorates this recently restored house which is set impressively on a raised lot. The cement steps, retaining wall, and curved path leading to the front porch are the originals. The house was built by a local entrepreneur, a man of great wealth who owned much of the land in the immediate area and raised horses near the hosue. c. 1890.

*OAK G-4*

3    Hogan House. 1870 E. 24th St. This sizeable Stick–Eastlake villa has stenciled four-leaf clovers in the bargeboard spindles above the corner porch, and triple-arched Italianate-style windows in the tower. The geometric stained glass in the entry hall is some of the best preserved in the East Bay. The original owner, Hugh Hogan, was a well-to-do lumberman; his obituary appropriately listed him as a "capitalist." 1890.

4    Taylor House. 1819 E. 24th St. All the hallmarks of the Stick style are present in this superb house, and the flanking palm trees in front are the original ones. The delicately stenciled Eastlake vine-patterns in the bargeboard are particularly appealing; so is the "wrap-around" corner porch, topped by a small gable. A man named Henry May once sold this entire block to Charles Lipman in 1868 for a $15 gold piece. Lipman later built the house and sold it to James Taylor. c. 1884.

5    Large Colonial Revival house. 2321 19th Ave. This home has an unusual "cupped," curved corner-portico, a Palladian window in the attic, red-stained shakes, and the original carriage house in back (visible from 24th Street). c. 1900–1905.

6    Raised-basement Italianate cottage. 2328 19th Ave. Note the hipped roof and the bracketed hood-molding above the double oak doors. It was restored recently. 1878.

7    Italianate, raised-basement cottage. 2306 19th Ave. This house, with its stickwork around the windows and small pediment in the roofline, may have been done by the same builder who designed number 2328. c. 1875–1880.

*OAK G-22*

8    Stick-style raised-basement cottage. 1836 E. 23rd St. The setting of this home is still farm-like, and the palm tree in front is the original. c. 1880–1890.

9    Queen Anne raised-basement cottage. 1930 22nd St. A wide, double attic-gable is decorated with Eastlake sunbursts and machine-cut ornament on the bargeboards. This is a well-done restoration. c. 1890–1895.

10    Queen Anne cottage. 2032 22nd St. Set high on a raised lot, this house still has its original rusticated-concrete retaining wall, as well as a terraced wooden stairway that leads up to the entry. c. 1890–1895.

11    Late-Victorian house. 2204 22nd St. This design contains an odd combination: an Italianate-style angled bay; a pedimented gable; a porthole window on the right corner; a Colonial Revival portico around the left corner; a square corner tower above the portico; and a wide Queen Anne turret on the left side. c. 1890.

12    Large Victorian house. 2227 22nd St. This stuccoed home has a square corner tower and an arched entry porch. c. 1880–1890.

*OAK G-25*

13     Late-Victorian house. 2242 22nd St. The square corner tower is topped by an odd-shaped roof and Romanesque-like arching around the right side and entrance. c. 1885–1895.

14     Two late-Victorian houses. 2205 and 2209 23rd Ave. at E. 22nd St. The small projecting corner turrets are topped by wooden finials, and the arched porches are Romanesque. Number 2209, which has been covered wth asbestos siding, has a Colonial Revival portico on the ground floor. Number 2205 retains its multitextured, shingle resurfacing. c. 1890–1895.

15     Late-Queen-Anne house. 2230 23rd Ave. There are carved garland freizes below the turret; a balustraded, terraced stairway; and banded, latticed windows around the right corner. The house is set high on a riased lot, with a four-foot concrete retaining wall. c. 1895–1900.

16     Small late-Victorian cottage. 2231 E. 23rd St. The attic window is indented, the squared bay is topped by a pyramidal turret, and the arched porch is Romanesque. c. 1895–1900.

17     Queen Anne cottage. 2340 E. 23rd St. at Inyo. This nice home has good ornamentation. c. 1890–1895.

18     Large, unusual Queen Anne house. 2376 E. 23rd St. Note the "derby hat" turret, recessed corner entry, Doric columns across the front, and chimney that runs up the middle of the front through a diminutive, third-floor balcony. c. 1890–1895.

19     Colonial Revival house. 2400 E. 22nd St. at 24th Ave. The wide turret is above a deep, Ionic-columned, "wrap-around" porch. c. 1900.

20     Late-Victorian house. 2238 24th Ave. There are Colonial Revival and half-timber details, and an open porch on the second floor of the tower. c. 1900.

21     Two large late-Victorian houses. 2400 and 2406 E. 23rd St. at 24th Ave. There are rounded Queen Anne corner turrets and mock half-timbering in the

high-peaked gables. Number 2400 has a deep, "wrap-around," Colonial Revival porch. 1895–1900.

22      Queen Anne house. 2320 24th Ave. Abounding in robust ornamentation of all shapes and textures, especially on the extremely lacy spindlework of the side porch, this house is what the Queen Anne style is all about. Note the machine-cut scrollwork frieze above the Palladian window in the main gable, and the stucco, almost-Baroque floral frieze around the tall, narrow turret. To complete the picture, the palm tree in front is the original one. c. 1885–1895.

23      Stick–Eastlake villa. 2326 24th Ave. The open, arched tower (to the side) was stripped of much ornament when the siding was added. c. 1885–1895.

24      Italianate mansion. 2212 E. 27th St. This immense, richly ornamented structure has a stenciled four-leaf-clover pattern in the bargeboard (similar to 1807 East 24th Street), split pilasters at the corners, and a square entry-porch with incised floral patterns on its curved brackets. Impressively sited on a high, raised lot, this is one of Oakland's finest Italianate houses. c. 1870–1880.

*OAK G-24*

## Detour — Worth a Side Trip

25      U-shaped tract of excellent Spanish-Colonial-style bungalows. Castello and Cordova Sts. at Fruitvale, just west of Freeway 580. Jack Scammel, a developer/architect, built these homes from orchard land he purchased during the Depression. Their exterior designs vary, and they have such unusual features as ship and owl weathervanes brightly stenciled shutters, and multicolored concrete slabs along their entry paths (c. 1934–1939). Across the street at 3148 Fruitvale is an excellent late-Queen-Anne house with a "wrap-around," Colonial Revival porch, a Palladian window, a wide corner-turret, and a curve-topped dormer set in the pyramidal roof. Once possessing a much larger lot planted with extensive rose gardens, this house was used in the early 1900s by the governor, as a summer residence. Jack London was a frequent guest (c. 1890–1900).

26      Antonio Peralta House. 2465 34th Ave. at Paxton, south of Fruitvale. This is the only home that a member of the Peralta family lived in that still stands. The design is almost midwestern-style Italianate, with paired, arched windows topped by shelf molding below a bracketed cornice, an a columned and balustraded porch across the front. 1870.

*OAK G-26*

# Oakland Tour H

## Fruitvale

### Tour Notes

The area now generally referred to as Fruitvale was once a district within the greater incorporated township of Brooklyn. In 1852, a group of pioneering entrepreneurs purchased the area as part of a large tract and began subdividing it into town lots. A number of enterprising farmers and horticulturists settled in the area along Sausal Creek and Fruitvale Avenue, and before long, many large orchards were being cultivated. The district got its name from those orchards. An early history of Alameda County tells us: "Fruit Vale is an avenue, immediately on the eastern border of the city, but carries no traffic except in fruits, being all private residences, with orchards and gardens attached."

The Fruitvale district finally became an incorporated part of the City of Oakland in 1909. Few of the residential streets have seen much architectural change since then. You still can find hundres of Victorian and Colonial Revival houses in different sizes and in varying states of repair in the area.

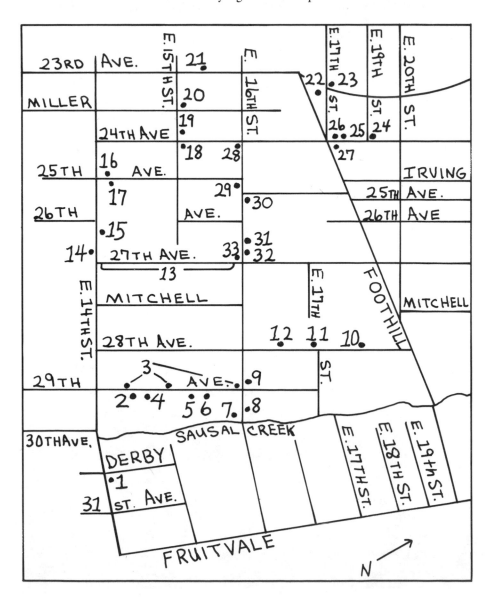

1     Fruitvale Medical Building. 3022 E. 14th Ave. at Derby. This is a Gothic Revival/Art Deco commercial building. c. 1930–1935.

2     A. E. Cohen House. 1440 E. 29th Ave. This stunning Stick villa is one of Oakland's truly great Victorian mansions, as well as a city landmark. The tall, squared corner tower with arched windows, the curved bargeboard, and the board-and-batten surfacing in the main gable are all hallmarks of this style. There is a touch of Eastlake detailing in the cut-out, four-leaf-clover designs of the miniature balconies and in the incised vine-patterns at the edges of the bargeboard and corner brackets. A. E. Cohen, the brother of the railroad magnate A. A. Cohen, received this house as a wedding present from his wife's family. 1882–1884.

3     Row of stucco California bungalows. 1400–1500 block of 29th Ave., odd side. Undoubtedly built as a tract, each house received varying treatment of its roof and porch. Numbers 1421 and 1451 are especially interesting. c. 1920–1930.

4     Brown Shingle house. 1448 29th Ave. There is an East Coast flavor to the latticed, glass-enclosed porch and the offset arrangement of windows in front. c. 1900–1910.

5     Brown Shingled house. 1524 29th Ave. Note the wide, projecting eaves, the second-story overhang, and the sophisticated handling of the casement windows in bands across the front bay and the enclosed second-floor side porch. The setting, a deep lot with birch and redwood trees, enhances the esthetic effect. c. 1900–1910.

6     Craftsman bungalow. 1534 29th Ave. This large bungalow has narrow clapboarding on the first floor and a large, shingled dormer with a walk-out porch in front. c. 1905–1915.

7     Linley House. 2939 E. 16th St. This impressive late-Victorian house has a high-peaked, Colonial Revival gable and a Classical garland frieze below the overhang. The corner turret has open, Romanesque arches flanked by columns, and the carved-oak, pilastered doorway is flanked by stained-glass panels and set in a deep side-portico with the same arching. A section of the wrought-iron fence remains in front. 1900.

8     Small "transitional" cottage. 2926 E. 16th St. This home has a Colonial Revival portico, and a Queen Anne turret and fish-scale shingles in the upper gable. c. 1900–1905.

*OAK H-1*

9     Brown Shingle house. 2840 E. 16th St. at 29th Ave. This unusual house has a "storybook" flavor, with its high-peaked front gable and wrought-iron scrollwork set into the front gates. c. 1906–1915.

10     Colonial Revival mansion. 1747 28th Ave. This stunning structure resembles Tara after the Civil War. It has massive Ionic columns and a heavy, broken pediment-and-ball finial above the door. c. 1900.

11     Tudor Revival house. 1649 28th Ave. Solid half-timbering and brick facing around the bottom of the first floor grace this twin-peaked home. c. 1915–1925.

12     Late-Victorian house. 1627 28th Ave. This home looks as though it jumped straight out of the pages of the *Scientific American Builder's Edition*. It has a wide overhang, underpinned with deep, curved brackets; various multipat-terned, decorative shingling in the front gable; a columned side-portico; and a second-floor niche in the left corner. c. 1897.

*OAK H-10*

13      Two rows of bungalows. 1400–1500 block of 27th Ave. These tree-shaded, pastel-colored stucco bungalows come in varying designs. c. 1920–1930.

14      St. Joseph's Home for the Aged. 2647 E. 14th St. The detailing on this huge, red-brick Georgian Revival building is precise, and its eight original palm trees still proudly adorn the immaculate grounds in front. Until this year, the building has been a rest home and hospital, but the building code now requires the patients to be moved, and the Catholic Church is selling the structure to a new tenant who, it is hoped, will keep it in its present condition. 1912.

15      Raised-basement Queen Anne cottage. 2570 E. 14th St. Note the "saw tooth" shingling in the gable. c. 1890–1895.

16      Primera Iglesia Bautista del Sur. 1421 25th Ave. This partially stuccoed, wooden Gothic Revival church has "saw tooth" shingling on a high-peaked gable, a triple-arched, square corner tower, and its original narrow clapboarding on the east side. c. 1890–1900.

17      Early-"Pioneer-box" house. 1430 25th Ave. Notice the tall, narrow, latticed windows and the long, bracketed porch. c. 1870–1880.

18      True Life Baptist Church. 2410 E. 15th St. Here is another partially stuccoed Gothic Revival church. This one has its original machine-cut Gothic trim on the tower, as well as most of its stained-glass windows. c. 1885–1895.

19      Two-story Stick–Eastlake house. 15th St. at 24th Ave., northeast corner. Recently restored, this house has Gothic arches, spindles on the porch, and an interesting plasterwork pattern in the gable. c. 1885–1895.

20      Large Spanish Colonial house. 2344 E. 15th St. A massive round tower projects from the front entryway. c. 1925–1935.

21      Late-Victorian house. 2527 23rd Ave. Recently restored with a good, pastel-colored paint job, this home blends Queen Anne and Stick–Eastlake ornament and has a set-back facade that recedes from the street in three stages. c. 1885–1895.

22      Primera Iglesia Bautista. 1660 23rd Ave. at E. 17th St. This fine Carpenter Gothic church has curved bargeboards over the Classic-columned entry porch and on the main gable. c. 1880–1890.

23      Church of Ebenezer. 1711 23rd Ave. at E. 17th St. This large Gothic Revival church has a tall, massive, open-arched corner tower, and a multitude of stained-glass windows below high-peaked gables. c. 1885–1895.

24      Large Stick–Eastlake/Queen Anne house. 2366 E. 19th St. Note the unusually fancy ornament on the porch and corner bays. c. 1890.

25      Queen Anne cottage. 1711 24th Ave. A small house with stickwork around the windows and neo-Classic columns on the porch. c. 1885–1895.

26      Stick-style house. 1703 24th Ave. Intricate, paneled patterns around the windows in the squared bay and above the porch adorn this charming house. The original palm tree and intact cast-iron fence around the lot create an air of antiquity. c. 1880–1890.

27      Serene late-Victorian wooden church. 1710 24th Ave. This church has stickwork around the wide-arched, stained-glass windows; it also has a solid, squared tower with a tall, metal finial capping its pyramidal roof. c. 1885–1895.

28      Raised-basement late-Victorian cottage. 1544 24th Ave. at E. 16th St. The blend of Queen Anne and Eastlake ornament is enhanced by a cheerful paint job. c. 1890–1895.

29      Simple Queen Anne house. 2503 E. 16th St. at 25th Ave. Note the stickwork on the tower and squared bay. c. 1890–1895.

30      Queen Anne raised-basement cottage. 2524 E. 16th St. at 25th Ave. A triple row of spindles adorns the porch. c. 1890–1895.

31      Queen Anne cottage. 2544 E. 16th St. The scrollwork design incised into the panel above the doorway is absolutely exuberant. c. 1890–1895.

32      Late-Victorian houses. 2600 E. 16th St. This design has narrow clapboarding, a deep-pedimented gable, and attached columns on the recessed corner porch. c. 1895–1900.

33      Colonial Revival house. 2621 E. 16th St. This pleasant, "boxy" house is set far back on its shaded lot. c. 1900–1910.

*OAK H-31*

## Detour — Worth a Side Trip

34      Mills College. (Take the MacArthur exit off Freeway 580 and follow the edge of campus until you reach the main auto gate. Pick up a brochure from the guard at the gate to get a list of the buildings on cmapus and their locations.) Of special interest are: Mills Hall (1871), the first building on campus — a French, mansard-roofed, Second Empire design on a stunning scale. Across the oval is Julia Morgan's clock tower, El Campanil (1904), one of her first designs. It is a personalized, concrete version of a Mission-style, open-arched bell tower. Down the road, toward the Seminary Avenue gate, is Kimball House (c. 1880–1890), a supremely ornate Bracketed Italianate building that was once part of a private estate, with heavy quoins on the projecting square bay in front and unusually intricate ornamentation around the windows and cornice. The rest of the campus is landscaped beautifully, and most of the other buildings are done in variations of the Spanish Colonial mode.

35      Dunsmuir House. (Take the 106th Ave. exit east off the 580 Freeway; go under the freeway; and turn up Peralta all the way to the top.) This is one of the East Bay's greatest Colonial Revival mansions. It was built in 1898 for the Dunsmuir family and used in a Hollywood film based on the family's tragic history. The large, exquisitely kept grounds and the massive portico extending toward the front drive give the house a southern ante-bellum look (Tara *before* the Civil War). The house is now open to the public as a convention center and a history museum from noon to 4 P.M. during mid-April to the end of September.

*OAK H 35*

# Piedmont

Population: 11,000. First settled: 1852, in the north end of town, around Dracena Park. Incorporated: 1907. Area: 1.8 square miles. Architectural characteristics: A handful of late-Victorian homes are scattered throughout the central area of the city, but most of the architecturally significant houses use the various Period Revival and Brown Shingle styles popular in those years (most were built between 1905 and 1930). Many homes by leading architects such as Julia Morgan and John Hudson Thomas are located in the neighborhoods to the east of Crocker and Highland Avenues.

### Areas Covered by Walking Tours
A: Central Piedmont
B: North Piedmont
C: Upper Piedmont

## Tour Notes

In the census of 1910, just three years after its incorporation as a city, Piedmont had no fewer than thirty-two millionaires among its residents, giving it the largest per-capita income level of all the communities of similar size in the United States. This remarkable fact helps explain the unusual number of grand residences, many fairly palatial, that overwhelm the first-time visitor.

This hilly community first began to be settled in 1852, when the Blair brothers purchased a tract of land from the Peralta family. The tract ran below Highland Avenue, roughly between Dracena Park, Oakland Avenue, and Grand Avenue. The Blairs used the property for cattle ranching, dairy farming, and rock quarrying; the section near Dracena Park provided much of the red-rock surfacing used for roads throughout the East Bay.

The Piedmont Springs Hotel was the next significant development in the area — between 1868 and 1870, it was built on the hot springs of what is now Piedmont Park, just behind the current high school, as a resort accommodation. Mark Twain was only one of many prominent guests who visited the hotel in its heyday to relax in its soothing baths and enjoy the sweeping vista of the Bay Area that its hilltop setting offered. There were several fires in the hotel, and in about 1893 it burned for the final time and went out of business.

In the 1870s and '80s, the hillsides began sprouting scattered settlements by "pioneer" residents. Among them was a Mr. Worcester, who built the first Brown Shingle house in the Bay Area (1876–1878). Although you can still find it at 575 Blair Avenue, it has been altered beyond recognition. Other early residents were the Craig and Wetmore families, whose homes still stand. In the late 1890s and early 1900s, residential development began on a modest scale along Oakland Avenue, and the side streets between Hillside and Highland were divided as lots and sold off. At this time, the area was still considered a suburb of Oakland.

The San Francisco earthquake of 1906 brought an influx of prominent families from across the Bay. These were people who had spent summers in the pleasant Piedmont hills and who now decided to build their new residences there. By the following year, the new community had grown enough to be incorporated as a city, and over the next few decades real estate speculation and advertising helped keep a steady stream of well-to-do homebuilders arriving in Piedmont.

At the city's inception, the founding fathers had decided that Piedmont should be a tranquil community, made up almost exclusively of residences, free from polluting industry and the hustle and bustle of commerce. Piedmont has thus remained a "city of homes," is the truest sense of the phrase. Almost no commercial or multi-unit development of any kind has occurred in these highland neighborhoods, which still present an early-twentieth-century architectural grandeur to the world. To stroll through the hills and dales of this comfortable community is to glimpse a bit of "paradise" on earth.

These notes were written with some information provided by June Rutledge of the Piedmont Historical Society.

## Tour Notes

Since Piedmont is almost exclusively a residential community, there is no downtown area in the traditional sense. However, the area around the city hall and along Oakland Avenue between Highland and El Cerrito can be called the town's central area. Most of the oldest remaining homes in Piedmont are located in this district. The late nineteenth century saw some scattered settlement here, and a handful of Victorian houses — including the oldest one remaining in Piedmont, at 342 Bonita Street — remain to attest to those early "pioneering" days. Between 1905 and 1915, several large mansions were built in various mixtures of Period Revival and Brown Shingle styles for wealthy professionals and businessmen. The civic center buildings around the city hall were erected around 1910 to 1930. The old high school was replaced with an "earthquake-proof" building in the 1970s, but except for that, there has been very little major construction in the area in recent decades.

This tour was prepared with information on some of the entries provided by Donald Church.

# Central Piedmont

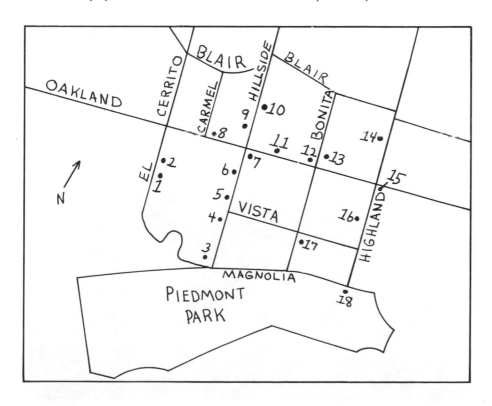

*PIED A-2*

1    Lanza House. 320 El Cerrito Ave. This large Tudor Revival house has massive beaming, a wide-angled gable, and a tapered chimney suggestive of John Hudson Thomas' early designs. The fine cast-iron fence, as well as the gates at the main entry and the driveway, have an Art Nouveau flavor to their scrollwork pattern. A sizeable stand of redwood trees lines the left-rear portion of the lot. 1911.

2    Brown Shingle house. 310 El Cerrito Ave. There is a sophisticated, East Coast quality to this home, with its high-peaked gables and dormers, volutes under the second-story overhang, and small-paned, leaded windows. The house is set high on a tidy lot with a brick garden wall, and urns flank the entry path. 1906.

3    Three-story Colonial Revival mansion. 365 Hillside Ave. at Magnolia. This massive, boxy home has a balustraded coach porch over the driveway, rusticated stone along the ground level, and pilasters at the corners. c. 1900–1910.

4    Tudor Revival house. 345 Hillside Ave. at Vista. This twin-gabled house, with its half-timbering and black-stained shingles, was built as a wedding "cottage" for the daughter of the Gorrill family, who lived next door. c. 1906.

5    Gorrill House. 337 Hillside Ave. Attributed to A. Page Brown (the architect of the San Francisco Ferry Building), this is a rare local example of a Tudor Revival mansion. Its three-story, rusticated-stone corner tower gives it a Romanesque touch. The leaded-glass windows and metal finial atop the tower are done nicely. Mr. Gorrill was a lumberman. 1896.

6    Barracloughs House. 321 Hillside Ave. This precise Colonial Revival mansion is done in the southern ante-bellum mode, and has an Ionic-colonnaded portico. c. 1895–1900.

7    Uhl House. 304 Hillside at Oakland Ave. This is a magnificent, multi-gabled Tudor Revival "manor" house, with touches of Jacobean style in its wide-paned bay windows and the pyramidal finials atop the gateposts. Commanding a spacious and exquisitely landscaped lot, the house used to be nicknamed "Grey Gables" before it was painted white. c. 1905–1910.

8    Colonial Revival cottage. 1719 Oakland Ave. This "cute" cottage has a low, hipped roof, an Art Nouveau stained glass window and a cast-iron fence. c. 1905.

*PIED A-4*

*PIED A-7*

9    Brown Shingle house. 225 Hillside Ave. Open tracery in a half-timbered pattern projects in front of the main gable of this unusual home. There are interesting balconies on the second-floor windows, as well as a rounded corner turret. 1905–1915.

10    Dutch Colonial Revival house. 214 Hillside Ave. This imposing home has a gambreled gable facing the street. An esthetic effect is created by the deep-brown, weathered shingling, which is offset by the white pediment-trim around the gable end, white shutters, and klinker-brick chimney. c. 1905–1915.

11    Raised-basement Queen Anne cottage. 1811 Oakland Ave. This is the oldest house left on upper Oakland Ave. c. 1890–1895.

12    Queen Anne cottage. 227 Bonita Ave. This gem has large, Eastlake-style sunburst panels, a hirsute, gargoyle-like face in the main gable, and finely coffered doors. 1889.

13    Brown Shingle house. 224 Bonita Ave. There is a distinct Craftsman flavor to the beaming on the gables and along the porch of this solid house. c. 1905–1915.

14    Late-Victorian-looking house. 225 Highland Ave. This home has an elongated "wrap-around," pillared porch; clapboards; and a miniature Palladian window in the gable. c. 1895–1905.

15    Transitional house. 1726 Oakland Ave. at Highland. This attractive home has a Queen Anne turret; a four-sided Colonial Revival porch; a sloping, "lean-to" roofline in back; high-peaked gables; and a mixture of shingled and clapboarded surfacing. This design resembles many of the designs of turn-of-the-century English architect, Charles Voysey. c. 1900–1910.

16    Modest whitewashed house. 311 Highland Ave. A Colonial Revival influence dominates this design with its shuttered, latticed windows, and a Midwest-style veranda. c. 1900–1910.

17    Wetmore House. 342 Bonita Ave. at Vista. The spindling across the veranda of this raised-basement, horizontal Stick–Eastlake-style Victorian house gives it an almost Steamboat Gothic look. A superb stained-glass window in the front door depicts scenes from rural life, and "urns of plenty" on pedestals flank the entry steps. One of Piedmont's first homes, Wetmore House is definitely its oldest remaining intact house. Originally part of a large farm, it had a twin house nearby, which has been incorporated into the structure of the Christian Science Church around the corner on Magnolia. Wetmore House is now a registered national historic place. 1878.

*PIED A-12*

18    Piedmont Park. Magnolia St. at Highland. At the Magnolia Street entrance to this lushly landscaped park, there is a Spanish-Baroque-style excedra dedicated to those citizens of Piedmont who died in battle in World War I. Note the face on the keystone in the middle. c. 1920.

# Piedmont Tour B

## North Piedmont

### Tour Notes

The rolling hillside streets that wind upward to the east of Highland Avenue and just below Crocker Avenue contain an outstanding collection of First Bay Tradition and Brown Shingle houses. Here can be seen some of the best work of such great Bay Area architects as Julia Morgan, John Hudson Thomas, and Louis Christian Mullgardt. The area was settled mostly in the years just following the incorporation of Piedmont (1907–1920), and the upper-middle-class and well-to-do clients who came here could afford to hire the best architects of the day to indulge their architectural fancies. A walk along these upland streets will be taxing on one's feet, but pleasing to the eyes and rewarding to the spirit of anyone who appreciates beautifully designed buildings.

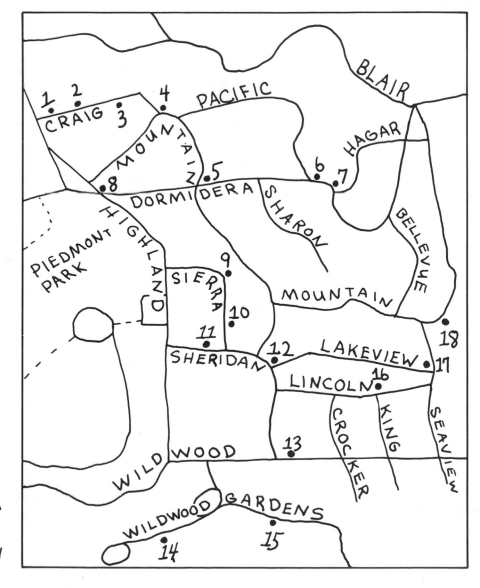

1    Tudor-Revival-genre house. 9 Craig Ave. This design is attributed to Julia Morgan. c. 1915.

*PIED B-16*

2     Juliet Alexander House. 19 Craig Ave. Charles W. Dickey, the same architect to design the Claremont Hotel in Berkeley, blended Mediterranean and neo-Classic elements here. Later additions to the house include a cloistered garden and a small chapel in the rear. 1915–1917; additions 1923–1933.

3     Large stuccoed house. 34 Craig Ave. The geometric ornament and Prairie School design almost certainly mark this as the work of John Hudson Thomas. c. 1916.

4     Craig House. 55 Craig Ave. In 1911, this red-stained, Stick–Eastlake house was moved from Highland Avenue to its current woodsy site. It is one of the "pioneer" homes in Piedmont, and the second-oldest house remaining in the city. 1879.

5     Clapboarded redwood house. 173 Mountain Ave. at Dormidera. The First Bay Tradition elements, especially the handling of the windows, evoke the work of John Galen Howard. c. 1905–1915.

6     Solid Brown Shingle house. 33 Dormidera Ave. c. 1910.

7     Hotel House. 43 Dormidera Ave. This is one of Louis Christian Mullgardt's most original designs. This rather enigmatic architect worked on the fringes of the First Bay Tradition; he died a poor and forgotten man. The house seems to be a blend of an oversized Craftsman bungalow and a Japanese teahouse. The clapboarding and banded windows show the Craftsman influence, while the stucco-and-timber upper story, with its shallow, gabled roof topped by wide, overhanging eaves, gives a Japanese effect. Mullgardt borrowed the sloping or "battered" walls on the lower section of the projecting right-hand pavilion from Tibetan monastery designs. They were the most characteristic feature of his domestic work. 1907.

*PIED B-7*

8     Piedmont Community Church. 400 Highland Ave. at Dormidera. This Mediterranean-style church has a touch of Mission Revival in the arcaded walkway in the middle. c. 1927.

9     Mediterranean Revival "bungalow." 45 Sierra Ave. Julia Morgan designed this home, which has banded windows. c. 1915–1925.

10     Mediterranean-style house. 49 Sierra Ave. Also designed by Julia Morgan, this one resembles number 45. Both were probably speculative housing. c. 1915–1925.

11     Tudor Revival house. Sierra Ave. at Sheridan, northwest corner. This sizeable house has an intricately decorated bargeboard. 1912.

*PIED B-12*

12      Tudor Revival/Mediterranean house. 117 Sheridan. Julia Morgan created this very refined design, which integrates a Tudor Revival peak-gabled form with her own blend of Mediterranean and original detailing. The lot is landscaped beautifully. c. 1915–1920.

13      Kelly House. 455 Wildwood Ave. at Sheridan. John Hudson Thomas designed this long, rambling house in a predominantly Mediterranean mode (note the white stucco walls and Mission-style arches), but there's also a touch of Prairie School flavor to its horizontal lines. This is one of Thomas' earliest and most spacious designs. 1910.

14      Frank C. Havens House. 101 Wildwood Gardens. Bernard Maybeck created this rare Piedmont design for Mr. Havens, Oakland's biggest turn-of-the-century developer. Over the years, Tiffany and Company and individual craftsmen steadily remodeled this original, First Bay Tradition, redwood house at the direction of Mr. Havens, who had a passion for all things oriental. Only the scalloped-arched coach porch is visible from the street. 1906; remodeling to c. 1940.

15      Small "rustic" cottage. 150 Wildwood Gardens. Note the "Log Cabin Revival" influence. c. 1930s.

16      Walter Lemert House. 37 Lincoln Ave. Copying a house in Normandy, Arthur Brown created this genuinely unique design with its blend of French Chateau turrets, its Egyptian Revival pylon chimney, and its Bulgarian-style cupola. 1909.

17      Knowland House. 65 Seaview Dr. at Lincoln. Julia Morgan created this baronial, Beaux Arts, neo-Classic mansion for the publisher of the *Oakland Tribune*. c. 1915–1925.

18      Fore House. 444 Mountain Ave. This unassuming, well-sited home most resembles a stuccoed Craftsman-style design. Note designer Louis Christian Mullgardt's hallmark — battered basement walls along the side. 1909.

*PIED B-17*

## Tour Notes

Probably the East Bay's most sumptuous neighborhood, the area of Piedmont east of Crocker Avenue can be called "upper" both in its altitudinal and socioeconomic levels. These steeply inclined avenues are graced by some of the largest and most impressive homes in the entire Bay Area. Some scattered residential development took place along Crocker and Seaview in the 1910s, where a number of Julia Morgan's homes, along with those by other First Bay Tradition architects, stand. But most of the homebuilding in the area took place in the 1920s and '30s, when wealthy immigrants to Piedmont built truly palatial mansions in whichever Period Revival styles suited their particular historic tastes. Be prepared for some really stunning sights as you explore these gilded uplands — and please, don't step on the lawns.

This tour was prepared with information on some of the entries provided by Robert Leefeldt and William B. Land.

# Upper Piedmont

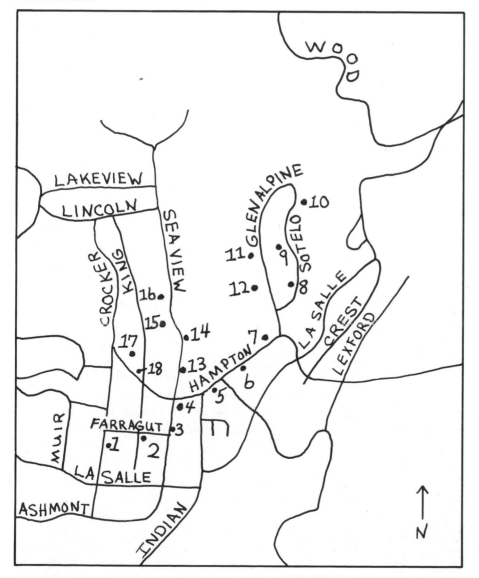

*PIED C-1*

*PIED C-5*

1    Reed House. 200 Crocker Ave. at Faragut. Julia Morgan designed an innovative, octagonal pavilion entry in this Italian-Renaissance-style house. Note the diamond-paned windows. The sensitive siting and attractive landscaping make excellent use of its corner lot. 1926.

2    James Lombard House. 62 Faragut Ave. This immense Tudor Revival house sits on a lot that takes up the entire block of Faragut, between King and Seaview. Julia Morgan's sophisticated handling of the sloping gable lines, fenestration, and massing of the chimneys transcends the usual stylistic repertoire of other Period Revival designs. 1915–1916.

3    Ayer House. 246 Seaview Ave. Another design by Julia Morgan, this eclectic, half-timbered house mixes Tudor and German-medieval elements on its finely crafted, exterior wood detailing. 1914.

4    Walter Starr House. 216 Hampton Rd. Julia Morgan used a basically Mediterranean Revival design, with unique Moorish "onion dome"-like wood tracery on the main windows. The landscaping creates a sense of serenity, and includes one of the original cement, dolphin-legged garden benches. 1911–1912.

5    Spanish Colonial Revival house. 320 Hampton Rd. at Indian Rd. This very fine home has a round corner turret and a superb, carved-stone, Spanish-Baroque-style entrance portal. c. 1920–1930.

6    French Chateau Revival house. 370 Hampton Rd. There are rounded turrets at either end, and fine metal grillwork and Gothic tracery on the facade of this pink stucco house. c. 1925–1930.

7    William St. Cyr Cavalier House. 401 Hampton Rd. at Glen Alpine. One of the largest Mediterranean Revival homes in the East Bay, its impressive facade has fitted stone arches and ornate, Renaissance-style detailing. c. 1920–1930.

8    Frank Buck House. 17 Sotello Ave. This Colonial Revival mansion was built for a prominent banker and U.S. senator from California. The front entrance, facing Sotello, is an unassuming Georgian-style facade; but facing the rear of the steeply sloping lot is a breathtaking, southern-ante-bellum-style, three-story portico with Egyptian papyrus-leaf capitals on its massive columns (partially visible from Glen Alpine Road below it). When Buck moved out of the house in 1940, the house was bought by Charles Lee Tilden (for whom Tilden Park was named). Tilden's widow occupied the house until her death in 1976, and after a period of vacancy the mansion was bought and restored lovingly by its current owners. c. 1924.

9    Whittier House. 23 Sotello Ave. This refined, Norman Revival, late-medieval-style house uses authentic materials and craftsmanship, from its slate roof down to the cobblestone driveway leading to its front door. Williamns and Westal built it for Whittier, a partner in the Dean, Whittier and Company stockbroker firm. 1930.

10    Dawson House. 75 Glen Alpine Rd. Designed by Albert Farr, this stately Louis XV, eighteenth-century-style French Chateau design has a properly imposing setting, high up on a wooded lot behind a massive gateway. c. 1924.

11    Fair House. 45 Glen Alpine Rd. This long, low-lying, "Elizabethan country manor"-style house was developed from what was originally a barn for a large farm tract. c. 1915–1920.

12    Sweetland Estate and Manor House. 11 Glen Alpine Rd. The largest house in the East Bay (forty-five rooms), this awesome behemoth of a mansion was built of solid, fitted stone in fifteenth-century Norman style. The slate-covered hipped roof, the Gothic, arched chapel and flower rooms projecting from

the ground floor, and the spiral-molded, clustered, columned chimneys are all authentic period features. The immense, superbly landscaped sloping lot completes the effect of baronial splendor. Frederick H. Reimers designed the house for Sweetland, the man who invented the automobile oil filter, electric timer, and electric-eye door opener. 1929.

*PIED C-8*

13     Moffatt House. 86 Seaview Ave. Willis Polk built this for a baron of the paper-products industry, Polk's characteristic mode is neo-Classic, but here he mixes the Baroque-style pedimented entryway with a horizontally oriented, Mediterranean-flavor, stuccoed facade and a low, clay-tiled roof. 1912.

14     French-Chateau-style house. 76 Seaview Ave. Attributed to Albert Farr, this bright pink, stone house could fit very nicely into any of the residential streets in Beverly Hills. c. 1925.

15     Italian-Renaissance-style house. 65 Seaview Ave. Julia Morgan supposedly designed this solid, straightforward home. c. 1915–1925.

16     McCandless House. 55 Seaview Ave. Built for a prosperous Hawaiian sugar merchant, this superb Tudor Revival manor house was done on an incredible scale. The red-brick facade is enhanced by a slate roof, stone quoining and window trim, and a multitude of pilastered chimneys. c. 1910–1915.

17     Herbert Hall House. 67 King Ave. Architect Clarence Tantau considered this to be his best designs. Its Spanish Colonial mode is characteristic of Tantau. 1930.

18     Greenwood House. 71 King Ave. Also by Clarence Tantau, this is probably the finest example of the Georgian Colonial Revival style in Piedmont. 1934.

## Detour — Worth a Side Trip

19     Mountain View Cemetery. 5000 Piedmont Ave. (Go west on Oakland Ave. to Grand; turn right up to Piedmont Ave; then turn right to the entrance.) This is by far the most fascinating cemetary in the East Bay. The beautifully landscaped grounds are covered with late-nineteenth-and early-twentieth-century grave markers and family crypts that represent every major architectural style popular in those years, from Gothic to high Renaissance. On your left as you approach the gates, at 4499 Piedmont Ave, is Julia Morgan's exquisitely designed Chapel of the Chimes, in Italian Renaissance and Gothic styles. c. 1920s.

*PIED C-12*

# Richmond

Population: 80,000. First settled: 1900, along the Santa Fe Railroad line in the Richmond flats. Incorporated: 1905. Area: 32.1 square miles. Architectural characteristics: The flatlands and hills have primarily wooden and stucco bungalows in Craftsman and Mediterranean styles. Some larger Colonial Revival houses are scattered near downtown, which has a number of neo-Classic and Streamlined Moderne commercial structures along MacDonald Avenue. Point Richmond has the greatest concentration of historic buildings in various late-Victorian and Classical Revival styles.

## Tour Notes

Richmond started relatively late, compared with other East Bay communities. Its development only began in 1900, when the Santa Fe Railroad laid a line through the flatlands to a terminal at Ferry Point. Industrial expansion got off to a brisk pace the following year, when Standard Oil began a refinery in the Potrero Hills. Out of that came the residential development of the area now known as Point Richmond. Richmond, the main settlement, began along the west end of Mac-Donald Avenue (named for the man who sold the land to the railroad and platted the new town). By 1905, Richmond and Point Richmond had grown together, and they were incoroporated as the City of Richmond. The new city soon expanded toward the hills to the east.

The city continued to grow at a slow but steady pace until World War II, when an influx of white and black immigrants came to work in the shipyards and armament plants. By 1945, the population had reached 100,000, but it slowly declined after the war, as the industries cut back and white middle-class residents who could afford to move left for the suburbs. The Point Richmond district originally was known as East Yard until it was incorporated into the city. Today, it still feels like an early-twentieth-century small town, and most of its turn-of-the-

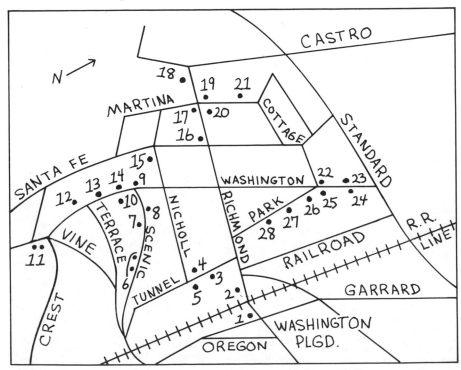

## Point Richmond

century buildings still stand. The three-sided "village square" at Washington and Park Place and the two oldest churches commanding the hilltop at West Richmond Avenue and Martina Street indicate the original rustic, almost mid-western flavor of this community most clearly. As you walk through these areas and along the side streets lined with wooden houses, you'll notice late-Victorian architectural features — even though this district did not begin to develop until after the Victorian Era had officially come to a close in 1901.

1      Municipal Natatorium. E. Richmond Ave. at S. Garrard. Made possible by a special bond issue, this natatorium — one of a vanishing breed — was built as the largest swimming pool in the East Bay. The style has a neo-Classic, late-Beaux-Arts flavor. Note the seahorse motifs in bas-relief panels across the frieze. 1924–1926.

2      J. G. Gerlach Building. 3 E. Richmond Ave. This type of restrained, neo-Classic, red-brick apartment building is common in big eastern cities. c. 1910.

3      Late-Victorian house. 229 Tunnel St. Note the stickwork and fish-scale shingles in the pediments. This was the second house on the block and served as a boarding house in World War II. 1901.

4      Colonial Revival cottage. 39 Nicholl Ave. Sited on a raised lot, this house has a recessed portico and leaded windows. c. 1905.

5      Late-Victorian cottage. 235 Tunnel St. This home uses the simple, planning-book type of high-peaked design that was popular at the time. c. 1901.

6      Two raised-basement cottages. 72 and 78 Scenic. Stick trim and latticework on the stairways enhance this house. c. 1900–1905.

7      Late-Victorian house. 84 Scenic. Note the stickwork, delicate spindles, and mansarded roofline. c. 1900–1905.

8      Turn-of-the-century cottage. 89 Scenic. This home has a hipped roof, stickwork, and a pleasant setting. c. 1900–1910.

9      Point Richmond Baptist Church. 304 Washington Ave. This late-Carpenter-Gothic-style church has an open upper deck at the top of its squared corner tower. c. 1906–1910.

10      Post-Victorian house. 319 Washington Ave. Despite its late date, there is a very Victorian feeling to the angled-bay corner, high-peaked gable and barge-board, and dovetailed corner spire. c. 1905–1907.

11      Two brown-shingled cottages. 505 and 509 Washington, above Crest. These two homes are of planning-book design and have a magnificent view of the Bay. c. 1910.

*RICH-1*

*RICH-16*

*RICH-27*

12      Raised-basement cottage. 428 Washington Ave. One of the earliest homes in this area, this has Stick—Eastlake decor on its door and porch. c. 1900.

13      Colonial Revival house. 323 Washington Ave. This hipped-roof home has a recessed portico on the second floor. c. 1905–1910.

14      Craftsman bungalow. 322 Washington Ave. This boxy home has an odd, low-angled roof, shingled brackets, and red-stained shingles. c. 1905–1915.

15      Transitional, raised-basement cottage. 123 Nicholl Ave. at Santa Fe. This odd cottage has an angled corner on a delicate, columned porch, topped by a turret. c. 1900–1905.

16      Our Lady of Mercy Catholic Church. W. Richmond Ave. at Santa Fe, northwest corner. This brown-shingled Gothic Revival church has a graceful tower and finely carved tracery on its front window. c. 1903.

17      First United Methodist Church. 400 W. Richmond Ave. at Martina. There's a distinctly midwestern flavor to this Romanesque Revival church, especially in the klinker-brick facade, round corner turret, and squared corner tower ending in a tall spire. 1906.

18      Turn-of-the-century boarding house. 409 W. Richmond Ave. This boxy house has stickwork and a pedimented gable filled with intricate, shingled patterns. 1901–1910.

19      Colonial Revival house. 402 W. Richmond Ave. at Martina. A fine brick facade, balustraded portico, quoining, and unusual wide-arched windows along the Martina Street side make this home interesting. 1906–1910.

20      Large Colonial Revival house. 322 W. Richmond Ave. at Martina. Note the wide, sloping, lean-to roofline; stickwork; recessed portico; porthole windows in the gable; and cast-iron railing on the cement retaining wall. c. 1901–1905.

21      Queen-Anne-style house. 126 Martina at Cottage. Built after the heyday of the style, this home has a full corner-turret and a glass-enclosed, delicately balustraded portico. The house is impressively sited on a high, raised lot that supports a large palm tree and the original carriage house (its hayloft faces Cottage Street). c. 1900–1905.

22      Hotel Mac. Washington Ave. at Cottage, northeast corner. This superb, red-brick Classical Revival building has large dentils and an egg-and-dart pattern below the cornice. Recently, the hotel was given a thorough restoration. 1911.

23      Neo-Classic apartment house. 18 Washington Ave. The exterior is done in stuccoed-over brick, and it has a stepped, false-front gable. c. 1910.

24      Wood-front store. 35 Washington Ave. Note the false-front Mission Revival-style gable. c. 1905–1915.

25      Wod-front store. 39 Washington Ave. This building has angled bays, Stick trim, and a bracketed cornice. This and number 35 probably were built at the same time by one developer. c. 1905–1915.

26      Neo-Classic brick commercial building. 111 Park Pl. at Washington. There is an indented wooden portico at the entry, and Dutch stepped-gables at either end. c. 1910.

27      Old City Hall. 145 Park Pl. This fine, red-brick, neo-Classic structure has inlaid, stone, stepped arches around the windows and entryways. Once a combined city hall, fire department, and jail (the cells still remain in back), it now serves as Richmond Fire Station Number One. 1910.

28      One-story wood-front store. 155 Park Pl. The large-paned, latticed, indented bay windows are used attractively. c. 1905–1910.

Population: 76,000. First settled: About 1848, in the area now known as the Heritage District. Incorporated: 1867. Area: 31.7 square miles. Architectural characteristics: Vallejo has more Greek Revival and Gothic Revival homes than any other East Bay community. Most of them are in the heights northeast of Mare Island Strait. A few hundred other Victorian buildings, covering the range of late-nineteenth-century styles, are also concentrated in this area. The downtown area still has a number of turn-of-the-century brick, stone, and wood commercial structures, primarily in various neo-Classic modes.

## Area Covered by the Walking Tour

Heritage District

## Tour Notes

Vallejo began its existence in 1848, as the intended site of the state capital, when General Mariano Vallejo, then a state senator, offered his land along the Carquinez Straits for development into the capital city. After five years of waiting in vain for a capitol building to be constructed, the legislature gave up and moved to Benicia in 1853. The following year, the U.S. government opened up the Mare Island Naval Base in Vallejo, which led to a gradual but steady influx of naval officers and other settlers to the residential district on the heights above the base.

Vallejo soon became the rail terminus for the entire Sacramento Valley, and during the 1870s it experienced a modest boom, although its boosters predicted that it eventually would surpass Oakland in size. But by 1880, the city had a respectable-sized population of 6,000, and it grew only moderately for the next several decades. Like many other Bay Area cities, Vallejo underwent a heady but short-lived boom during World War II, because of its shipyard facilities. After the war, it settled back into a less hectic residential and civic development.

# Vallejo Tour

## Heritage District

The city's Heritage District, east of downtown, is now designated as an official historic district, and has a sizeable concentration of nineteenth-century buildings in various styles. An exceptional number of Greek Revival, Gothic, and early Italianate-style cottages and houses remain in the area; and one of the finest brick Gothic Revival churches in the Bay Area (St. Vincent's Catholic Church) dominates the highest point in the district. As the following tour map shows, dozens of later-Victorian and early-twentieth-century buildings are also scattered throughout the pleasantly landscaped streets of the Heritage District, which are well worth exploring.

*VAL-1*

1    False-front Bracketed Italianate house.739 Ohio St. Note the refined detailing. c. 1870–1880.

2    Late-Italianate house. 614 Ohio St. The facade has Colonial Revival details. c. 1885–1895.

3    Italianate house. 1128 Marin St. This mansard-roofed house has a Gothic, high-peaked gable, and probably was stripped of much of its decoration when the fireproof siding was added. c. 1865–1875.

4    Gothic Revival cottage. 922 Sacramento St. The narrow lancet windows and pendant, flanked by carved trefoil patterns in the gable, are still visible on the street side of this stuccoed-over cottage. c. 1865–1875.

5    St. Vincent's Catholic Church. Sacramento and Florida Sts., northwest corner. This is a dignified, brick, Gothic Revival church with stone trim that recalls parish Gothic churches in rural England. The Gothic detailing on the tower and large, traceried, stained-glass windows in the transepts are especially graceful. This building replaced an earlier wood-frame structure that the congregation erected at Marin and Capitol Streets in 1855. The land for the current church was donated by General Mariano Vallejo's family. The main church was built between 1867 and 1870, and the small chapel at the back was added later.

6    Italianate/Colonial Revival house. 1012 Sutter St. Here is an unusual combination of styles in one house. The main floor, built in 1869, comes from an Italianate house and was brought here from Capitol Street in 1910, which is also when the imposing Colonial Revival front porch was added.

7    Queen Anne house. Sutter at Capitol St., northwest corner. This large, wide-turreted house has Colonial Revival details. c. 1895.

8    Wilson House. 728 Capitol St. Julia Morgan designed this large, Carftsman-style house, which has a Swiss-Chalet-style flavor. The elegantly carved detailing on the bargeboard is typical of the high craftsmanship Morgan used in her residential work. The only documented example of Morgan's work in Vallejo, the house has an incredible total of eleven fireplaces. 1909.

9    Gothic Revival cottage. 740 Capitol St. This house has a steeply pitched central gable; tall, narrow, shuttered windows; a square-pillared, midwestern-like veranda; and an angled bay on the right sidc. This residence was built elsewhere and then moved here. 1860–1862.

10    Cast-iron railings along the sidewalk. 733 Capitol St. c. 1890.

11    Small, Italianate-style cottage. 803 Capitol St. at Napa. Once this was part of a 700-acre estate. c. 1872.

12    Abbot House. 639 Virginia St. This large, Italianate-style farmhouse has ample grounds. it was brown-shingled in 1920. The original Gothic-gabled, red-stained, board-and-batten barns behind the house are visible from Georgia Street. 1868.

*VAL-8*

13    Commander Orr House. 626 Virginia St. This is an example of a very late Greek Revival house, with a wide portico, tall, latticed windows, and an Italian-ate flavor to the detailing in the gable. It was occupied for many years by a navy commander at Mare Island. 1869.

14    Eastern-style Gothic Revival villa. 928 Sutter. This is an extremely rare type of Gothic design for California, with lacy eyelet bargeboards on its gables and a central, spired tower. The arched tracery and delicate pendant on the right side-gable are very nice. Allegedly, the house was used in its early years as a private riding school for daughters and wives of well-to-do officers at the nearby military bases in Vallejo and Benicia (though this has never been substantiated). The shingling was added later. c. 1866.

15 & 16    Two late-Queen-Anne houses. 600 and 610 Georgia St. c. 1890–1895.

17    John Wilson House. 705 Georgia St. at Napa. This large Queen-Anne/ Eastlake-style house has an impressive array of ornament, and recalls many of the Newsom brothers' designs. c. 1885–1895.

18    High-peaked Colonial Revival house. 720 Georgia St. c. 1895–1905.

19    Unusual Queen-Anne/Colonial-Revival-style apartment house. 806 Georgia St. c. 1895.

20    Greek Revival house. 842 Georgia St. One of the oldest homes remaining in Vallejo, this has hollow, squared, two-story columns across the front. Extensive "neo-Georgian" remodeling of the doors and windows was done recently. c. 1855–1865.

21    Italianate house. 912 Georgia St. The design is unique to Vallejo. c. 1870.

22    Queen Anne cottage. 915 Georgia St. 1895.

23    Transitional late-Victorian house. 740 York St. at El Dorado. Queen-Anne- and Brown-Shingle-style features are combined. c. 1895.

24    Queen Anne house. 738 York St. An arcaded, curved corner porch was recently restored to its original appearance (it lost its ornament over twenty years ago). 1895.

25    Queen Anne cottage. 747 York St. c. 1890–1895.

26    Queen Anne cottage. 626 York St. c. 1890–1895.

27    "Pioneer box." 610 Sutter St. This clapboarded house has split pilasters and wide, square-latticed windows. c. 1860s.

*VAL-5*

*VAL-6*

28     Transitional early-Italianate house. 532 York St. The facade has a Greek-Revival-style pillared porch. c. 1860–1870.

29     Late-Victorian townhouse apartments. 524–528 York St. This building was done in the Queen Anne mode. c. 1890–1900.

30     Small, Italianate-style, "shotgun" house. 523 York St. at Napa. One of the few of its kind left in Vallejo, this house has an elongated, narrow design that can best be viewed from Napa Street. c. 1870s.

*VAL-9*

**Detour — Worth a Side Trip**

31    Mare Island Naval Station. Just east of downtown, across Mare Island Strait. (Go east along Georgia St. to Santa Clara St.; turn right up to Tennessee St.; then go left until it turns into the Mare Island Causeway and joins the island.) One of the first naval bases in the western United States, Mare Island was purchased by the U.S. government in 1853, and occupied by the navy under David Farragut in 1854. The many fine military barracks include: the 1901 Federal-Revival-style Walnut Avenue Quarters; Quarters 133 at 340 7th Street (c. 1870); and Quarters M-1 at 1242 Cedar Avenue (1869). The gem of the island is St. Peter's Chapel at Walnut and Cedar — the oldest navy chapel in the U.S. Built of redwood in 1901, it has priceless, Tiffany stained-glass windows. Get permission to view these buildings from the administration building on Walnut Avenue at 7th Street.

32    Port Costa. (Go south across the Carquinez Toll Bridge and look for the Port Costa exit sign on your right; follow the signs about three miles to the town.) This old railroad and shipping dock town was founded in 1879. A number of interesting buildings remain from its late-nineteenth-century heyday, including: a two-story "Pioneer" house next to 132 Canyon Lake Drive (c. 1880); a Gothic Revival church with a nice tower at Prospect and Canyon Lake Drive (c. 1890s); a rusticated-stone Romanesque Revival commercial building at the end of Canyon Lake Drive on the left (1897); and the Post Office and Warehouse Building, the first fireproof building in Contra Costa County (1886).

*VAL-17*

# Part IV

## Supplementary Information

*2601 Hillcress Ave., Berkeley, c. 1901*

# A Guide to Historical Groups and Research Sources in the East Bay

The best single, overall source for property records of communities in Alameda County is the County Hall of Records, Room 101, in the County Courthouse at 13th and Fallon streets in Oakland. Here you will find microfilm records of all property deed transactions that occurred in the county since 1853. These records will show who the original owner of a particular piece of property was, when it was bought, from whom, and for how much money. Victorian-Era buildings were usually constructed shortly after a subdivided lot was purchased, so it is possible to make an educated guess about the date of a given nineteenth-century structure (not until 1900 were exact records of building construction kept systematically, in this area). Bring the address of a building you are interested in and as much information about the previous owners as you can gather. To get that information, you can talk with the current owner, or with any title company in the appropriate city — its personnel will research deed transactions for you as far back as they can. Then go to the person at the front desk in Room 101 for instructions on how to look up the original deed.

For buildings constructed after 1900, the best source of information is usually the city planning or building permit departments that are located in various city halls. Building permits are kept on file, and they usually give the exact date of construction, cost, original owner (and sometimes the architect), and any later alterations for specific buildings in that city, by address. The years for which these records have been kept vary, but generally most cities in the east Bay began compiling fairly systematic records shortly after the 1906 earthquake.

Another good source of reference material is the library collections on architectural history. Many of the larger East Bay libraries have these. The California Room at the Oakland Public Library Main Branch, 125 14th Street, has an excellent collection of material on the history of East Bay neighborhoods, including many photographs of buildings, dated with the year in which the picture was taken. The Bancroft Library at U.C. Berkeley has a set of Platt Books for Berkeley, dating from 1907, with owners' names attached to lots. It also has a fine collection of old photographs of buildings from all over the Bay Area. If the Berkeley, Alameda, Piedmont, Hayward, and Vallejo city libraries don't have smaller collections in their own files, they can tell you where to find them. Finally, the U.C. Environmental Design Library in Wurster Hall has microfilm copies of the *California Architect and Building News* from about 1880 through 1901. These list a number of construction notices for buildings in the state. Several other old, bound periodicals on the shelves have illustrated articles on noteworthy buildings that were constructed since the late nineteenth century.

The following is a list of many of the historic societies and preservation groups existing in the East Bay. All these keep some kind of historic records on buildings in their communities. A number of them, as indicated, conduct extensive architectural surveys of the neighborhoods they serve. Volunteers for such research are greatly appreciated.

*Vine Street near Walnut, Berkeley, c. 1880*

## Alameda

Alameda Architectural and Historical Survey
Department of City Planning, Advance Planning Section
Woody Minor, Coordinator
Alameda City Hall
Santa Clara and Oak Streets
Alameda, CA 94501

Alameda Historical Society
George Gunn, Curator
Alameda Public Library
22624 Santa Clara Avenue
Alameda, CA 94501
Open Saturdays, 11 A.M. to 4 P.M.

Alameda Victorian Preservation Society
P.O. Box 1677
Alameda, CA 94501

## Berkeley

Berkeley Architectural Heritage Association
P.O. Box 7066, Landscape Station
Berkeley, CA 94707
(BAHA is conducting an architectural heritage survey. Write Leslie Emmington or Anthony Bruce at
	the above address to get information.)

Oceanview Neighborhood Preservation Association
Stephanie Manning, Survey Coordinator
2107 5th Street
Berkeley, CA 94710

## Hayward

Hayward Area Historical Museum
22701 Main Street
Hayward, CA 94541

## Kensington

Louis Stein Photographic Collection
360 Rugby Avenue
Kensington, CA 94708
(Mr. Stein has one of the finest private collections of historic photographs of Berkeley and Kensington
	buildings in the Bay Area.)

## Oakland

Brooklyn Neighborhood Preservation Association
c/o Peter Carlson
1937 8th Avenue
Oakland, CA 94606
(This groups has just been granted funds for an architectural survey and can use volunteer help.)

Camron-Stanford House
Elizabeth Cohen, Director
1418 Lakeside Drive
Oakland, CA 94606
(The Camron-Stanford House Association has a free, excellent walking-tour booklet, *The Heart of
	Oakland: A Walking Guide to Lake Merritt*.)

Oakland Landmarks Commission
Planning Department, City Hall
14th and Washington Streets
Oakland, CA 94606
(The Planning Department has a helpful booklet, *Rehab Right*. It's free to Oakland residents, and
available to others from the State Office of Historic Preservation at a small fee.)

## Piedmont

Piedmont Historical Society
June Rutledge, President
358 Hillside Avenue
Piedmont, CA 94610

## Vallejo

Vallejo Historical and Naval Museum, in Old City Hall
734 Marin Street
Vallejo, CA 94590

## Statewide Organizations

California Heritage Council
680 Beach Street, Room 351
San Francisco, CA 94109

California Historical Society
2090 Jackson Street
San Francisco, CA 94109
(The Historical Society has an excellent collection of historic photographs of streets and buildings
throughout the state.)

Californians for Preservation Action
P.O. Box 2169
Sacramento, CA 95810

State Office of Historic Preservation
P.O. Box 2390
Sacramento, CA 95811

## National Organizations

National Trust for Historic Preservation
Western Regional Office
681 Market Street
San Francisco, CA 94103

The Victorian Society in America
The Atheneum, East Washington Square
Philadelphia, PA 19106

In addition, the various chambers of commerce and city planning department
offices in each of the cities covered in this book have information — and, often,
printed booklets — on locations of various historic buildings in their communities.

# Reading List of Architectural Heritage Books

### Books on General Architecture in America

*Grieff, Constance. *Lost America.* Vols. 1 and 2. 1973.

*Haas, Irvin. *America's Historic Houses and Restorations.* 1966.

Smith, Kidder, for American Heritage. *Architecture in America.* 1976.

Wren, Tony, and Elizabeth Mulloy for the National Trust for Historic Preservation. *America's Forgotten Architecture.* 1976.

### Books on Specific Architectural Styles and Historic Areas

Andrews, Wayne. *American Gothic: Its Origins, Trials, and Triumphs.* 1975. P.

*Newcomb, Rexford. *Franciscan Mission Architecture of Alta California.* 1973. P.

*Scully, Vincent, Jr. *Modern Architecture.* 1961, revised 1974.

Wright, Frank Lloyd, *In Cause of Architecture,* 1975.

### Books on Bay Area Architecture

*Bernhardi, Robert. *Buildings of Berkeley.* 1971. P.

*Bohn, Dave. *East of These Golden Shores.* 1971. P.

*Bruce, Curt, and Aidala, Thomas. *Great Houses of San Francisco.* 1974.

Ehrich, Benjamin B. *Photographic Guide to the University of California.* 1969. P.

*Freuderheim, Leslie. *Building with Nature: Roots of the San Francisco Bay Region Style.* 1974.

*Gebhard, David, *et al. *Architecture in the San Francisco Bay Area and Northern California.* 1973, revised 1976. P.

*Olwell, Carol, and Judith Waldhorn. *A Gift to the Street: San Francisco Victorians.* 1976. P.

*Pettit, George. *Berkeley: The Town and Gown of It.* 1973.

*Richey, Elinore. *Remain to Be Seen: Historic Houses in California Open to the Public.* 1973.

*Richey, Elinore. *The Ultimate Victorians: On the Continental Side of the Bay.* 1971.

*San Francisco for Junior League and Chronicle Books. *Here Today.* 1975.

The Foundation for San Francisco's Architectural Heritage and California Living Books. *Splendid Survivors.* 1979. P.

*Waldhorn, Judith Lunch, and Sally Woodbridge. *Victoria's Legacy.* 1978. P.

*Woodbridge, Sally, *et al. *Houses of the Bay Area.* 1976.

* indicates that the book is available at the Berkeley and Oakland libraries.     P. indicates that the book is available in paperback.

*Walnut and Hearst, Berkeley, c. 1890*

# Glossary of Architectural Terms

*adobe*   Mud bricks used by Spanish and Mexican settlers to construct their homes and missions; or any house built during Spanish and/or Mexican periods, using adobe as the major building material.

*allegorical sculpture*   Sculptural details on a building that symbolize the culture that built it or the purpose of the building. Used heavily on Beaux Arts structures.

*apse*   A section of a building that is semicircular in shape. Usually projecting from the east end, as in Gothic- and Romanesque-style buildings. (See p. 35)

*arabesque panel*   A decorative panel that consists of a flat surface with a design etched around it, with a sunken part offset by a color wash.

*arcade*   A row of arches supported by columns or squared pillars. (See p. 38)

*Art Nouveau*   A design movement originating in France and popular c. 1890–1920 that used curved lines and bright blue and red tones in architectural and decorative detailing — for example, stained glass.

*atrium*   A small courtyard in the front part of a building. An atrium is covered along the sides and usually open to the sky in the middle. Common in Roman houses.

*balustrade*   A row of miniature pillars, or balusters, usually used as support for banisters on a stairway or as decoration in front of a window. (See p. 31)

*banded*   As in windows or columns. An arrangement of a specific architectural feature in a tightly spaced row.

*bargeboard*   A decorative piece or attached pieces of wood lining the eaves of a steeply pitched gable. Used primarily in Gothic architecture. (See p. 30)

*Baroque*   A style, popular in Europe c. 1600–1800, which lavishly used Classical motifs with boldly stated lines and massing.

*basilica*   An Early Christian style of church, consisting of a nave, aisles on the side, and often an apse at the far end.

*battening*   Thin "weather strips" of wood covering the board surface of a wood-frame building, as in Gothic Revival churches (often called *board-and-battening*).

*battered*   Sloping slightly inward, as in battered walls.

*Bauhaus*   A German school of architecture originating in the 1920s that used clean, sweeping lines and modern materials such as glass and steel, especially on the "glass-and-steel" skyscrapers now prevalent in the U.S. cities.

*bay*   A unit of wall surface divided by large vertical features, such as a slanted or angled projection with windows (that is, a slanted bay window). (See p. 30)

*Beaux Arts style*   See Part II, "Major Styles of Historic Architecture."

*belfry*   A bell tower, as in Mission-style churches.

*beveled glass*   Glass with a cut, angled edge around its perimeters, as in beveled-glass windows.

*blind*   An architectural feature directly behind which is a blank wall surface, as in blind balcony or blind arch.

*Bracketed Italianate style*   See Part II, "Major Styles of Historic Architecture."

*bracket*   A piece of wood or stone projecting from a vertical surface to give support to a horizontal feature, such as a cornice. In Victorian times, brackets often were fancily carved and used decoratively. (See also corbel.) (See p. 31)

*Brown Shingle style*   See Part II, "Major Styles of Historic Architecture."

*bungalow*   A small one-and-one-half-story house with a low-lying Main floor and a shallow basement. In California, the two main types are the wood-frame Craftsman bungalow and the stucco Mediterranean bungalow.

*buttress*   A vertical support along a wall surface, used commonly in Gothic architecture. Two main types are clasping (attached to the wall along its entire length) and flying (detached from the wall along most of the length, connecting only at the top). (See p. 35)

*Byzantine style*   A style originating in Constantinople in the fifth century A.D., using round arches, multiple domes, and brightly colored mosaic scenes.

*canted bay*   A pointed bay with two sides projecting at 45-degree angles.

*capital*   The upper portion of a column, usually sculpted in one of the four classic orders: Corinthian, Doric, Ionic, or Roman Composite.

*carillon*   A group of bells arranged in order, usually suspended at the top of a bell tower.

*Carpenter Gothic Style*   The Gothic Revival style, rendered entirely in wood.

*Chicago School*   A group of turn-of-the-century Chicago architects who developed the early steel-frame construction that was first used on skyscrapers. (Also refers to the type of building they invented.)

*Churin style*   Short for Churriguera, an 18th-century Spanish Baroque architect, and/or the personal mode he developed, which used lavish and highly ornamented scrollwork and other neo-Classic motifs as decorative details.

*clapboarding*   Overlapping wooden boards used as exterior wall surfacing. (See p. 37)

*Classic, neo-Classic motifs*   Design elements borrowed from ancient Classical architecture; primarily, columns or pilasters, cornices, triangular pediments, and the four decorative orders of Greek and Roman capitals. In neo-Classic architecture, these forms are borrowed more freely and used more loosely.

*clerestory*   A row of windows (usually, pointed-arched) along the upper portion of the central walls of a building, as in the nave of a Gothic cathedral.

*coach porch*   A floorless porch along the side of a large house. Originally, it served as a shelter for passengers alighting from a coach.

*coffered*   Indented with square or rectangular recessed panels, as on the surface of a coffered ceiling or dome. (See p. 34)

*Colonial Revival style*   See Part II, "Major Styles of Historic Architecture."

*Concrete Brutalism*   The use of concrete construction in plain, alternating surfaces (that is, "concrete as sculpture").

*corbel*   A block of stone projecting from a wall as a horizontal support, or a block of decoratively carved wood supporting the lower end of an interior archway. Used in many Victorian homes. (See p. 37)

*Corinthian*   A classical Greek order consisting of a column with a high base; a slender, fluted (ridged) shaft; and an ornate capital with stylized, carved acanthus leaves. (See p. 31)

*cornice*   A decorative horizontal ledge projecting at a right angle from the top of a roof, doorway, or window and usually lined with brackets, dentils, or corbels. (See p. 31)

*crenelation*   A parapet (originally defensive, later used decoratively) consisting of alternating raised portions separated by evenly spaced gaps, as in Gothic-style buildings.

*cresting*   Ornamental ironwork placed at the roofline or above the porch or projecting bay window.

*cupola*   A small (usually single-story) turret-like room projecting above a roofline. Thus, it has no base of its own. (See p. 32)

*cutout vertical box*   A contemporary house design (c. 1960 to present) that uses a slanting roofline and stark wooden walls in a box-like massing.

*dentil*   A square or rectangular block of wood or stone decorating the underside of a cornice. (See p. 29)

*Doric*   The first and simplest of the Greek orders, consisting of a column with no base; a relatively short, fluted shaft; and an undecorated lip or rim around the upper end. (See p. 29)

*dormer*   A vertical projection from a sloping roofline that supports one or more windows. (See p. 35)

*Dutch Colonial style*   An Early American house style imported from Holland, generally having a gabrel roof, dormer windows, and a front and/or rear door that opens in two parts.

*eave*   The lowest end of a sloping roof that projects over the walls. (See p. 37)

*egg-and-dart frieze*   A type of decoration along a frieze that uses alternating oval and ridge shapes.

*Egyptian Revival*   A style, especially popular in the 1920s and 1930s, using slanted pavilions, projecting slabs, massive columns, and other elements borrowed from Ancient Egyptian architecture.

*engaged column*   A column that is attached along its rear portion to the surface behind it.

*españada*   A Baroque-style, curved, false-front gable originating in Spain and used frequently in Mission-style buildings. (See p. 38)

*esplanade*   A double-terraced stairway leading up to an entrance. Originally used on Renaissance-style buildings.

*exhedra*   A curved, recessed, decorative structure with a seat.

*facade*   The exterior of a building at its front or back, usually containing an entrance.

*fanlight*   Radiating tracery decoration in a half-moon-shaped piece of glass, usually used above a door as a transom.

*Federal style*   An Early American architectural style (c. 1780–1850) that used decorative lintels above windows, fanlights above doors, low-hipped roofs, and tall, narrow chimney stacks.

*fenestration*   The treatment of windows in the design of a building.

*finial*   A decorative end piece, found in a variety of shapes, and usually placed at the peak of a roofline or on a gatepost. (See p. 30)

*fish-scale shingles*   Wood shingles in a semicircular shape resembling fish scales, commonly found on Queen-Anne-style Victorian houses. (See p. 33)

*foliated capital*   The top of a column or pilaster using compressed, stylized leaf and vine patterns.

*fountain-spray motif*   An Art Deco design using a stylized spray of water as a finial.

*French Chateau style*   Buildings using French Renaissance elements such as rounded corner turrets, Gothic-arched tracery around windows, heavy stone or stone-like walls, and decorative iron grillwork.

*French Provincial mode*   Buildings using any variety of domestic styles of architecture such as small chateaus, found in outlying areas of France.

*French Second Empire*   An ornate nineteenth-century style of architecture using Renaissance elements such as round-arched windows and porticos, combined with a mansard roof and iron cresting.

*fretwork shingling*   Squared shingles that alternate in a rising and falling pattern.

*frieze*   A horizontal band across the top of a wall or porch, often decorated with carved or molded designs. (See p. 29)

*gable*   A section at the end of a roof that usually is triangular in shape but that, by extension, can be curved. "Miniature" gables often are used decoratively above doors and porches. (See p. 30)

*gambrel*   A double-angled gable on a roofline, rising steeply at the bottom and bending to a shallow pitch at the top.

*gargoyle*   A decorative figure carved from wood or stone that projects from the surface of a building and usually displays an ugly countenance. In Medieval times, gargoyles were intended to scare away evil spirits.

*Georgian Colonial mode*   An Early American architectural style (c. 1700–1780) that used arches with keystones, latticed windows, and neo-Classic elements such as pilasters, porticos, pediments, and Palladian motifs.

*Gothic Revival*   See Part II, "Major Styles of Historic Architecture."

*Greek Revival*   See Part II, "Major Styles of Historic Architecture."

*Half-timbered*   A Medieval construction technique using joined wood, timber framing exposed on the facade and filled in with stucco or similar material. Later, mock timbering was used on the surface to create a decorative effect. (See p. 38)

*Hansel and Gretel style*   See Part II, "Major Styles of Historic Architecture."

*hipped roof*   A roof with four low-sloping sides. Similar to a pyramid but ending in a flat or ridged top instead of a point. (See p. 29)

*hood*   A projecting, flat-topped, decorative piece above a door or window. Usually supported by brackets.

*incised panel*   A decorative wooden panel with lightly carved, indented scrollwork or other patterns. Common on Stick–Eastlake and Queen-Anne-style Victorian houses.

*Ionic*   A classical Greek order consisting of an elegantly molded base; a tall, slender, fluted shaft; and a capital with a spiral or scrollwork design, called a volute.

*Islamic arch*   A wide, pointed arch used mostly decoratively as an opening on a porch or doorway, originating in the Moslem architecture of the Middle Ages.

*Italianate style*   See Part II, "Major Styles of Historic Architecture."

*Jacobean Revival*   An imitation of a seventeenth-century English style of architecture, using brick walls, chimneys lining the end walls, and a blend of alternating curves and rising steps on the gables.

*keystone*   The central stone at the top of a round arch, which holds the other stones in place. (See p. 39)

*klinker brick*   Rough-surfaced, dark-colored brick that was popular as decorative surfacing on the facades of brick buildings c. 1895–1940.

*lancet window*   A window with sections of glass outlined in decorative patterns of lead. Most commonly, diamond shaped.

*lintel*   A solid piece of wood or stone across the top of a window or doorway that provides support for the weight above. (See p. 29)

*loggia*   A roofed-over open arcade along the side of a building.

*Mannerism*   A European architectural style that came after the High Renaissance and just before the Baroque styles, which consisted chiefly of neo-Classic motifs rendered in overblown, unnatural proportions.

*mansard roof*   A roof design with four steeply sloped sides and multiple dormer windows (that is, the attic and top floor are combined within the roofline).

*medallion*   A usually circular-shaped decorative recess in a wall, often embellished with some bas-relief design.

*Mediterranean Revival mode*   See Part II, "Major Styles of Historic Architecture."

*Monterey-style balcony*   A projecting wooden-railed balcony along the upper floor of a two-story stucco or adobe building.

*Moorish style*   A Medieval Spanish architectural style using Islamic pointed arches and glazed tile insets.

*Mother Goose style*   An exaggerated half-timber mode, similar to the Hansel and Gretel style.

*nave*   The central, rectangular portion of a church, flanked by aisles and ending at the crossing (if there are transepts).

*New England saltbox*   An Early American house design that used wood-frame construction, usually clapboarding, as surfacing, and a long, sloping roofline that was extended in the rear to cover a low, single-story lean-to addition in the back.

*Norman Revival style*   One of the more popular Period Revival styles, using real or mock half-timbering, hipped roofs (often covered with slate), latticed windows, and a mix of stucco and brick as surfacing.

*palazzo*   An Italian Renaissance palace using thick masonry walls, round-arched windows and doors, and often a tall, square observation tower extending above the roofline.

*Palladian motif*   An opening, most often a window, in the facade of a building. This motif consists of a central round-arched section and two rectangular flanking wings, usually framed by pilasters. Though named after the Renaissance Italian architect Palladio, it was not actually invented by him. (See p. 35)

*parapet*   A wall, roughly chest-high, along the top of a roof or a porch. Originally used to provide defense for sentries; later used decoratively.

*Parish Gothic church*   A modest, small-scale, Gothic-style church, like those found in the rural parishes of England.

*patina*   A thin green rust that develops on the surface of bronze and copper. Often seen on copper-lined roofs.

*pavilion*   An ornamental building (usually on the same grounds as a main residence), such as a summer house; or the part(s) of a building that is higher than the rest, that is, the center or wings. (See p. 30)

*pediment*   The enclosed gable end (usually triangular-shaped) of a house or neo-Classic style building, or any enclosed triangular- or curved-shaped decorative feature on a building. (See p. 29)

*pendant*   A narrow hanging decoration, usually pointed at the bottom and suspended from the peak of a gable and often intersected with a crossbar, as in Stick- and Gothic-style houses.

*pent eaves*   Eaves that are bent inward at the top.

*Period Revival styles*   See Part II, "Major Styles of Historic Architecture."

*pilaster*   A flat or squared version of a column. Often used solely as decoration along a wall. (See p. 32)

*Pioneer house*   See Part II, "Major Styles of Historic Architecture."

*pipestem column*   A tall, slender, attached column used decoratively, usually at the corners of an angled bay window.

*portico*   A colonnaded porch that is not as wide as the facade of the building from which it projects. (See p. 32)

*post-and-beam*   A construction technique in which upright posts projecting horizontal beams at right angles.

*Prairie School*   See Part II, "Major Styles of Historic Architecture."

*pyramidal roof*   A roof design with four sloping sides reaching a point, like a pyramid.

*Queen Anne style*   See Part II, "Major Styles of Historic Architecture."

*quoins*   Blocks of stone, usually rectangular-shaped or alternating with squares, used to line the corners of a building for decorative effect. In Victorian houses, wooden imitations often were used. (See p. 31)

*raised-basement cottage*   See Part II, "Major Styles of Historic Architecture."

*rampart*   A wall surrounding a building or portion of it, originally used for defensive purposes.

*Regency style*   An early-nineteenth-century architectural style popular in England and parts of France, which used neo-Classic Georgian elements with a Palladian motif around the entrance.

*Renaissance style*   A grouping of architectural modes popular in Europe during the Renaissance that all freely borrowed ancient Classical elements for decorative as well as structural purposes.

*Roman Composite style*   The fourth classic order of column invented by the Romans, this combined the Ionic volute with the Corinthian acanthus leaf on its capital.

*Romanesque Revival*   See Part II, "Major Styles of Historic Architecture."

*rose window*   A large, round, stained-glass window with tracery, used in Romanesque- and Gothic-style churches.

*rotunda*   A round building, usually domed. By extension, often used to refer to a round wing of a larger building.

*rusticated stone*   Wall masonry that has been chiseled so that it has a rough, antique appearance. Commonly used on Romanesque-style buildings. (See p. 35)

*sawn decoration*   Wooden decorative panels with ornamental patterns cut out by a jig saw. Common in Victorian homes.

*saw-tooth shingling*   Shingles with sharply pointed ends.

*scarfillo paneling*   Concrete decorative panels with patterns exposed by etching out around them and using a color wash in the etched places, similar to arabesque panels. Often used on Art Deco buildings.

*Scientific American Builder's Edition*   A periodical popular at the turn of the century that illustrated designs for numerous varieties of "transitional"-style cottages.

*scrollwork*   Carved, sawn, or molded decorative panels with neo-Classic, curved, ornamental patterns.

*Second Empire style*   See mansard.

*setback*   The portion of a building that is set on a recessed plane from the main facade.

*shotgun house*   A Victorian house without a hallway, all of whose rooms are arranged in direct succession from front to back.

*sideboarding*   The most common type of wood plank exterior surfacing. Horizontal boards are laid one above the other and separated by a narrow groove. (See p. 31)

*Spanish Colonial style*   See Part II, "Major Styles of Historic Architecture."

*spindlework*   Slender, round pieces of wood arranged in decorative patterns on Queen Anne and other late-Victorian-style homes, usually along the top of a porch. (See p. 34)

*split-planed gable*   A high-peaked gable in which the bottom half is on a recessed plane from the upper half.

*Steamboat Gothic style*   Any use of ornate sawn-wood decorative trim across a porch or veranda, similar to the deck of a Victorian steamboat.

*stepped arcade*   A row of arches arranged on an inclined plane, as along a stairway on the side of a building.

*Stick style*   See Part II, "Major Styles of Historic Architecture."

*Stick–Eastlake style*   See Part II, "Major Styles of Historic Architecture."

*stickwork*   Wood plank decorative trim used on the exterior of many later Victorian-style homes, especially along the corners and around the window frames of Stick-style houses. (See p. 31)

*Streamlined Moderne*   See Part II, "Major Styles of Historic Architecture."

*Stupa-shaped tower*   Originally derived from buddhist relic chambers in India. By extension, any four-sided windowless spire that has curved, tapering sides and a rounded top.

*sunburst panel*   In Victorian architecture, a decorative wood panel with a radiating sunburst pattern, derived from the interior-decoration motifs of English designer Charles Eastlake. (See p. 34)

*Swiss Chalet style*   A house design borrowed from traditional Alpine homes, using massive wood framing; shingled, clapboarded, or half-timbered exterior surfacing; extended, decoratively carved roof beams; and wide, overhanging eaves.

*terra cotta*   Hard-baked clay, usually molded into tiles and colored and glazed, as on the facade of Art Deco buildings.

*Torrigate arch*   In traditional Japanese architecture, an archway consisting of two upright posts spanned across the top by a beam that extends over both sides.

*tracery*   Decorative trim in wood or stone over the surface of a stained-glass window, originally used in Gothic churches. By extension, any Gothic-style decorative wood trim over the surface of a door or panel, as used in Victorian Gothic Revival.

*transept*   The wings of a cruciform (or cross plan) church at right angles to the nave.

*transitional cottage*   A late-nineteenth- or early-twentieth-century house that displays characteristics of both Queen Anne and Colonial Revival styles.

*trefoil*   A three-leaf-clover motif, from Gothic architecture.

*Tudor Revival*   See Part II, "Major Styles of Historic Architecture."

*turned baluster*   A baluster molded by turning it on a lathe. Commonly used on stairways and gateposts.

*turret*   A small tower, usually used as a decorative feature, with a variety of spire shapes on top such as a "witch's hat," etc. (See p. 33)

*veranda*   A wide porch extending across the front of a house.

*vigas*   The Spanish term for heavy protruding beams, as used along the roof of California missions. (See p. 38)

*villa*   The Italian term for a large country house. In Victorian times, any large picturesque home, usually with a tower or cupola.

*volute*   A spiral-shaped decorative piece, such as on the capital of an Ionic column or a bracket.

*wainscoting*   A band of decorative wood paneling around the bottom or lower part of the walls of a room. In fancier homes, often coffered and waist high.

*workingman's cottage*   A small Victorian house with one main floor and modest ornament.

*W.P.A.*   The Works Progress Administration building program, inaugurated under Franklin D. Roosevelt's New Deal, which, during its existence (1935–1942), built thousands of public buildings in a style that came to be called W.P.A. Moderne. (See also Part II, "Major Styles of Historic Architecture.")

*ziggurat*   A Babylonian stepped pyramid, adopted as a building form for many Art-Deco-style buildings.

*Zigzag Moderne*   See Part II, "Major Styles of Historic Architecture."

# Index

The following structures are listed in chronoligical order from earliest to latest styles, and divided alphabetically by town within each style. For each structure, the name of the building is given first, then the address, the date, and the architect (if known). An indication of where the building is included in a walking tour is given by the name, entry, and page number of the tour.

## Spanish Colonial Styles c. 1790s–1850

### Missions

#### Mission San Jose

Friar's Residence of the Mission San Jose, Mission Blvd., c. 1810, by Father Lausen; Fremont Tour B, Entry 5.

### Adobes

#### Martinez

Martinez Adobe, on the grounds of the John Muir Estate at 4 Alhambra Rd., 1848; Detour on Benicia Tour, Entry 35.

#### Niles

Vallejo Adobe, on the grounds of the California Nursery at Nursery Ave., 1843; Fremont Tour A, Entry 10.

## Greek Revival Style

### Benicia
1. Fischer House (originally a hotel), 137 West G St., 1848; Entry 24.
2. Masonic Hall, 110 West J St., 1850; Entry 10.
3. Old State Capitol, First and West G Sts., 1852; Entry 23.
4. Commandant's House, Benicia Industrial Park, 1860; Detour, Entry 34.
5. Enlisted Men's Barracks, Benicia Industrial Park, c. 1870; Detour, Entry 34.

### Berkeley

1607 5th St., "Pioneer" cottage, c. 1865–1875; Tour J. Entry 22.

### Oakland
1. 777 W. 8th St., "Pioneer" cottage, c. 1860s; Tour D, Entry 33.
2. 1028 Adeline St., mid-Victorian house (Greek Revival porch), c. 1870–1875; Tour C, Entry 47.

### Vallejo
1. 842 Georgia St., c. 1855–1865 (remodeled 1950s); Entry 19.
2. Commander Orr House, 626 Virginia St., 1869; Entry 13.
3. 532 York St., c. 1860–1870; Entry 27.

## Victorian Styles 1837–1901

### Gothic Revival, c. 1840s–1900±

#### Alameda
1. Gothic Revival cottage, 1238 Versailles Ave., c. 1852; Tour D, Entry 21.
2. Immanuel Lutheran Church, 1420 Lafayette St., 1891, by F. Kraft; Tour B, Entry 25.

#### Benicia
1. Walch Cottage, 235 E. L St., 1849; Entry 1.
2. St. Paul's Episcopal Church, 1st and E. J Sts., S.E. corner, 1858–1860; Entry 15.
3. Gothic Revival church, 135 W. J St., c. 1870s; Entry 8.

## "Pioneer Boxes," c. 1860–1890

### Berkeley

1. 834 Delaware St., c. 1855–1865; Tour J., Entry 10.
2. 1607, 1609 5th St., c. 1865–1875; Tour J, Entry 22.
3. Chego House, 1809 4th St., 1877; Tour J, Entry 15.
4. Charles Schnelle House, 1924 19th St., 1878; Tour J, Entry 3.
5. Alphonso House, Plaza at Delaware between 5th and 6th Sts., 1878; Tour J, Entry 12.
6. 913 Hearst Ave., c. 1880; Tour J, Entry 8.
7. 1942 Hearst, c. 1875–1885; Tour A, Entry 14.
8. 749 Cedar, c. 1880s; Tour J, Entry 17.
9. Paschold House, 1647 6th St. at Virginia, 1886; Tour J, Entry 26.
10. 1020 Addison at 10th, c. 1880–1890; Tour K, Entry 18.
11. 2317 8th St., c. 1880s; Tour K, Entry 25.
12. Commercial building, 892 University, c. 1875–1885; Tour K, Entry 13.
13. 2407 10th St., c. 1880; Tour K, Entry 38.

### Fremont

1. Sim Cottage, Shinn Historic Park, 1269 Peralta Blvd., 1850; Tour A, Entry 1.
2. 44342 Mission Blvd., c. 1870s; Tour B, Entry 9.
3. 44352 Mission Blvd., c. 1870s; Tour B, Entry 10.
4. Shinn House, Shinn Historic Park, 1269 Peralta Blvd., 1876; Tour A, Entry 1.

### Hayward

1. Portuguese Hotel, 22801 Mission Blvd., c. 1880; Entry 1.

### Oakland

1. 8th St. at Castro, S.E. corner, c. 1860s; Tour B, Entry 27.
2. 1781 W. 8th St., c. 1860–1870; Tour D, Entry 33.
3. 741 and 710 Henry St., c. 1865–1875; Tour D, Entry 22.
4. 1821 W. 7th St., c. 1865–1875; Tour D, Entry 35.
5. 1035 8th Ave., c. 1865–1870; Tour F, Entry 47.
6. 1223 12th Ave., c. 1870s; Tour F, Entry 39.
7. 1120 and 1124 E. 8th St., c. 1870s; Tour F, Entry 41.
8. 1430 25th Ave., c. 1870–1880; Tour H, Entry 17.
9. 622 E. 10th St., c. 1870s; Tour F, Entry 50.
10. 832 W. 21st. St., c. 1870s; Tour B, Entry 15.
11. 815, 825, 835 Grand St., c. 1870s; Tour B, Entry 15.
12. 2015 Filbert St., c. 1870–1880; Tour B, Entry 15.
13. 1706 W. 8th St. at Willow, c. 1870–1880; Tour D, Entry 28.
14. 714 Pine St., c. 1870s; Tour D, Entry 36.

### Vallejo

1. 610 Sutter St., c. 1860s; Entry 26.
2. 80 Canyon Lake Dr., c. 1880; Detour, Entry 3.

## False-Front "Pioneer" Buildings, c. 1860–1890

### Alameda

2156 San Antonio Ave., c. 1870s; Tour B, Entry 18.

### Benicia

1. 166 W. H St., c. 1870s; Entry 21.
2. Commercial building, 401 1st St., c. 1880s; Entry 29.

### Berkeley

1. Jose de Joaquin de Silva House, "Pioneer" Italianate, 1824 5th St., 1878; Tour J, Entry 14.
2. 1504 5th St., c. 1875–1885; Tour J, Entry 20.
3. O'Keefe Saloon, 1723 6th St., 1878; Tour J, Entry 28.

4. 743 Addison at 5th St., c. 1875–1885; Tour K, Entry 4.
5. Christ Chapel Church ("workingman's"-style library), 2016 7th St., 1879; Tour K, Entry 11.
6. Walter Mork Metal Works Co., 844 University, c. 1880–1890; Tour K, Entry 12.
7. Mount Emory Batpist Church, Bancroft Way at 7th, S.E. corner, c. 1880–1890; Tour K, Entry 28.
8. Commercial building, 1001 Channing at 9th., c. 1880–1890; Tour K, Entry 33.
9. Yellow House Restaurant, 2377 Shattuck Ave., 1886; Tour F, Entry 23.

### Emeryville

Vernetti's Town House, 5862 Doyle St., c. 1885–1895; Entry 10.

### Fremont

1. 37364 Niles Blvd., c. 1875–1885; Tour A, Entry 8.
2. Commercial building, 43279 Mission Blvd., c. 1875–1885; Tour B, Entry 3.
3. Commercial building, 44377 Mission Blvd., c. 1880s; Tour B, Entry 12.

### Oakland

1. "Flat-front" houses, 1524 and 1510 Center St., c. 1870s; Tour D, Entry 4.
2. "Pioneer" Italianate, 1765 W. 8th St., c. 1870–1880; Tour D, Entry 32.
3. "Shotgun house," 1625 13th Ave., c. 1870s; Tour F, Entry 25.
4. Commercial building, 1241 13th Ave., c. 1875–1885; Tour E, Entry 37.
5. "Pioneer" Italianate, 1130 E. 8th St., c. 1870s; Tour F, Entry 41.
6. Last Chance Saloon, c. 1880; Tour B, Detour, Entry 44.

### Richmond

1. Commercial building, 39 Washington Ave., c. 1905–1915; Entry 25.
2. Commercial building, 155 Park Place, c. 1905–1910; Entry 28.

### Vallejo

"Shotgun" house, 523 York St. at Napa, c. 1870s; Entry 29.

## Raised-Basement Italianate Cottages, c. 1865–1885.

### Alameda

1. 2306 Alameda Ave., c. 1870s; Tour C, Entry 10.
2. 2310 Alameda Ave., c. 1870s; Tour C, Entry 11.
3. 1214 Oak St., c. 1875–1880; Tour C, Entry 8.
4. 1220 Regent St., c. 1875–1885; Tour D, Entry 8.

### Berkeley

1. Hillegass House, 2601 Parker St., 1868; Tour H, Entry 3.
2. Wooley House, 2509 Haste St., 1876; Tour G, Entry 5.
3. Heywood House, "workingman's" cottage, 1808 5th St., 1878; Tour J, Entry 14.
4. Velasca House, 2109 5th St., 1878; Tour K, Entry 5.
5. Cooley House, 914 Hearst, c. 1875–1880; Tour J, Entry 7.
6. 939 Addison St., c. 1880–1890; Tour K, Entry 20.
7. Wilson House, 2415 Blake St., 1885; Tour H, Entry 17.
8. Farallones Institute (Ehret House), 1516 5th St., 1886; Tour J, Entry 10.
9. 2100 6th St. at Addison, c. 1890s; Tour K, Entry 8.

### Oakland

1. 868 and 871 W. 21st St., c. 1865–1875; Tour C, Entry 13.
2. Antonio Peralta House, 2465 34th St., 1870; Tour G, Entry 26.
3. 1909 Filbert St., c. 1870s; Tour C, Entry 20.
4. 1022 5th Ave., c. 1870–1880; Tour F, Entry 55.
5. 1524 11th Ave., c. 1870s; Tour F, Entry 30.

6. "Workingmen's cottages," 1604, 1608, 1614 12th Ave., c. 1870–1880; Tour F, Entry 24.
7. 2328 19th Ave., 1878; Tour G, Entry 6.
8. 2306 19th Ave., c. 1875–1880; Tour G, Entry 7.
9. 1085 W. 12th St., c. 1875–1880; Tour C, Entry 42.
10. 1034 W. 10th St., c. 1875–1880; Tour C, Entry 45.
11. 1027 Adeline St., c. 1875–1880; Tour C, Entry 48.
12. 623 18th St., c. 1875–1885; Tour B, Entry 2.
13. "Workingman's" cottage, 1421 W. 17th St., c. 1880s, Tour D, Entry 2.
14. 1447 13th Ave., c. 1880–1890; Tour F, Entry 26.

### Vallejo

1. 1012 Sutter St., 1869; Entry 6.
2. 803 Capitol St., c. 1872; Entry 11.

## Italianate Villas, c. 1870–1885

### Benicia Area

1. Clock Tower, Benicia Arsenal (stone "palazzo" style), 1859; Detour, Entry 34.
2. John Muir House, 4 Alhambra Rd. in Martinez, 1884; Detour, Entry 35.

### Berkeley

1. Napoleon Byrne House, 1301 Oxford St., 1868; Tour B, Entry 18.
2. 1930 Delaware at Bonita, c. 1880–1890; Tour A, Entry 12.

### Hayward

Meek Mansion, Boston at Hampton Rd., 1869; Detour, Entry 17.

### Oakland

1. Pardee Mansion, 672 11th St., at Castro, 1868; Tour B, Entry 24.
2. 970 W. 21st St., c. 1870s; Tour C, Entry 16.
3. De Fremery House, Adeline between 17th and 18th sts., (no tower), 1860 or 1867; Tour C, Entry 36.
4. 1521 9th St., (no tower), c. 1865–1875; Tour D, Entry 15.
5. 2212 E. 27th St., (no tower), c. 1870–1880; Tour G, Entry 24.

### Vallejo

1128 Marin St., c. 1865–1875; Entry 3.

## Bracketed Italianate House, c. 1865–±1890

### Alameda

1. Anthony House, 1630 Central Ave., 1876; Tour A, Entry 2.
2. 900 Grand Ave., c. 1878; Tour A, Entry 25.
3. 2225 San Antonio Ave., c. 1875–1880; Tour C, Entry 1.
4. 1420 Broadway, c. 1880–1890; Tour D, Entry 16.
5. 452 Santa Clara, c. 1890; Tour E, Entry 15.

### Berkeley

1. Hanscom House, 1525 Walnut St., 1875; Tour A, Entry 3.
2. 2010 10th St., c. 1870–1880; Tour K, Entry 15
3. Alfred Bartlett House, Blake at Fulton, N.E. corner, 1877; Tour H, Entry 24.
4. 1612 Edith St., c. 1880; Tour A, Entry 23.
5. 2120 Sacramento St., c. 1880s; Tour K, Detour, Entry 41.
6. Boone Academy, 2035 Durant Ave., 1884–1890; Tour F, Entry 22.
7. 2248 Dwight Way, c. 1880–1890; Tour H, Entry 13.
8. 1425 Oxford, c. 1890; Tour A, Entry 19.
9. George Wilkes House, 835 Delaware St., 1891; Tour J, Entry 11.

### Italianate and Neo-Classic Commercial Structures, c. 1860–1890

#### Benicia

1. 636 1st St., c. 1880s; Entry 26.
2. Classic Revival, 718 1st St., c. 1890s; Entry 22.

#### Berkeley

Channing at San Pablo, S.W. corner, c. 1880–1890; Tour K, Entry 37.

#### Oakland

1. Wilcox Block, 9th and Broadway, S.W. corner, c. 1860–1868; Tour B, Entry 36.
2. Washington at 9th St., S.E. corner, 1865–1879, by William Stokes; Tour B, Entry 38.
3. Delger Block, Broadway between 10th and 9th Sts., 1868–1882; Tour B, Entry 33.
4. Dunn's Block, 721 Washington St., 1875; Tour B, Entry 40.
5. 461 and 477 9th St., c. 1875; Tour B, Entry 37.
6. Peniel Mission, 722 Washington St., c. 1875; Tour B, Entry 41.
7. Dahlke's Bar, 7th and Broadway, N.W. corner, c. 1875; Tour B, Entry 42.
8. Nicholl Block, Washington and 9th St., N.E. corner, 1875–1876; Tour B, Entry 35.
9. Portland Hotel, 476 9th St., 1877, by William Stokes; Tour B, Entry 34.
10. Washington at 8th St., S.W. corner, c. 1875–1880; Tour B, Entry 39.
11. Chester at W. 8th St., S.E. corner, c. 1880s; Tour C, Entry 21.

### Mansard Roof or "Second Empire" Style, c. 1860–1885

#### Alameda

Croll's Bar, 1400 Webster at Central, 1879, wing added c. 1889; Tour E, Entry 6.

#### Berkeley

South Hall, U.C. Campus, 1870–1873, by David Farquharson; Tour E, Entry 9.

#### Fremont

Sisters of St. Dominic Convent, south wing, behind Mission San Jose, c. 1880; Tour B, Entry 6.

#### Oakland

Mills Hall, Mills College, 1871; Tour H, Detour, Entry 34.

### Stick-Style Buildings, c. 1870–±1895

#### Alameda

1. Moffitt House, 911 Grand St., 1870; Tour A, Entry 24.
2. 1419 Union St., c. 1870–1880; Tour B, Entry 3.
3. Miller House, 1012 Grand St., 1880–1882; Tour A, Entry 17.
4. 903 Grand, c. 1880–1890; Tour A, Entry 26.
5. Siegfried House, 2044 Alameda Ave., c. 1870–1880; Tour B, Entry 23.
6. 2221 Central Ave., c. 1880–1890; Tour C, Entry 18.
7. 2115 Park Ave. W., c. 1885–1895; Tour D, Entry 2.
8. Stick/Queen Anne, 1224 Park Ave. E., c. 1875–1885; Tour D, Entry 6.
9. 1203 Regent St., c. 1880–1895; Tour D, Entry 9.
10. 1202 Versailles Ave., c. 1880–1890; Tour D, Entry 22.
12. 1439 5th St., c. 1880–1890; Tour E, Entry 18.
13. 1437 5th St., c. 1885; Tour E, Entry 19.
14. Queen Anne with Colonial Revival elements, 1237 Park Ave. W., c. 1890; Tour D, Entry 1.
15. 424 Santa Clara Ave., 1895; Tour E, Entry 13.

## Stick and Stick–Eastlake Villas, c. 1875– ±1895

### Oakland

1. A. E. Cohen House, 1440 29th Ave., 1882–1884; Tour H, Entry 2.
2. Hogan House, 1870 E. 24th St., 1890; Tour G, Entry 3.
3. 2242 22nd St., c. 1885–1895; Tour G, Entry 13.
4. 2326 24th Ave., c. 1885–1895; Tour G, Entry 23.

## Stick–Eastlake Buildings, c. 1875–±1895

### Alameda

1. 1193 Park Ave. W., c. 1880–1890: Tour D, Entry 3.
2. 1416 Broadway, c. 1880–1890; Tour D, Entry 15.
3. "San Francisco Stick" elements, 1602 San Antonio, 1889; Tour A, Entry 15.
4. Queen Anne elements, 1206 Broadway, c. 1885–1895; Tour D, Entry 10.
5. 1354 Broadway, c. 1885–1895; Tour D, Entry 13.
6. Queen Anne elements, 342 Santa Clara Ave., c. 1885–1895; Tour E, Entry 12.
7. 1018 Paru St., 1890; Tour A, Entry 14.
8. 1001 Grand St., 1891, by Charles Shaner; Tour A, Entry 20.
9. Queen Anne elements, 912 Lafayette St., c. 1894; Tour B, Entry 11.
10. 2165 San Jose Ave., c. 1890–1895; Tour B, Entry 19.
11. Queen Anne elements, 2250 San Antonio Ave., c. 1890; Tour C, Entry 4.
12. 1411 5th St., c. 1890–1895; Tour E, Entry 17.

### Benicia

1. 124 W. H St., c. 1876; Entry 20.
2. 715 W. 3rd St., c. 1880–1890; Entry 19.
3. 121 E. J St., c. 1885–1890; Entry 12.

### Berkeley

1. 2320 7th Ave., c. 1880s; Tour K, Entry 27.
2. 2329 6th St., c. 1880–1890; Tour K, Entry 31.
3. Italianate elements, 1019 Addison at 10th St., c. 1880–1890; Tour K, Entry 40.
4. 2320 Blake St., c. 1885–1889; Tour H, Entry 20.
5. 1708 Shattuck Ave., c. 1885–1895; Tour A, Entry 7.
6. Andrew Weir House, 2163 Vine St. at Oxford, c. 1885–1895; Tour B, Entry 21.
7. 2638 Parker St., c. 1890; Tour G, Entry 23.
8. Lizzie Hume House, 243 Ellsworth St., 1892; Tour H, Entry 10.
9. 2115 6th St., c. 1885–1895; Tour K, Entry 6.
10. 2230–2232 8th St., c. 1890; Tour K, Entry 23.
11. 832 Bancroft, c. 1890; Tour K, Entry 29.
12. 2321 6th St., c. 1885–1895; Tour K, Entry 30.
13. 2155 and 2157 Vine St., c. 1890–1895; Tour B, Entry 22.
14. 2027 Hearst St., c. 1890–1895; Tour A, Entry 15.
15. Warren Cheney House, 2241 College Ave., U.C. Campus, c. 1895; Tour E, Entry 33.
16. 2020–2012 Dwight Way, c. 1895–1900; Tour F, Entry 28.

### Emeryville

5894 Beaudry, c. 1890–1895; Entry 12.

### Fremont

Farmhouse, 39270 Mission Blvd., c. 1880–1890; Tour B, Entry 17.

### Hayward

1. Old Mohr Home, farmhouse, Hesperian Blvd., just north of Chabot College, 1886; Entry 19.
2. McConaughy House, farmhouse, 18701 Hesperian Blvd., 1886; Entry 18
3. 750 B Street, c. 1890s; Entry 6.

**Oakland**

1. 1036 Adeline St., c. 1875–1885; Tour C, Entry 49
2. Commercial building, W. 7th at Peralta, N.E. corner, c. 1875–1885; Tour D, Entry 25.
3. 1626, 1622, 1618, 1614 Castro St., c. 1880–1890; Tour B, Entry 7.
4. Queen Anne elements, 1416 Castro St., c. 1880s; Tour B, Entry 14.
5. 1010 and 1014 Castro St., c. 1880–1890; Tour B, Entry 25.
6. Rowhouses, Peralta at W. 12th, S.E. corner, c. 1880–1890; Tour D, Entry 8.
7. Commercial building, W. 8th at Peralta, N.E. corner, c. 1880s; Tour D, Entry 24.
8. Gothic elements, 1796 W. 8th St. at Pine, c. 1880s; Tour D, Entry 34.
9. 2112 10th Ave., c. 1886; Tour F, Entry 13.
10. Queen Anne elements, 2304 9th at E. 23rd., by Newsom, 1887; Tour F, Entry 12.
11. "Wokingman's" cottages, 1730–1704 10th Ave., 1887; Tour F, Entry 19.
12. Commercial building, 11th Ave. at E. 12th St., S.E. corner, c. 1880–1890; Tour F, Entry 33.
13. Commercial building, 12th Ave. at E. 12th St., N.E. corner, c. 1880–1890; Tour F, Entry 33.
14. Italianate elements, 1454 9th St. at Center, c. 1880–1890; Tour D, Entry 18.
15. 696 10th St. at Castro, c. 1890; Tour B, Entry 26.
16. 769 W. 19th St., c. 1885–1895; Tour C, Entry 3.
17. Queen Anne elements, 1527 Union St. at 16th., c. 1885–1895; Tour C, Entry 37.
18. 932, 922, 916 E. 11th St., c. 1885–1895; Tour F, Entry 44.
19. 817, 809, 803 E. 11th St. at 8th Ave., c. 1885–1895; Tour F, Entry 46.
20. Queen Anne elements, 1014 5th Ave., c. 1885–1895; Tour F, Entry 56.
21. 1635 E. 22nd St., c. 1885–1895; Tour G, Entry 1.
22. Gothic elements, 15th St. at 24th Ave., N.E. corner, c. 1885–1895; Tour H, Entry 19.
23. 2527 23rd Ave., c. 1885–1895; Tour H, Entry 21.
24. Queen Anne elements, 2366 E. 19th St., c. 1890; Tour H, Entry 24.
25. Queen Anne elements, 822 6th Ave., c. 1890–1895; Tour F, Entry 52.

**Piedmont**

1. Wetmore House, 342 Bonita Ave. at Vista, 1878; Tour A, Entry 17.
2. Craig House, 55 Craig Ave., 1879; Tour B, Entry 4.

**Richmond**

428 Washington Ave., c. 1900; Entry 12.

# Queen Anne Style, c. 1880–±1900

### Alameda

1. 1001 Morton St., c. 1885–1895; Tour A, Entry 10.
2. 815 Grand St., c. 1885–1895; Tour B, Entry 27.
3. Commercial building, 1431 Webster St. at Taylor, c. 1885–1895; Tour E, Entry 5.
4. 1015 Morton St., c. 1890; Tour A, Entry 8.
5. 1007 Morton St., c. 1890; Tour A, Entry 9.
6. 1000 Paru St., c. 1890; Tour A, Entry 12.
7. 2019 San Antonio St., c. 1890; Tour B, Entry 16.
8. 1226 Park Ave. E., c. 1890; Tour D, Entry 7.
9. 1240 Broadway, c. 1890; Tour D, Entry 11.
10. 1244 Broadway, c. 1890; Tour D, Entry 12.
11. 1412 Broadway, c. 1890; Tour D, Entry 14.
12. 2700 Central Ave., c. 1890; Tour E, Entry 9.
13. 543, 547 Taylor St., c. 1890; Tour E, Entry 9.
14. 1117 Morton St., 1891, by Charles Shaner; Tour A, Entry 5.
15. 2103 San Jose Ave. at Willow, 1891, by Charles Shaner; Tour B, Entry 21.
16. 2258 San Antonio Ave., c. 1891; Tour C, Entry 6.
17. Stick–Eastlake elements, 1135 Morton St., c. 1893; Tour A, Entry 4.
18. 1023 Morton St., c. 1890–1895; Tour A, Entry 7.
19. Colonial Revival elements, 1400 San Jose Ave., c. 1890–1895; Tour A, Entry 11.

23. 902 Peralta at W. 9th, c. 1890; Tour D, Entry 14.
24. 718 Henry St., c. 1890; Tour D, Entry 22.
25. Commercial building, Gothic details, 1249 E. 12th St., c. 1885–1895; Tour F, Entry 38.
26. 812 6th Ave., c. 1885–1895; Tour F, Entry 52.
27. 546 E. 11th St. at 6th Ave., c. 1885–1895; Tour F, Entry 53.
28. 2302 17th Ave. at 23rd St., c. 1890; Tour G, Entry 2.
29. 1824 West St. at 19th, c. 1890–1895; Tour C, Entry 2.
30. 1930 Filbert St., c. 1890–1895; Tour C, Entry 19.
31. 918 E. 18th St. at Myrtle, c. 1890–1895; Tour C, Entry 24.
32. 1409 W. 17th St. at Cypress, c. 1890–1895; Tour D, Entry 1.
33. Eastlake details, 1028 Peralta St., c. 1885–1895; Tour D, Entry 9.
34. Hiram Tubbs House, 544 E. 14th St. at 7th Ave., c. 1890–1895; Tour F, Entry 1.
35. 1937 8th Ave., c. 1892; Tour F, Entry 7.
36. 1940 and 1950 9th Ave., c. 1890–1895; Tour F, Entry 8.
37. 2035 10th Ave., 1893–1894; Tour F, Entry 16.
38. 1930 10th Ave., c. 1890–1895; Tour F, Entry 17.
39. 1200 block of E. 15th St. at 12th Ave., c. 1890–1895; Tour F, Entry 28.
40. 1104 E. 8th St., c. 1890–1895; Tour F, Entry 41.
41. 954 E. 11th St. at 10th Ave., c. 1890–1895; Tour F, Entry 43.
42. 1930 22nd St., c. 1890–1895; Tour G, Entry 9.
43. 2032 22nd St., c. 1890–1895; Tour G, Entry 10.
44. Romanesque elements, 2205, 2209 23rd Ave. at E. 22nd, c. 1890–1895; Tour G, Entry 14.
45. 2340 e. 23rd St. at Inyo, c. 1890–1895; Tour G, Entry 17.
46. 2376 E. 23rd St., c. 1890–1895; Tour G, Entry 18.
47. 2570 E. 14th, c. 1890–1895; Tour H, Entry 15.
48. Eastlake elements, 1544 24th Ave. at E. 16th St., c. 1890–1895; Tour H, Entry 28.
49. 2503 E. 16th St. at 25th Ave., c. 1890–1895; Tour H, Entry 29.
50. 2524 E. 16th St. at 25th Ave., c. 1890–1895; Tour H, Entry 30.
51. 2544 E. 16th St, c. 1890–1895; Tour H, Entry 31.
52. 629 W. 18th St., c. 1895; Tour B, Entry 3.
53. 1631 Myrtle St., c. 1895; Tour C, Entry 26.
54. 1710 Filbert St., c. 1895; Tour C, Entry 33.
55. 1400 block of W. 8th St., c. 1895; Tour D, Entry 19.
56. 1222 11th Ave., c. 1895; Tour F, Entry 31.
57. 1734 Grove St. at 18th, c. 1890s; Tour B, Entry 4.
58. 3148 Fruitvale Ave., c. 1890–1900; Tour G, Entry 25.
59. Colonial Revival elements, 1228, 1222 Union St., c. 1895–1900; Tour C, Entry 39.
60. Romanesque elements, 2231 23rd Ave., c. 1895–1900; Tour G, Entry 16.
61. 2230 23rd Ave., c. 1895–1900; Tour G, Entry 15.
62. Colonial Revival elements, 2400, 2406 E. 23rd St. at 24th Ave., c. 1895–1900; Tour G, Entry 21.
63. 1627 28th Ave., c. 1897; Tour G, Entry 12.
64. Colonial Revival elements, 2238 24th Ave., c. 1900; Tour G, Entry 20.
65. Linley House, Colonial Revival elements, 2939 E. 16th St., 1900; Tour H, Entry 7.

### Piedmont

1. 227 Bonita Ave., 1889; Tour A, Entry 11.
2. 1811 Oakland Ave., c. 1890–1895; Tour A, Entry 11.
3. 225 Highland Ave., c. 1895–1905; Tour A, Entry 14.

### Richmond

1. 235 Tunnel St., c. 1901; Entry 5.
2. Mansard roof, 84 Scenic, c. 1900–1905; Entry 7.
3. 319 Washington Ave., c. 1905–1907; Entry 10.
4. Colonial Revival Elements, 123 Nicholl Ave., c. 1900–1905; Entry 15.
5. 126 Martina at Cottage, c. 1900–1905; Entry 21.

### Vallejo

1. John Wilson House, Eastlake details, 705 Georgia St. at Napa, c. 1885–1895; Entry 16.

2. 600 and 610 Georgia St., c. 1890–1895; Entry 15.
3. 747 York St., c. 1890–1895; Entry 24.
4. 626 York St., c. 1890–1895; Entry 25.
5. Apartments, 524–528 York St., c. 1890–1895; Entry 28.
6. Colonial Revival elements, Sutter at Capitol St., N.W. corner, c. 1895; Entry 7.
7. Colonial Revival elements, 806 Georigia St., c. 1895; Entry 18.
8. 915 Georiga St., 1895; Entry 21.
9. 740 York St. at Eldorado, c. 1895; Entry 22.
10. 738 York St., 1895; Entry 23.
11. Two cottages, 90 Canyon Lake Dr., c. 1890s; Detour, Port Costa, Entry 31.

# Miscellaneous Victorian Sites
## c. 1840s–1900

### Alameda

1. Late-Victorian house, 2254 San Antonio Ave., c. 1890–1895; Tour C, Entry 5.
2. Rooming house, 503 Santa Clara Ave., c. 1890–1895; Tour E, Entry 21.

### Benicia

Benicia Arsenal Grounds, Guard House, (1872), Powder Magazine (1857), Camel Barns (1853–1854); Detour, Entry 34.

### Berkeley

1. Cast-iron railings, Cedar between Oxford and Walnut, c. 1890; Tour A, Entry 2.
2. Late-Victorian house, 1415 Arch St., 1897; Tour B, Entry 10.
3. Hitching post, 1300 Arch St. (in front), c. 1890s; Tour B, Entry 16.
4. Lillian Bridgeman House and Studio, 1715 La Loma Ave., 1899, 1908; Tour D, Entry 1.
5. Jensen House, 1675 La Loma Ave., 1894; Tour D, Entry 4.
6. Sutch House, 1731 La Verada Rd., c. 1890–1900; Tour D, Entry 7.
7. Peterson House, "coaching inn," 1631 La Verada Rd., 1895; Tour D, Entry 8.
8. Leuschner Observatory (in ruins), U. C. Campus, original wing, 1885, by Clinton Day; Tour E, Entry 23.
9. Garage, Milvia at Addison St., N.E. corner, c. 1885–1890; Tour F, Entry 1.
10. Eastlake/Colonial Revival house, 2014 Channing Way, c. 1895; Tour F, Entry 25.
11. Conestoga wagon wheels, lot on 4th St. between Virginia and Cedar, c. 1890s; Tour J, Entry 16.
12. Water tower, 6th St. between Cedar and Virginia, c. 1890s; Tour J, Entry 25.
13. Feeney's Wire Rope Factory, 600 Addison, c. 1875; Tour K, Entry 1.

### Fremont

1. Cast-iron fence, 36967 Niles Blvd., c. 1870s; Tour A, Entry 9.
2. Victorian farm buildings, 32860 Alvarado–Niles Rd., c. 1885–1895; Tour A, Entry 15.
3. Old Mission San Jose graveyard, grounds of Old St. Joseph's Church, c. 1820s–1900; Tour B, Entry 2.
4. Late-Victorian farmhouse, 41252 Mission Blvd., c. 1890; Tour B, Entry 14.

### Oakland

1. Late-Victorian house, 665 W. 16th St., c. 1895; Tour B, Entry 8.
2. Victorian duplex, 663 15th St., c. 1890–1895; Tour B, Entry 13.
3. Oakland Ensemble Theater, 660 13th St., 1890, by A. Page Brown; Tour B, Entry 18.
4. Brick warehouses, Jack London Square, c. 1875–1885; Tour B, Entry 44.
5. Log cabin, Jack London Square, c. 1890s; Tour B, Entry 44.
6. Late-Victorian house, 1003 W. 12th St. at Filbert, c. 1885–1890; Tour C, Entry 43.
7. Late-Victorian duplex, 1701 17th St., at Peralta, c. 1880–1890; Tour D, Entry 3.
8. Late-Victorian house, 726 Henry St., c. 1895; Tour D, Entry 22.
9. Late-Victorian house, iron fence, 1448 Madison St., c. 1890; Tour E, Entry 10.
10. Schilling Gardens and gate, 19th St. north of Jackson, 1894; Tour E, Entry 20.
11. Late-Victorian house, 1121 7th Ave., c. 1890; Tour F, Entry 49.
12. Late-Victorian house, 2204 22nd St., c. 1890; Tour G, Entry 11.
13. Late-Victorian house, 2227 22nd St., c. 1880–1890; Tour G, Entry 12.
14. Late-Victorian house, 2600 E. 16th St., c. 1890–1895; Tour H, Entry 32.

# Transitional Era c. 1890–1915

## Romanesque Revival, c. 1886–±1915

Colonial
Revival
Houses
c. 1895–±1915

## Craftsman Bungalows and Brown Shingle Houses
### c. 1890s–±1920

7. Craftsman, 2908 Russell Ave., c. 1910; Tour I, Entry 13.
8. Craftsman, 2900 Russell Ave., c. 1910; Tour I, Entry 14.

### Emeryville

Brown Shingle, 1249, 1253 Stanford St. at Beaudry, c. 1905–1915; Entry 18.

### Fremont

Craftsman, 3330 Alvarado–Niles Rd., c. 1905–1915; Tour A, Entry 12.

### Kensington–Thousand Oaks

1. Craftsman, Alameda at Thousand Oaks Blvd., S.E. corner, c. 1910; Entry 23.
2. Craftsman, 726 Arlington Ave., c. 1910–1920; Entry 15.
3. Navitzky House, Log Cabin elements, 15 Sunset Dr., 1930; Entry 5.

### Oakland

1. Brown Shingle, 1183 W. 12th St., c. 1900–1910; Tour C, Entry 40.
2. Brown Shingle, 1148 29th Ave., c. 1900–1910; Tour H, Entry 4.
3. Brown Shingle, 1524 29th Ave., c. 1900–1910; Tour H, Entry 5.
4. Craftsman, 1534 29th Ave., c. 1905–1915; Tour II, Entry 6.
5. Brown Shingle, 2840 E. 16th St. at 29th Ave., c. 1906–1915; Tour H, Entry 9.

### Piedmont

1. Brown Shingle, 310 El Cerrito Ave., 1906; Tour A, Entry 2.
2. Brown Shingle, 33 Dormidera Ave., c. 1910; Tour B, Entry 6.
3. Brown Shingle, 225 Hillside Ave., c. 1905–1915; Tour A, Entry 9.
4. Craftsman, 224 Bonita Ave., c. 1905–1915; Tour A, Entry 13.
5. Craftsman, 173 Mountain Ave., at Dormidera, c. 1905–1915; Tour B, Entry 5.
6. Craftsman with Log Cabin elements, 150 Wildwood Gardens, c. 1930s; Tour B, Entry 15.

### Richmond

1. Brown Shingle, 505, 509 Washington Ave., c. 1910; Entry 11.
2. Craftsman, 322 Washington Ave., c. 1905–1915; Entry 14.

---

# Buildings by First Bay Tradition Architects
## c. 1890s–1930s

Included in this section are a number of Beaux-Arts-style buildings by Bay Area architects (primarily, John Galen Howard) and Prairie-Style buildings (mostly by John Hudson Thomas). They can be found within each architect's section.

## Bernard Maybeck

### Berkeley

1. Keeler Cottage, 1770–1790 Highland Pl., 1895, rear addition 1902, remodeled c. 1925; Tour C, Entry 9.
2. Town and Gown Club, 2401 Dwight Way at Dana St., 1899; Tour H, Entry 16.
3. Gifford McGrew House, 2601 Derby at Hillegass Ave., 1900; Tour G, Entry 20.
4. Faculty Club, U.C. Campus, 1902–1903 (later additions by Warren Perry, 1914, 1925, and Downs and Lagorio, 1959); Tour E, Entry 14.
5. Hillside Club, 2286 Cedar St., 1906 (rebuilt 1924, by Mark White); Tour B, Entry 6.
6. Senger House, 1321 Bayview Pl., 1907; Tour B, Entry 12.
7. Schneider–Kroeber House, 1325 Arch St., 1907; Tour B, Entry 14.
8. Oscar Mauer Studio, 1772 Le Roy Ave., 1907; Tour C, Entry 7.
9. Lawson House, Prairie elements, 1515 La Loma Ave., 1907; Tour D, Entry 10.
10. Atkinson House, 2735 Durant Ave., 1909; Tour G, Entry 8.
11. First Church of Christian Science, Dwight at Bowditch, 1910 (Sunday School by Henry Gutterson, 1927); Tour G, Entry 1.

12. E. C. Priber House, 1709 La Loma Ave., 1910; Tour D, Entry 2.
13. Randolph School, 2700 Belrose Ave., 1911; Tour I, Entry 2.
14. Matthewson Studio House, Prairie elements, 2704 Buena Vista at La Loma Ave., 1915; Tour D, Entry 11.
15. Cedric Wright House, 2515 Etna St., 1921; Tour G, Entry 17.
16. Gannon House, 2780 Buena Vista Rd., 1924; Tour D, Entry 18.
17. Maybeck "Sack" House, 1711 Buena Vista Rd., 1924; Tour D, Entry 13.
18. 1 Maybeck Twin Dr., c. 1925–1935; tour D, Entry 15.
19. Tufts House, 1733 Buena Vista Rd., 1931; Tour D, Entry 14.
20. Wallen Maybeck House, 2751 Buena Vista Rd., 1933; Tour D, Entry 6.

### Kensington–Thousand Oaks

1. Jones House, 1827 San Juan Ave., 1916; Entry 25.
2. Jerolemon House, 168 Southhampton Rd., 1923; Entry 12.

### Piedmont

Frank C. Havens House, 101 Wildwood Gardens, 1906; Tour B, Entry 14.

## Julia Morgan

### Berkeley

1. Prof. Charles M. Bayley House, Piedmont at Durant, N.W. corner, 1905; Tour G, Entry 9.
2. St. John's Presbyterian Church, College Ave. at Derby, 1908; Tour G, Entry 19.
3. Houses, 2531, 2535 Etna St., c. 1910; Tour G, Entry 18.
4. Girton Hall, U.C. Campus, 1911; Tour E, Entry 17.
5. Hatfield House, 2695 Le Conte Ave., 1912; Tour C, Entry 10.
6. Hobart Hall, 2600 Dwight Way at Bowditch, 1918–1920; Tour G, Entry 2.
7. Elliott House, Georgian Revival, 1 Eucalyptus Rd., 1919; Tour I, Entry 36.
8. House, 1600 Arch St. at Cedar, 1920; Tour C, Entry 28.
9. Hearst Memorial Gymnasium for Women, Beaux Artes style, U.C. Campus, 1925, assisted by Bernard Maybeck; Tour E, Entry 32.
10. Seldon Williams House, 2821 Claremont Blvd. at Avalon, 1928; Tour I, Entry 5.
11. Berkeley City Club, 2315 Durant Ave., 1929; Tour H, Entry 2.

### Kensington–Thousand Oaks

1. Ralph Elste House, 1937 Thousand Oaks Blvd., 1915; Entry 30.
2. McGregor House, 1962 Yosemite Rd, 1920; Entry 17.

### Oakland

1. El Campanile, Mills College Campus, 1904; Tour H, Entry 34.
2. Y.W.C.A., 1515 Webster at 15th St., 1915; Tour A, Entry 18.

### Piedmont

1. Walter Starr House, 216 Hampton Rd., 1911–1912; Tour C, Entry 4.
2. Ayer House, 246 Seaview Ave., 1914; Tour C, Entry 3.
3. James Lombard House, Tudor Revival, 62 Faragut Ave., 1915–1916; Tour C, Entry 2.
4. Tudor Revival house, 9 Craig Ave., c. 1915; Tour B, Entry 1.
5. House, 117 Sheridan, c. 1915–1920; Tour B, Entry 12.
6. House, 45 Sierra Ave., c. 1915–1925; Tour B, Entry 9.
7. House, 49 Sierra Ave., c. 1915–1925; Tour B, Entry 10.
8. Knowland House, Beaux Artes, 65 Seaview Dr., c. 1915–1925; Tour B, Entry 17.
9. 65 Seaview Ave., c. 1915–1925; Tour C, Entry 15.
10. Reed House, 200 Crocker Ave. at Faragut, 1926; Tour C, Entry 1.
11. Chapel of the Chimes, 4499 Piedmont Ave., 1928; Tour C, Entry 19.

### Vallejo

Wilson House, 728 Capital St., 1909; Entry 8.

# John Hudson Thomas

### Albany

Prairie Style house, 975 Ventura at Sonoma, c. 1915–1920; Entry 33.

### Berkeley

1. Walter Chowen house, 94 The Uplands, 1908; Tour I, Entry 21.
2. Hall House, 51 Oakvale Ave., 1908; Tour I, Entry 28.
3. Dubrow House, 123 Parkside Dr., 1909; Tour I, Entry 31.
4. Dungan House, 41 Oakvale Ave., 1911; Tour I, Entry 27.
5. Merrill House, Prairie elements, 10 Hillcrest Ct., 1911; Tour I, Entry 34.
6. Johnson House, 2 Hillcrest Ct., 1912; Tour I, Entry 35.
7. Kidd House, Priaire elements, 95 The Plaza Dr., 1913; Tour I, Entry 29.
8. Sellander House, Prairie elements, 35 Oakvale Ave., 1914; Tour I, Entry 26.
9. Loring House, Prairie Style, 1730 Spruce St., 1914; Tour B, Entry 2.
10. Hume Castle, 2900 Buena Vista Rd., 1928; Tour D, Entry 20.

### Kensington–Thousand Oaks

1. Murdock House, Prairie elements, 1874 Yosemite Rd., 1911; Entry 21.
2. Spring Mansion, Beaux Artes, 160 San Antonio Ave., 1912; Entry 11.
3. Sill House, Prairie elements, 1936 Thousand Oaks Blvd., 1913; Entry 19.
4. Four houses, 1941–1947 Yosemite Rd., 1928; Entry 18.
5. John Hudson Thomas House, 31 Norwood Ave., c. 1930; Entry 4.

### Piedmont

1. Kelly House, Prairie elements, 455 Wildwood Ave. at Sheridan, 1910; Tour B, Entry 13.
2. Lanza House, Tudor Revival, 320 El Cerrito Ave., 1911 (attributed to Thomas); Tour A, Entry 1.
3. Prairie Style house, 34 Craig Ave., c. 1916; Tour B, Entry 3.

# John Galen Howard

### Berkeley

1. Hearst Mining Building, Beaux Artes, U.C. Campus, 1902–1907, assisted by Julia Morgan; Tour E, Entry 20.
2. Hearst Greek Theater, U.C. Campus, 1903, assisted by Julia Morgan; Tour E, Entry 19.
3. Cloyne Court, 2600 Ridge Rd. at Le Roy, 1904; Tour E, Entry 2.
4. Leuschner Observatory, U.C. Campus, 1904; Tour E, Entry 23.
5. California Hall, Beaux Artes, U.C. Campus, 1905; Tour E, Entry 6.
6. North Gate Hall, U.C. Campus, 1906 (additions by Walter Stileberg 1936, Howard Moisel 1952 and 1950); Tour E, Entry 22.
7. Senior Men's Hall, U.C. Campus, 1906; Tour E, Entry 15.
8. Claremont Court Gates, Claremont Blvd. at Russell, 1907; Tour I, Entry 9.
9. University Library, Beaux Artes, U.C. Campus, 1907–1917; Tour Tour E, Entry 7.
10. Sather Gate, Beaux Artes, U.C. Campus, 1908–1910; Tour E, Entry 2.
11. Euclid Apartments, 1865 Euclid Ave. at Hearst, 1912; Tour C, Entry 1.
12. Durant Hall, Beaux Artes, U.C. Campus, 1912; Tour E, Entry 5.
13. Agriculture Building, Beaux Artes, U.C. Campus, 1912; Tour E, Entry 27.
14. Sather Tower, U.C. Campus, 1913–1917; Tour E, Entry 8.
15. Naval Architecture Building, U.C. Campus, 1914; Tour E, Entry 21.
16. Wheeler Hall, Beaux Artes, U.C. Campus, 1916–1918; Tour E, Entry 4.
17. Hilgard Hall, Beaux Artes, U.C. Campus, 1916–1918; Tour E, Entry 28.
18. Gilman Hall, Beaux Artes, U.C. Campus, 1917; Tour E, Entry 13.
19. Women's Faculty Club, U.C. Campus, 1923; Tour E, Entry 16.
20. Stephens Hall, U.C. Campus, 1923; Tour E, Entry 11.
21. Le Conte Hall, Beaux Artes, U.C. Campus, 1924; Tour E, Entry 12.
22. Haviland Hall, Beaux Artes, U.C. Campus, 1924; Tour E, Entry 24.

### Ernest Coxhead

#### Alameda

Greenlease House, 1724 Santa Clara Ave., 1882–1894; Tour B, Entry 1.

#### Berkeley

1. Beta Theta Pi House, 2607 Hearst Ave., at Le Roy, 1893 (additions, 1909), by Coxhead and Coxhead; Tour C, Entry 2.
2. Phoebe Apperson Hearst House, 2368 Le Conte Ave. (and guest house behind), 1900; Tour C, Entry 23.
3. Freeman House, "Allenoke," 1765–1769 Le Roy Ave. at Ridge, 1904–1906, by Coxhead and Coxhead; Tour C, Entry 4.
4. Allenoke Carriage House, 2533 Ridge Rd., 1904, by Coxhead and Coxhead; Tour B, Entry 5.
5. Brackenridge House, 10 Encina Pl., 1906; Tour I, Entry 24.
6. Van Sant House, 6 Encina Pl., 1906; Tour I, Entry 25.

## Buildings by Other First Bay Tradition Architects
### c. 1890s–±1930

#### Berkeley

1. Paget Gorill House, 2727 Dwight Way at Etna, 1891, by Willis Polk; Tour G, Entry 16.
2. Moody House, 1755 Le Roy Ave., 1896, by A. C. Schweinfurth; Tour C, Entry 8.
3. First Unitarian Church, U.C. Campus, 1898, by A. C. Schweinfurth; Tour E, Entry 31.
4. Benjamin Wheeler House, 1820 Scenic Ave., 1900; Tour C, Entry 14.
5. Colonel Greenleaf House, 2610 College Ave., 1902, by Albert Dodge Coplin; Tour G, Entry 24.
6. Fred Wallace House, 1340 Arch St. at Rose, 1905, by Mark White; Tour B, Entry 11.
7. Reese House, 1705 La Loma, 1905, by E. A. Hargreaves; Tour D, Entry 3.
8. Claremont Park Co. Gates, Claremont Ave. at The Uplands, 1905, by W. C. Hays; Tour I, Entry 20.
9. Thorsen House, 2307 Piedmont Ave., 1908, by Green and Green; Tour G, Entry 11.
10. St. Clement's Episcopal Church, 2837 Claremont Blvd., 1908, by Willis Polk; Tour I, Entry 8.
11. Gertrude White House, 99 The Plaza Dr., by Harris Allen, 1913; Tour I, Entry 30.
12. Thomas Brown House, 2753 Buena Vista Rd., 1914, by W. C. Hays; Tour D, Entry 17.
13. McDuffie House, 3016 Avalon Ave., 1915, by Henry Gutterson; Tour I, Entry 6.
14. House, 1322 Bayview Pl., c. 1924, by Henry Gutterson; Tour C, Entry 14.
15. Foulds House, 1600 Euclid Ave., 1928, by Henry Gutterson; Tour C, Entry 14.

#### Kensington–Thousand Oaks

1. Mark Daniels House, 1864 Yosemite Rd., 1914, by Jeffery Bangs; Entry 22.
2. Cooper House, 1831 San Juan Ave., c. 1915, by W. C. Hays; Entry 27.
3. Leavens House, 1900 Yosemite Rd., 1923, by Walter Sittleberg; Entry 20.

#### Piedmont

1. Hotel Hosue, 43 Dormidera Ave., 1907, by Louis Christian Mullgardt; Tour B, Entry 7.
2. Fore House, 444 Mountain Ave., 1909, by Louis Christian Mullgardt; Tour B, Entry 18.
3. Walter Lemert House, 37 Lincoln Ave., 1909 by Walter Brown; Tour B, Entry 16.
4. Moffatt House, 86 Seaview Ave., 1912, by Willis Polk; Tour C, Entry 13.
5. Juliet Alexander House, 19 Craig Ave., 1915–1933, by C. W. Dickey; Tour B, Entry 2.

## Beaux Arts Neo-Classic Buildings
### c. 1890s–±1930

#### Alameda

1. Old Post Office, Central Ave. at Park Ct., 1912, by John Knox Taylor; Tour C, Entry 13.
2. Wells Fargo Bank, 1442 Webster St., 1917; Tour E, Entry 4.
3. Alameda High School, 2000 Central Ave., 1926; Tour C, Entry 17.
4. Alameda Library, 2264 Santa Clara Ave., 1936; Tour C, Entry 19.

#### Berkeley

1. University House, U.C. Campus, 1902, by Albert Pissis; Tour E, Entry 25.

## Mediterranean Revival Styles, c. 1900–±1940

# Period Revival Era

## c. 1900–±1940

This category includes Mission Revival, stucco bungalows, Italian, Renaissance Revival, Spanish Colonial, and general Mediterranean styles, as indicated in each entry.

20. Spanish Colonial house, 1645 Scenic Ave., c. 1925–1935; Tour C, Entry 27.
21. Mason–McDuffie Building, Mediterranean elements, 2101 Shattuck Ave at Addison, 1928, by Walter H. Ratcliff, Jr.; Tour F, Entry 7.
22. International Students' House, Mediterranean and Mission Revival elements, Piedmont at Bancroft Way, 1928, by George Kelham; Tour G, Entry 10.
23. California School for the Blind, auditorium, Mission Revival with Art Deco elements, Derby at Belrose, 1930, by James B. McDougall; Tour I, Entry 1.
24. Worth Ryder House, Spanish Colonial and Italian Renaissance elements, 2772 Hilgard Ave., by owner, c. 1930s; Tour D, Entry 9.

### Emeryville

1. California Syrup and Extract Co., Italian Renaissance elements, 1230 Powell St., c. 1920–1930; Entry 8.
2. Westinghouse building, Mission Revival, Powell at Peladeau St., n.w. corner, 1924; Entry 2.

### Fremont

1. "Joe's Corner" Bar, Spanish Colonial, J St. at Niles Blvd., S.W. corner, 1920; Tour A, Entry 2.
2. Ellsworth Building, Moorish Revival, 37597 Niles Blvd., 1926; Tour A, Entry 4.
3. Dominican Convent, north wing, Spanish Colonial, behind Mission San Jose, c. 1930s; Tour B, Entry 7.

### Hayward

1. All Saints Catholic Church, 2nd at E St., N.E. corner, 1909–1910; Entry 13.
2. Pratt Mortuary, Mission Revival, 1044 C St., c. 1925–1935; Entry 14.

### Kensington–Thousand Oaks

1. Italian Renaissance Revival house, 1853 San Juan Ave., c. 1920; Entry 28.
2. Anson Blake House, Italian Renaissance villa, 70 Rincon Rd., 1922, 1924, by Walter Bliss; Entry 2.
3. Spanish Colonial Revival house, 54 Norwood Ave., c. 1925–1935; Entry 3.
4. "Southwest Revival" house, 322 Arlington Ave., c. 1925–1935; Entry 10.
5. Sunset View Mausoleum, Sunset View Cemetery, Renaissance style, Sunset at Franciscan St., 1927; Entry 6.
6. Pharmacy Building, Spanish Colonial style, 299 Arlington Ave., 1928, by William R. Yelland; Entry 9.
7. Nachtreib House, Spanish Colonial style house, 111 Southhampton Rd., 1928, by Warren Perry; Entry 13.

### Oakland

1. John Missionary Baptist Church, Spanish Baroque style, 1909 Market at 19th St., c. 1905–1915; Tour C, Entry 7.
2. Masonic Temple, Mission Revival, 1433 Madison at 15th St., 1908, by O'Brien and Warner; Tour E, Entry 11.
3. Allison Apartments, Mediterranean, 1560 Alice, c. 1910–1920; Tour E, Entry 4.
4. Alician Apartments, Mediterranean, 1450 Alice St., c. 1915–1925; Tour E, Entry 2.
5. Darien Apartments, Mediterranean, 1505 Jackson St., 1915–1925; Tour E, Entry 6.
6. Commodore Apartments, Mediterranean, 1501 Madison St., c. 1915–1925; Tour E, Entry 8.
7. Pearson Realty Office, Italian Renaissance style, 401 15th St. at Franklin, c. 1915–1925; Tour A, Entry 12.
8. Swan's Market, Mediterranean details, 10th St. between Washington and Clay, 1917; Tour B, Entry 32.
9. Duel Brae Apartments, Mediterranean, 1445 Lakeside Dr., 1917; Tour E, Entry 15.
10. U.S. Post Office, Spanish Colonial style, 15th St. at Franklin, S.E. corner, c. 1920; Tour A, Entry 13.
11. Stucco bungalows, 1400–1500 block of 29th Ave., c. 1920–1930; Tour H, Entry 3.
12. Stucco bungalows, 1400–1500 block of 27th Ave., c. 1920–1930; Tour H, Entry 13.
13. Myrtle Arms Apartments, Mediterranean, 176 15th St., 1922; Tour E, Entry 7.

14. Spanish Colonial house, 2344 E. 15th St., c. 1925–1935; Tour H, Entry 20.
15. Spanish Colonial bungalows, Castello and Cordova Sts. at Fruitvale, c. 1934–1939; Tour G, Entry 25.

### Piedmont

1. W.W. I Memorial, Spanish Baroque style excedra, Piedmont Park, Magnolia St. at Highland, c. 1920; Tour A, Entry 18.
2. Spanish Colonial Revival house, 320 Hampton Road, c. 1920–1930; Tour C, Entry 5.
3. William St. Cyr Cavalier House, Mediterranean style, 401 Hampton Rd. at Glen Alpine, c. 1920–1930; Tour C, Entry 7.
4. Piedmont Community Church, Mediterranean Revival with Mission-style elements, 400 Highland Ave., 1927; Tour B, Entry 8.
5. Herbert Hall House, Spanish Colonial style, 67 King Ave., 1930, by Clarence Tantau; Tour C, Entry 17.

### Richmond

1. Commercial building, Mission-style detail, 35 Washington Ave., c. 1905–1915; Entry 24.

## Other Period Revival Buildings, c. 1900–±1940

These listings include Tudor, Georgian, Gothic, and other twentieth-century Revival styles, as indicated in each entry.

### Alameda

1. Tudor Revival house, Paru at Central St., S.E. corner, 1898 addition c. 1930; Tour A, Entry 3.
2. Tudor Revival house, 1100 Grand St., c. 1915–1925; Tour A, Entry 16.
3. Hansel-and-Gretel-style house, 912 Grand St., c. 1920–1930; Tour A, Entry 23.

### Albany

1. Norman Revival bungalow, 1315 Washington St., c. 1925–1935; Entry 3.
2. Norman Revival bungalow, 1090 Peralta St., c. 1925–1935; Entry 21
3. Tudor Revival bungalow, 1041 Ordway, c. 1925–1935; Entry 30.
4. Georgian Revival house, 1330 Washington St., c. 1930s; Entry 4.
4. Tudor Revival house, 732 Ramona St., c. 1930; Entry 5.

### Berkeley

1. Bay Commons, Georgian Revival, Berkeley Way at Bonita, S.E. corner, 1905; Tour A, Entry 18.
2. Campbell House, Jacobean Revival, 2815 Claremont Blvd., 1909, by Patterson Ross; Tour I, Entry 3.
3. Douglas House, Tudor Revival house, 35 Parkside Ave., 1910, by Albert Farr; Tour I, Entry 22.
4. Cutter House, Tudor Revival house, 1314 Arch St., 1910–1912; Tour I, Entry 15.
5. Tudor Revival house, 2721 Belrose Ave., c. 1910–1920; Tour I, Entry 3.
6. Tudor Revival house, 2851 Russell Ave., c. 1910–1920; Tour I, Entry 15.
7. Burke House, neo-Tudor house, 2911 Russell Ave., 1914, by D. J. Patterson; Tour I, Entry 12.
8. Dominican School of Philosophy and Religion, Tudor Revival, 2401 Ridge Rd., 1923, by Stafford Jory; Tour C, Entry 17.
9. Norman Revival apartments, 2317 Le Conte Ave., c. 1924; Tour C, Entry 21.
10. Holbrook Hall, Pacific School of Religion, Gothic Revival, 1798 Scenic Ave., 1924, by Walter H. Ratcliff, Jr.; Tour C, Entry 24.
11. First Congregational Church, Georgian Revival, Dana St. between Durant and Channing, 1924, by Horace Simpson; Tour H, Entry 7.
12. Kofoid Hall, Louis XIII style, 2369 Le Conte Ave., c. 1925; Tour C, Entry 22.
13. Graduate Theological Union, Georgian Revival, 2465 Le Conte Ave., c. 1925; Tour C, Entry 15.

14. Georgian Revival house, 1609 Spruce St., c. 1925–1935; Tour B, Entry 4.
15. Tupper and Reed Music Store, Hansel and Gretel style, 2277 Shattuck Ave., 1926, by William R. Yelland; Tour F, Entry 20.
16. Normandy Village, Hansel and Gretel style with Norman elements, 1817–1839, 1781–1783 Spruce St., 1927–1928, by William R. Yelland; Tour B, Entry 1.
17. Smith House, Regency style, 2812 Russell Ave., by William Wurster; Tour I, Entry 18.
18. Berkeley Day Nursery, Norman Revival, 2031 6th St., 1927, by Walter H. Ratcliff, Jr.; Tour K, Entry 9.
19. Church Divinity School of the Pacific, Gothic Revival, 2449 Ridge Rd., 1929, by Walter H. Ratcliff, Jr.; Tour C, Entry 16.
20. Bowles Hall, Tudor Revival, U.C. Campus above Gayley Rd., 1929, by George Kelham; Tour E, Entry 17.
21. University Christian Church, Gothic Revival, Scenic Ave. between Le Conte and Virginia, 1931, by Walter H. Ratcliff, Jr.; Tour C, Entry 4.
22. Moses Hall, Tudor Revival, U.C. Campus, 1931, by George Kelham; Tour E, Entry 10.
23. Tudor Revival apartment houses, 1810–1916 Arch St., c. 1930s; Tour C, Entry 30.
24. Georgian Revival house, 2274 Cedar St., c. 1935; Tour B, Entry 5.

## Emeryville

1. Dutch Revival commercial building, 1520 Powell St., c. 1915–1925; Entry 1.
2. Georgian Revival office building, 1475 Powell St., c. 1920–1930; Entry 3.

## Fremont

Mater Dei Shrine, Gothic Revival, Dominican Convent grounds, 1923; Tour B, Entry 8.

## Hayward

Green Shutter Hotel, Georgian Revival, B St. at Main, S.E. corner, c. 1915–1925; Entry 8.

## Kensington–Thousand Oaks

1. Tudor Revival house, 611 Arlington Ave., c. 1915–1925; Entry 14.
2. Georgian Revival house, 261 Arlington Ave., c. 1925–1935; Entry 8.
3. Tudor/Jacobean Revival house, 1966 Yosemite Rd., 1926, attributed to Timothy Pfleuger; Entry 16.
4. Tudor Revival house, 686 San Fernando Ave., c. 1930 by Edwin L. Snyder; Entry 29.

## Oakland

1. Skyscraper with Renaissance-style details, 13th St. and Broadway, N.E. corner, c. 1900–1905; Tour A, Entry 25.
2. 7th Ave. Baptist Church, Dutch Renaissance Revival, 1740 7th Ave., c. 1900–1905; Tour F, Entry 5.
3. Tudor Revival house, 1494 Alice, c. 1905–1915; Tour E, Entry 3.
4. White Building, Gothic Revival, 15th St. at Franklin, S.E. corner, c. 1910–1920; Tour A, Entry 17.
5. St. Joseph's Home for the Aged, Georgian Revival, 2647 E. 14th St., 1912; Tour H, Entry 14.
6. Cathedral Building, French-Gothic-Chateau-style skyscraper, Telegraph at Broadway, 1913, by Benjamin G. McDougall; Tour A, Entry 8.
7. Tudor Revival house, 1649 28th Ave., c. 1915–1925; Tour H, Entry 11.
8. Cook's Union Hall, Georgian Revival, 1608 Webster St., c. 1920–1930; Tour A, Entry 16.
9. Oakland Tribune Building, French-Chateau-style skyscraper, 13th St. at Franklin, S.E. corner, 1923, by Edward T. Foulkes; Tour A, Entry 21.
10. Gothic Revival office building, 8th St. at Harrison, N.W. corner, c. 1925; Tour A, Entry 25.
11. Fruitvale Medical Building, Gothic Revival with Art Deco elements, 3022 E. 14th Ave., c. 1930–1935; Tour H, Entry 1.
12. West Coast Furniture, Gothic Revival, 1520 Broadway, 1932; Tour A, Entry 11.

---

# Early Modern Era c. 1906–±1950

## Prairie School Buildings, c. 1906–±1930s

## Art Deco and Streamlined Moderne Styles, c. 1925–±1950

# Miscellaneous Early-Twentieth-Century Structures

## c. 1900–1930

*Bancroft and Fulton, Berkeley, c. 1910*

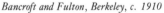